Public Management: Old and New

D1602547

Discussion of public management reform has been riveted by claims that a new paradigm, a business-like New Public Management, is replacing traditional, bureaucratic government on a global scale. By examining the evolution of managerial structures, practices, and values in France, Germany, the United Kingdom, and the United States, *Public Management: Old and New* reveals how public management reform in any country is inevitably shaped by that country's history.

This original new book illuminates the historical, institutional, and political factors that are essential to understanding contemporary public management practices and reform processes. Laurence E. Lynn, Jr. argues that constitutions and constitutional institutions, legislatures, and courts regulate the evolution of managerialism and that the triumph of democracy, not of capitalism, is the most influential of recent global developments shaping public management reform.

Indispensable for all students of public management, administration, and policy, this influential and insightful text offers a breadth of understanding and a unique perspective on public management today. It is an original addition to the bookshelves of all those interested in gaining a broad institutional perspective on their field.

Laurence E. Lynn, Jr. is the George H. W. Bush Chair and Professor of Public Affairs at the Bush School of Government and Public Service, Texas A&M University. He has received the H. George Frederickson Award and the Dwight Waldo Award for lifetime contributions to public administration and management scholarship.

Public Management: Old and New

Laurence E. Lynn, Jr.

WITHDRAWN
UTSA LIBRARIES

Routledge
Taylor & Francis Group

NEW YORK AND LONDON

First published 2006 in the USA and Canada
by Routledge
270 Madison Ave, New York, NY 10016

Simultaneously published in the UK
by Routledge
2 Park Square, Milton Park, Abingdon, Oxon OX14 4RN

Routledge is an imprint of the Taylor & Francis Group, an informa business

© 2006 Laurence E. Lynn, Jr.

Typeset in Perpetua and Bell Gothic by
Keystroke, Jacaranda Lodge, Wolverhampton
Printed and bound in Great Britain by
MPG Books Ltd, Bodmin, Cornwall

Library of Congress Cataloging in Publication Data
Lynn, Laurence E, 1937–
Public management: old and new/Laurence E. Lynn.
    p. cm.
Includes bibliographical references and index.
ISBN 0–415–28729–4 (hard cover) — ISBN 0–415–28730–8 (soft cover)
1. Public administration. 2. Public administration—Case studies. I. Title.
JF1351.L96 2006
351—dc22   2006011914

British Library Cataloguing in Publication Data
A catalogue record for this book is available from the British Library

ISBN10: 0–415–28729–4 (hbk)
ISBN10: 0–415–28730–8 (pbk)

ISBN13: 978–0–415–28729–6 (hbk)
ISBN13: 978–0–415–28730–2 (pbk)

Contents

Preface   ix

Milestones in the history of public management   xiii

1 Public management comes of age   **1**

Introduction   1

Administration, management, and governance   4

    The idea of administration: inordinate magnitude and difficulty   5

    The idea of management: finding the light   6

    A distinction without a difference   8

    A distinction with a difference?   10

Public management or public *management*?   12

Plan and method of the book   15

Notes   17

2 History and contemporary public management   **19**

Introduction   19

Pathways of change   20

Public management: a three-dimensional view   24

    Structure and process   24

    Craft   27

    Institutionalized values   29

Public management in France, Germany, the United Kingdom, and the
United States: overviews   32

    France   32

    Germany   33

    United Kingdom   35

    United States of America   36

Notes   38

3   Old public management: Continental traditions   **40**

Introduction   40
Pre-Westphalian public administration   40
Absolutism and the modern state   43
   Sovereignty and administration   44
   Administrative science   46
State, bureaucracy, and *Rechtsstaat*   48
   The imperial bureaucracy   49
   Rechtsstaat   52
Survival, reconstruction, and the welfare state   55
   The interregnum   55
   Reconstruction and social welfare   56
Continental legacies   58
Notes   60

4   Old public management: British traditions   **62**

Introduction   62
An unwritten constitution   64
Creating administrative capacity   67
   Intellectual preparations   67
   A modern civil service – and bureaucracy   68
   The rule of (common) law   72
War and welfare   73
   Strengthening governance   73
   Science and ethics   74
British legacies   76
Notes   77

5   Old public management: American traditions   **79**

Introduction   79
Revolutionary public administration   80
   Founding views   80
   Pre-bureaucratic America   82
An American invention   84
   European influence   85
   A pragmatic response   88
   Scientific management   92
   The New Deal   95
From New Deal to Great Society   97

American legacies   99
Notes   101

6   New Public Management: reform, change, and adaptation   104

     Introduction   104
     The birth of managerialism   105
     Reinventing American government   108
     Something new in Europe   114
         Great Britain   117
         Continental Europe   121
             Germany   121
             France   124
         The European Union   127
     A disaster waiting to happen?   129
     Managerialism in perspective   131
     Notes   132

7   New Public Management: delegation and accountability   136

     Introduction   136
     Perspectives on accountability   138
     Old Public Administration vs. New Public Management   142
     The political economy of accountability   145
         The new political economy   146
         The chain of delegation   147
         Horizontal democracy   152
     Tensions   154
     Notes   154

8   Of wine and bottles, old and new   157

     Introduction   157
     Old bottles   160
         Old Public Administration   160
         Path or punctuation?   162
             A narrative of continuity   162
             A narrative of change   163
     New wine   165
         Convergence or differentiation?   167
         What is happening in theory?   169
     Managerialism in historical perspective   173

CONTENTS

Internationalizing the profession	176
New bottles?	178
Notes	180
References	183
Index	204

Preface

The writing of this book began with an idea for a title and a few basic convictions: that public management is a nexus where politics, law, and administration necessarily engage each other; that the comparative study of public management is essential to understanding its importance as an institution of governance; that a study of public management must be both historical and analytical, both descriptive and theoretical; and that public management as a subject of teaching and research must be recognized as having multiple dimensions, including its structures of authority, its practices or craft, and its institutionalized values.

These convictions were formed as I participated in discussions of the most recent hot topic in the field of public management reform. A "New Public Management" (NPM) emphasizing incentives, competition, and results is, it has been argued by many scholars and practitioners, displacing the obsolete "Old Public Administration," with its emphasis on politically supervised hierarchy – "command and control" – and on compliance with rules of law. Of course, there are critics on both normative and empirical grounds of this narrative of transformation. As this book appears, moreover, the NPM fevers have begun to subside, and the talk, now more sober and less breathless, is of governance, participatory democracy, networks, and other "paradigms" of public management.

Rather than simply note the passing of yet another ephemeral managerial fashion, in the manner, say, of Japanese management, planning–programming–budgeting, scientific management, and cameralism, the widespread popularity of NPM's narrative of reform invites reflection on what the subject of public management ought to be about. This issue has been central in American professional discourse since the emergence of the field of public administration beginning in the latter nineteenth century. "Managerialism" is a much newer idea in Europe, however, and there are tendencies in Europe, as well as among many in the United States, to view public management narrowly: as an operational function of government that can as readily be "reformed" as can personnel administration, budgeting or auditing. To the contrary, the argument of this book is that public management is deeply rooted in national (and, increasingly, international) politics, law and institutionalized values. The "NPM narrative," with its "out-with-the-old, in-with-the-new" imperative, offers an opportunity to understand how, why, and with what consequences the view of public management elaborated in this book is, and always has been, the correct one.

Though its perspective is broadly historical, this book was not written for historians, who will immediately note its reliance on secondary, English-language sources. Though it compares public management in four countries, it was not written for country specialists or even for comparativists, who will immediately note that more detailed descriptions and comparisons of the governments included in this study, as well as of a much broader array of governments, are available. (The magisterial works of E. N. Gladden (1972a, 1972b) and S. E. Finer (1997) are prominent among them.) As an American, I am myself acutely aware of omitted levels of detail and insight concerning my own government that are important to a deep understanding of American government and public management. Though its concern is with political institutions, the book was not written for political scientists, who will note the limited attention devoted to the kinds of theoretical considerations that are central to their research.

The audience for this book is, rather, students of management and, especially, of public management. My intention is to provide in a single volume description and analysis at a level of detail sufficient to illuminate the historical, institutional, and political contexts that shape contemporary public management and that are essential to understanding public management reform processes and their consequences.

The intellectual approach here is, as noted, broadly institutional in that it traces the evolution of those durable governmental structures, conventions, practices, and beliefs that enable and constrain public management policy and practice. The central argument is that public management without its institutional context is "mere" managerialism, that is, an ideology which views management *principia probant, non probantur* as a technocratic means to achieve the end of effective governmental performance without regard for the powerful influences of specific institutional contexts and circumstances on its structures, practices, and values. From an analytic perspective, management must, I argue, be understood as endogenous to each country's political economy, and each country's political economy must be understood as a resultant of path-dependent, dynamic processes subject to occasional "punctuations" or discontinuous changes that affect their specific character.

For source materials, I have cast my net as widely as possible for resources available in English. Owing to the World Wide Web, such materials now include what were once regarded as "fugitive sources," including reports, unpublished manuscripts, and innumerable websites that make available research reflecting various motives and perspectives. At the risk of imparting a tone that occasionally seems derivative because of numerous quotes and citations, my general purpose has been to integrate the contributions of the most insightful scholarship bearing on public management into a coherent analytical account of how the field has evolved.

During the writing of this book, I confronted the challenge of creating coherent narratives from many specialists' accounts with two handicaps. First, as an American, my basic grasp of European governments and the subtleties of their politics is bound to be limited, and I anticipate having to wince when those neglected subtleties are pointed out. Second, the fact that I was trained as an economist and have found that thinking like one is especially insightful no doubt unduly limits my appreciation for insights from fields of scholarship and from epistemologies other than those with which I am most familiar. My goal, however, has been neither to try to beat specialists at their own game nor to present either a revisionist account of administrative history or an account that over-privileges the perspectives of the sub-discipline of political economy. Rather, the goal has been to make accessible, in coherent form, to an Anglophone audience the insights that now reside in countless national and specialized niches in the literature. It is my insecurities that account for my tendency to let the specialists speak in their own words rather than everywhere putting up inadequate paraphrases.

Inevitably I have drawn on my own earlier papers and on the research on which they are based, notably:

- 1993. "Management sans Manageurs: Les Fausses Promesses des Reformes Administratives." *Politiques et Management Public* 11: 45–65.
- 1996. "Reforma Administrativa desde una Perspectiva Internacional: Ley Pública y la Nueva Administración Pública." *Gestión y Política Pública* 5: 303–18.
- 1998. "A Critical Analysis of the New Public Management," *International Public Management Journal* 1: 107–23.
- 1998. "The New Public Management: How to Transform a Theme into a Legacy." *Public Administration Review* 58: 231–37.
- 1999. "Public Management in North America." *Public Management* 1: 301–10.
- 2001. "The Myth of the Bureaucratic Paradigm: What Traditional Public Administration Really Stood For." *Public Administration Review* 61: 144–60.
- 2001. "Globalization and Administrative Reform: What Is Happening in Theory?" *Public Management Review* 3: 191–208.
- 2002. "Novi Trendi v Javnem Menedzmentu (Recent Trends in Public Management)." In *Vec neposredne demokracije v Sloveniji – DA ali NE – Novi trendi v javnem menedzmentu*. 131–50. Ljubljana, Republika Slovenija: Drzavni Svet Republike Slovenije.
- 2003. "Public Management." In B. G. Peters and J. Pierre, eds., *Handbook of Public Administration*. 14–24. Thousand Oaks, CA: Sage.
- 2004. "Reforma a la Gestión Pública: Tendencias y Perspectivas (Public Management Reform: Trends and Perspectives)." In María del Carmen Pardo, ed., *De la Administración Pública a la Gobernanza*. 105–28. Mexico City: El Colegio de México.
- 2005. "Public Management: A Concise History of the Field." In E. Ferlie, L. Lynn, Jr. and C. Pollitt, eds., *Handbook of Public Management*. 27–50. Oxford: Oxford University Press.
- 2005. "Introduction to a Symposium on Public Governance" (with Carolyn J. Hill, Isabella Proeller and Kuno Schedler). *Policy Studies Journal* 33: 203–11.

I hope that this book is appropriate for use as a primary or a supplementary text for courses in public management at the graduate and advanced undergraduate level. I have also endeavored, at the risk of some redundancy, to structure key chapters, notably Chapters 1, 2, 6, 7, and 8, so that they can be assigned as supplementary, stand-alone readings.

Finally, a preliminary note on usage is in order. I argue in this book (as I do elsewhere) that no authoritative distinction can be drawn between the concept of administration and that of management despite considerable scholarly effort to make such a distinction. I also argue, as noted above, that public management is not confined to "what managers do" or to governmental operations. It comprises the structures of formal authority, the practices of those in managerial roles, and the institutionalized values that infuse choice and decision making throughout government. The history of public administration, which encompasses the emergence and evolution of structures of authority, of "best practices" and of institutionalized values, is also, therefore, a history of public management. In other words, the chapters of this book dealing with what some call Old Public Administration in France, Germany, the United States, and the United Kingdom are about public management every bit as much as the chapters that discuss NPM and the managerialism of recent years.

Though I was tempted to use the term public management throughout the book, such usage would no doubt have irritated readers for whom the term public administration is not only acceptable but historically appropriate and accurate. Where I thought the context called for it, I used the term public administration. Where either term would have been appropriate, I used the term public management.

Laurence E. Lynn, Jr.
College Station, Texas, USA

Milestones in the history of public management

Fourth century BCE	Shen Pu-hai governs in north-central China, codifies principles of administration
124 BCE	Founding of imperial university in China to inculcate the values and attitudes of public service
529	First draft of the Code of Justinian I promulgated, summarizing Roman law
1154–1189	English common law established during the reign of Henry II
1231	Frederick II of Lower Italy and Sicily promulgates statutes at Melfi adumbrating modern bureaucracy
1640–1688	Absolutist regime of Frederick William (The Great Elector) of Brandenburg (later Prussia) establishes public service as a duty to the people, not the ruler
1648	Treaty of Westphalia creates European community of sovereign states
1688	The Glorious Revolution reconstitutes British monarchy with curtailed powers
1760	Johann von Justi publishes authoritative cameralist treatise *Die Grundfeste zu der Macht und Glückseligkeit der Staaten*
1787	United States Constitution incorporates elected executive, separation of powers; papers now known as *The Federalist* published
1789	Revolution in France promulgates Declaration of the Rights of Man, establishes principle of national (as opposed to royal) sovereignty
1804–1814/15	Reign of Napoleon Bonaparte marked by promulgation in 1804 of the influential *Code Napoléon*, which codified civil law, and influential administrative reforms
1829–1837	US president Andrew Jackson initiates spoils system as basis for public personnel selection
1836	Henry Taylor publishes *The Statesman*, the first modern book devoted to public administration

1848	Continental revolutions accelerate movement toward political democracy and *Rechtsstaat*
1853	Northcote–Trevelyan Report accelerates progress toward the professionalization of the British civil service
1883	The Pendleton Act initiates movement toward American civil service reform
1900	Frank J. Goodnow's *Politics and Administration: A Study in Government* makes seminal case for the administrative state
1911	Publication of Frederick W. Taylor's *Principles of Scientific Management* inaugurates the scientific management movement
1947–1948	Criticisms by Robert A. Dahl, Herbert S. Simon, and Dwight Waldo undermine the authority of "traditional public administration," laying foundations for "intellectual crisis"
1960–1978	Successive American administrations promote PPBS, MBO, ZBB, and other executive tools of management reform
1979–1990	Government of British prime minister Margaret Thatcher launches the "New Public Management" movement
1992	David Osborne and Ted Gaebler's book *Reinventing Government* popularizes the idea and many principles of public management reform
1990–2006	Influenced by New Public Management, the field of public management becomes international and comparative

Chapter 1

Public management comes of age

INTRODUCTION

Effective management of public organizations – departments, agencies, bureaus, offices – is vital to the success of government programs, policies, and regimes, and perhaps even of democracy itself.[1] Although generally accepted around the world, this seemingly sensible statement would have been only barely intelligible within the public administration profession as recently as the 1970s.[2] From a subject widely regarded as "new" only a generation ago, public management is now a field of policy making, practice, and scholarship which enjoys international recognition. "Public management" and "public management reform," along with concepts and terms of art associated with them, have entered the languages of practical politics, scholarship and instruction.

A number of factors impelled the rapid growth of interest in public sector management. Among the most prominent were the national economic crises of the 1970s and 1980s, which opened disconcerting gaps between government outlays and revenues and suggested the need for more tight-fisted management of public agencies. Other contributing factors included heightened expectations for effective government on the part of citizens around the world following the end of the Cold War; growing interdependence within the global economy, which increased pressures for efficient regulation and reliable and frugal administration of government functions (Caiden 1991, 1999); and the growing popular appeal of neo-liberal, that is to say, business-and-market-oriented, ideologies, policies, and political programs intended to reduce the scale, scope, and fiscal appetite of governments. The era of generous, unmanaged, rule-governed social provision, of the welfare state, was, it was widely argued, history.

As forces and ideas threatening the status quo of national welfare state governments gathered momentum, the ideology of managerialism and strategies for public management reform became a priority of the international community, including the Organization for Economic Cooperation and Development (OECD), the World Bank, the United Nations Development Program, the European Commission, the Inter-American Development Bank, and many other regional bodies, as well as of bilateral aid donors, trade partners, and non-governmental organizations (NGOs), with "unmistakable impact" (Common 1998, 61). Among such organizations, as well as among many national advocates for governmental improvement, the belief took hold that external pressures for change had created new opportunities for public management reforms by national governments (Fuhr 2001). National and international public management consultancies began to proliferate and flourish, sustaining the momentum for change, and academic interest in these developments burgeoned.

Because improving public management in more than specifically technical ways virtually always requires active political and expert support, neologisms that incite approval, such as "new public management," "reinventing government," and "state modernization and reform," entered the vocabularies of policy makers, practitioners, and scholars world-wide. Surveyed by the OECD, few countries failed to report deliberate efforts at governmental improvement, and most claimed actual, albeit largely uncorroborated, achievements (OECD 1994, 1995, 1996). Discussions of public management that were once confined within national boundaries are now the subjects of a thriving international discourse featuring comparative analysis, evaluation, and lesson-drawing.

These developments have spawned new programs of public-management-oriented teaching and research and, as well, have energized, although not in any coordinated way, academic fields concerned with various aspects of the subject. The disciplines of political science, economics and sociology, policy subfields such as health, education, public welfare, and information technology, professional fields such as financial management, personnel management, and accounting, and private-sector-oriented fields such as organization studies, management, and non-governmental or non-profit sector studies have come to be viewed as intellectual resources for the study and practice of public management, and their practitioners regularly participate in international public management forums. The sense of urgency about public management reform and the casting of a wide net to capture useful ideas are thought by many to have thrown the traditional field of public administration into crisis by revealing the inadequacy of its intellectual apparatus for addressing twenty-first-century problems of resource allocation, coordination and control (Kettl 2002).

Of particular interest to public management specialists are the insistent claims by many scholars, policy makers, and public officials that the field of public management has crossed a historical watershed. A new paradigm of public management emphasizing incentives, competition, and performance – termed New Public Management or, more generally, managerialism – is said by many to be displacing traditional public administration's reliance on rule-based hierarchies overseen by the institutions of representative democracy, a development with profound implications for democracy itself. The mantra has grown in volume: the bureaucratic paradigm is dead; long live quasi-markets and quangos, flattened hierarchies and continuous improvement, competitive tendering and subsidiarity. Other anti-traditional paradigms emphasizing, for example, deliberative democracy, or networked relationships and partnerships – joined-up government – or "governance" are also claimed to be gaining in popularity in national, state, and local governments around the world. A grand, global isomorphism of governmental structures and practices is thought by many to be well under way.

2

These remarkable claims and developments and their implications for public management thought, policy, and practice are the subject of this book. Although the impressively growing literature of public management records the views of numerous skeptics and critics of recent developments (discussed further in Chapter 6), there have been relatively few systematic attempts to examine managerialism's central premise: that the field of public management is experiencing a historical transformation that is realigning the relationships between the state and society, between government and citizen, between politics and management. The book's primary questions are these: In the light of the long history of public administration and management in organized societies, are claims on behalf of such a transformation credible? What is actually new, and to what extent is "the new" changing in fundamental ways not only public management policies and practices but the field's intellectual and institutional infrastructure? To the extent that we can discern significant continuity in the managerial institutions of mature democracies, what are the implications of such a reality for the prospects of further managerial reform?

The argument of this book is that the old and the new, that is, public management's historical and contemporary structures, practices, and institutions, are so intimately interrelated that answers to the foregoing questions require an understanding of the paths and patterns of national institutional development. While reform, change, and adaptation of contemporary national administrative systems may be nearly universal, it follows centuries of reform, change, and adaptation that have resulted in national institutions whose function is to guarantee a certain stability and continuity in democratic governance. To imagine that such institutions can be overturned in a generation is an unwarranted conceit. The past constrains and shapes the present and constrains the future in comprehensible ways.

The heart of the book is an examination and analysis of public management, old and new, in the United States, the United Kingdom, France, and Germany. Intellectual boundaries for this inquiry must first be laid, however. These boundaries are the subject of the first two chapters of the book. (The plan and method of the remaining six chapters are outlined at the end of this chapter.)

Because the very idea of a new public management conveys the notion of divergence from past practice – from "traditional public administration" – the question arises as to how the history of a rapidly obsolescing field can be relevant to understanding contemporary developments. Public administration was "then"; public management is "now." Moreover, because a premise of contemporary managerialism is that the functional distinction between the public and private sectors is, and ought to be, breaking down – that public and private management are, or at least ought to be, increasingly indistinguishable – the question arises as to how a history of institutions formed when industrial capitalism was rudimentary at best can be relevant to understanding governance in an era of transcendent global capitalism and stateless enterprises, instantaneous communications, and the extensive interpenetration of public and private sectors.

3

The present chapter takes up two issues related to these questions: the relationship between "administration," "management," and a third, more recent and related concept, "governance" and the distinguishability of public and private management. Concerning the first of these issues, the conclusion is that it is generally impossible to establish, either historically or conceptually, a definitive distinction between administration and management; in effect, the history of public administration is a history of public management, a notion that many readers, especially in Europe, may find uncongenial or unhelpful. While governance may yet emerge as a distinction with a difference, such a conclusion is as yet premature. Concerning the second of these issues, the conclusion is that a distinction between public and private management is virtually axiomatic; the two sectors are constituted in fundamentally different ways, one through sovereign mandate, the other through individual initiative enabled but not mandated or directed by the state.

In the light of these conclusions, Chapter 2 discusses why and how history matters to a proper interpretation of contemporary developments in public management. Using social science concepts such as path dependency and punctuated equilibrium, an initial conclusion is that there have emerged inextricable links between the past and present of public management that, as illustrated by the four countries discussed in this book, both ensure the fundamental continuity of national institutions and enable change, adaptation, and reform without debilitating disruption, albeit – and this is fundamental – on different terms in different countries. Next, a concept of public management emphasizing three dimensions – structures, practices, and institutionalized values – is set forth in some detail to provide a framework for interpreting the specific character of both continuity and change. Reference to these three dimensions will be made throughout the book.

ADMINISTRATION, MANAGEMENT, AND GOVERNANCE

The terms "public administration," "public management," and "public governance" entered academic discourse more or less in that order. They are sometimes used as if they were virtually interchangeable, sometimes held to be conceptually distinct. Unfortunately, the considerable intellectual effort that has been devoted to differentiating them has failed to converge on a conventional scheme of conceptualization and usage, largely because each of the three terms itself lacks a definitive conceptualization.

In the most general sense, both "administration" and "management" when referring to the public sector seem to encompass methodical efforts to accomplish the goals of sovereign authority. Yet as already noted, public management has been widely acknowledged on both sides of the Atlantic to represent a new approach to governing, a new ideology, or perhaps a new paradigm. In sorting out this issue, it will be helpful to review briefly the evolution of each of the two ideas.[3]

The idea of administration: inordinate magnitude and difficulty

The general notion of administration as methodical effort associated with securing the goals of sovereign authority is of ancient origin, as is awareness, or, as it might be termed, "common knowledge" (Hood and Jackson 1991b) or "practice wisdom," of the techniques of administration.[4] However, it is in the literature of cameralism – a theory of managing natural and human resources in a way most lucrative for the ruler and his interests, and the precursor of modern administrative science – that one finds systematic recognition of the idea of administration that anticipates later intellectual developments.

Motivated in part by hostility to the kind of manipulative and opportunistic advice to rulers associated with Machiavelli, cameralism identified "techniques and objects of administration" for state domains the use of which would stabilize and increase the ruler's powers (Tribe 1984, 268). The term *polizei* (referring to the maintenance of internal order and welfare) was defined as "activity of interior state administration . . . which is established as an independent means for achieving general objectives of the state, without consideration for the individual and without waiting until its service is specifically called for" (F. Rettig quoted by Anderson and Anderson 1967, 169). According to Georg Zincke, perhaps the foremost cameralist academic scholar, "a prince needs genuine and skillful cameralists. By this name we mean those who possess fundamental and special knowledge about all or some particular part of those things which are necessary in order that they may assist the prince in maintaining good management in the state" (quoted by Lepawsky 1949, 99; Small 1909, 253).[5]

Early usages of the term "administration" in the English language were primarily descriptive and only implicitly conceptual. In 1836, Sir Henry Taylor, in a book, *The Statesman* (1958), which has been termed "the first modern book to be devoted to the subject of public administration," argued that without "administrative measures" we have but the potentiality of government (quoted by Dunsire 1973, 10). John Stuart Mill wrote that "freedom cannot produce its best effects, and often breaks down altogether, unless means can be found of combining it with trained and skilled administration" (Mill 1861, quoted by Dunsire 1973, 73). In *The Science of Law* (1874), Sheldon Amos (quoted by Fairlie 1935, 19–20) said that administration consists

> in selecting a vast hierarchy of persons to perform definite work; in marking out the work of all and each; in taking such measures as are necessary to secure that the work is really done; and in supplying from day to day such connections or modifications as changing circumstances may seem to suggest. . . . In a very complete and advanced condition of society . . . the task of administration is one of inordinate magnitude and difficulty, but it is only a subordinate agency in the whole process of government.

One writer referred to administration as occurring at "the lower ranges" of government (Fairlie 1935).

5

The term "administration" began to find its way into technical dictionaries, especially those concerned with the law. Bouvier's *Law Dictionary* (first published in 1839), at the end of its article on the administration of estates, gives a brief definition of the administration of government: "The management of the affairs of the government; the word is also applied to the persons entrusted with the management of public affairs" (quoted by Fairlie 1935, 14–15). Black's *Law Dictionary*, first published in 1891, defined "the administration of government" as "the practical management and direction of the executive department, or, of the public machinery or functions" (quoted by Fairlie 1935, 25). Note the habit of dictionaries (also true of the *Oxford English Dictionary*) of using each of the terms "management" and "administration" to define the other, a habit that, as already noted, originated with seventeenth-century cameralists.

The most systematic attempts to define administration in the English language were associated with identifying the activity of administration with respect to the emergent field of administrative law. "It is only since the last decade of the nineteenth century," says John Fairlie (1935, 3), "that the terms 'public administration' and 'administrative law' have come to receive extended recognition in English-speaking countries. In this recent development, Frank J. Goodnow was the first important leader [whose work] marked the beginning of fuller recognition and more extended study of public administration in the United States" (Fairlie 1935, 25).[6] Goodnow, according to Fairlie, saw administration as "the entire activity of the government, exclusive of that of the legislature and the purely judicial work of the courts" (quoted by Fairlie 1935, 25).

Early American public administration textbooks, which were attempting to give shape to an emergent field, necessarily offered definitions and conceptualizations of administration. Leonard White differentiated administrative law as concerned with the protection of private rights from public administration as concerned with the efficient conduct of public business (Fairlie 1935, 36).[7] According to W. F. Willoughby (1927), "[i]n its broadest sense, [administration] denotes the work involved in the actual conduct of governmental affairs, regardless of the particular branch of government concerned. . . . In its narrowest sense, it denotes the operations of the administrative branch only" (quoted in Fairlie 1935, 35). To Ernest Barker (1944, 3), administration was "the sum of persons and bodies who are engaged, under the direction of government, in discharging the ordinary public services which must be rendered daily if the system of law and duties and rights is to be duly 'served'."[8]

The idea of management: finding the light

As already noted, the term "management" appeared early in the discussion of state administration as virtually synonymous with administration. Management as a distinctive idea did not begin to emerge until the nineteenth century, with "[e]xplicit theorizing . . . perhaps most noticeable in the US, which industrialized later and even faster than Germany or the UK" (Pollitt 1990, 12). The term initially tended to characterize those activities associated with providing direction to the large-scale corporate organizations associated with industrial capitalism. It was extended by analogy to government.

The flowering of the scientific management movement (discussed further in Chapter 5), given impetus by the publication of Frederick W. Taylor's *The Principles of Scientific Management* in 1911 and by the unprecedented managerial challenges of World War I, instigated a widening interest in general management and administration.[9] Taylorites insisted that management could be a true science and should be universally applied, a view that was influential on both sides of the Atlantic (Pollitt 1990). The popularity of the idea was reinforced in Europe by the work of Henri Fayol, the French manager-engineer, who "fathered the first theory of management through his principles and elements of management" (Wren 1987, 179). It was Taylor, however, who attracted the mass audience and his followers who gave international currency to the term "management."

In the United States, a regulatory proceeding, the Eastern Rate Case Hearings, and the Taylorite arguments of Louis Brandeis to the hearing examiners brought notions of scientific management and a thirty-year-old industrial "management movement" into contact with each other (Person 1977 [1926]). Thereafter, references to "management" proliferated in literature and professional discussion in both the public and the private sectors. Frederick Cleveland, the Progressive reformer closely associated with American bureaus of municipal research, made frequent early use of the term. By 1931, John Gaus was referring to the techniques of public management, largely as a result of the codified knowledge of city administration – an increasing number of cities were under the administration of "city managers" – that was being accumulated and disseminated by bureaus of municipal research around the country.

In a 1933 book written under the sponsorship of President Herbert Hoover's Committee on Social Trends, Leonard White titled a chapter "Management Trends in the Public Service," trends which he termed "the New Management."[10] By this term, he meant the emergence of "a contemporary philosophy of administration" – today one might say an ideology of administration – favoring consolidation of the administrative power of the elected chief executive and of the city manager. For an exemplary statement of this philosophy, he cites a series of principles put forward in 1931 by a state governor: "consolidation and integration in departments of similar functions; fixed and definite assignments of administrative responsibility; proper coordination in the interests of harmony; executive responsibility centered in a single individual rather than a board" (White 1933, 144). In most of his published work, especially in the 1940s and subsequently, Fritz Morstein Marx, a sometime government official, repeatedly used the term "public management" (Morstein Marx 1940, 1948, 1949).

A management movement had also arisen in Great Britain, beginning with Charles Babbage's 1832 book *On the Economy of Machinery and Manufactures*, but with important differences from the American ideology.[11] According to John Child (1969, 23), British management thought, a "comprehensive body of knowledge," serves both ideological and scientific functions: a "legitimatory" function of securing the social recognition and approval of managerial authority (by claiming appropriate social values for management) and a technical function of searching for practical means of rendering managerial authority maximally effective (by statements of effective managerial techniques). In a similar vein, Rosamund Thomas (1977) argues that British thought sought to unify scientific thinking and ethical thinking, in contrast to what she saw as America's narrower preoccupation with a science of administration.[12]

Perhaps the most coherent expression of the British managerial school was Oliver Sheldon's *The Philosophy of Management* (1979 [1924]).[13] "The responsibility of management," he argues, "is a human responsibility, occasioned rather by its control of men than its application of technique. . . . The responsibility of management resides in the fact that the industry which it directs is composed of human as well as material elements" (1979 [1924], 72–3). He continues (1979 [1924], 74, 75):

> [Management] must operate in some direct relation to the community. . . . [M]anagement is here used in a generic sense, and that in proportion as the workers are consulted, proffer suggestions and skill, or even knowingly and willingly assist in production, the workers themselves share with management the same responsibility. . . . Management is finding the light of a new spirit glinting from the pinnacles of its corporate task. That spirit is the spirit of service – the conception of industrial management as a social force directing industry to the service of the community.

Following World War II, British Treasury official J. R. Simpson argued that "it is essential to the preservation of democracy that the executive arm of government should attain a high standard of efficiency and effectiveness. That will require public management of a higher order, dynamic in character and ever striving for improvement" (Simpson 1949, 106). He defined management as "a single entity and all its parts are interdependent. . . . Organization and methods and personnel cannot be treated as separate independent elements in management. . . . [T]he maintenance and development [of good management] can be guided and stimulated from the top" (Simpson 1949, 100).

Following management movements initiated by the challenges of industrial capitalism, the idea of public *management* had become firmly rooted in both the United States and Great Britain by the 1940s, although, unlike the term administration, its use was still more idiosyncratic than systematic and often looked on askance by those of a more orthodox temper.

A distinction without a difference

What of the relationship between these two great ideas, administration and management, which have crossed paths for centuries? There have been efforts to finesse the issue, the coinage of President Franklin Roosevelt's Committee on Administrative Management and the efforts simply to join "public administration and management" as a singular noun, but they have gained little acceptance. More influential have been efforts to establish clear distinctions. Unfortunately, they have ultimately been no more successful.

Some distinctions are intended to be descriptive or objectively analytical. Sheldon described management as a generic function divided into three aspects: administration, management in the narrower sense, and organization (Sheldon 1979 [1924]). Administration, according to Sheldon, is "the determination of a top-level policy, the co-ordination of the major aspects of the business, and the control of management proper" (quoted by Pollard 1974, 102); management in the narrower sense contributes nothing except performance. Henri Fayol reversed the order of subordination: "It is important not to confuse *administration* with *management*. To manage . . . is to conduct [an organization] toward the best possible use of all the resources at its disposal . . . [i.e.] to ensure the smooth working of the . . . essential functions. Administration is only one of these functions" (quoted by Wren 1979, 232).[14]

Other scholars have held that, of the two concepts, administration is original and primary, public management is novel and subordinate or specialized. In their *Public Management: The Essential Readings*, for example, Steven Ott, Albert Hyde, and Jay Shafritz (1991) argue, as do James Perry and Kenneth Kraemer (1983) and Hal Rainey (1990), that "*Public management* is a major segment of the broader field of public administration. . . . Public management focuses on public administration as a profession and on the public manager as a practitioner of that profession." According to Ott, Hyde and Shafritz (1991, ix), public management

> is the part of public administration that overviews the art and science of applied methodologies for public administration program design and organizational restruc-turing, policy and management planning, resource allocations through budgeting systems, financial management, human resources management, and program evaluation and audit.

For still others, the two terms are virtually synonymous. In Roscoe C. Martin's view, by 1940, "administration was equated with management" (Martin 1965, 8). In assaying mid- to late nineteenth-century antecedents to Woodrow Wilson's famous 1887 essay "The Study of Administration," Paul Van Riper (1990, 8) notes "that the words *administration* and *management* have been treated here as synonymous." According to James Stever (1990), Marshall Dimock, who accorded more respect to the work of Ordway Tead, Mary Parker Follett, Elton Mayo, Chester Barnard, and Phillip Selznick than most traditional public administration scholars, saw administration as an integrative activity that shapes society, the science and art of putting institutions together; the terms "manager" and "administrator" were used interchangeably in his work. More recently, Christopher Pollitt and Geert Bouckaert (2004) and Laurence Lynn (2005) have held that the two ideas are for all practical purposes indistinguishable.

One possible conceptual difference between "administration" and "management" lies in the differing underlying assumptions concerning those institutional phenomena that should be assumed as given and those that should be assumed to be malleable and, thus, the object of managerial attention, in a given situation. As Theo Toonen and

Jos Raadschelders (1997, 6) put it, terms such as managerialism, neo-managerial, and the managerial angle imply "within structure/system. . . . The new public management tradition seems more focused on efficiency and effective management control *within a given context of policy and institutional constraints*." Mark Moore (1984) used the same assumption in differentiating the "new" American public management movement and its craft perspective (see Chapter 6) from its more traditional predecessors and their structural perspective. In short, administration might be said to embrace political-administrative institutions as a whole, whereas management is concerned with the organizations that conduct the actual operations of government within an institutional framework.

That particular distinction is arbitrary and problematic, however. If the idea of public management is held to be a subject that is analytically separable from its institutional context, with its historical development and traditions, then the creators of knowledge for the field of public management will be likely to ignore institutional issues that have a vital bearing on the practice of public management and the success of public management reform. In other words, *no* distinction is better than that particular distinction.

A distinction with a difference?

Public management is, as will be discussed in Chapter 6, a sharply contested idea which, like the term "administrative management" before it, may yet fail to achieve permanent status as a paradigm of scholarship and practice. For some, public management is irredeemably associated with "managerialism," an ideologically motivated effort to substitute corporate sector values and instrumental notions of efficiency for an ethical commitment by the state and its officers to service and collective justice, in the process transforming active citizens into passive consumers. For others, public management invites an undue focus on actors in managerial roles to the exclusion of the organizations and institutions and systems that constrain and enable managerial behavior. For still others, for whom government is about politics and policy, public management is nothing more than traditional public administration with a fashionable new label, a domain for technocrats and mavens of government operations: the public sector equivalent of industrial engineering. Devolution, globalization, and hyper-pluralism are examples of the tectonic forces that are forcing revolutionary change on administrative practice, argues Donald Kettl (2002), who concludes that governments must have new theories to explain and guide practice.

The ambiguous status of public management is one reason why a new term, "governance," is coming into use to characterize the domain within which both "traditional" public administration and New Public Management, or managerialism, are to be found. This term has already achieved wide popularity with American and European scholars as well as with international organizations, who view it as encompassing administrative arrangements that envelop or even lie outside traditional governments and hierarchies.

10

Many within the field have begun to embrace the idea of "governance" as an organizing concept (Garvey 1997; Heinrich, Hill and Lynn 2005; Kettl 2000, 2002; Peters and Pierre 1998; Rhodes 1996; Salamon 2002). The momentum behind this idea has reached the point that George Frederickson and Kevin Smith (2003, 225) can suggest that governance has become "a virtual synonym for public management and public administration."

The intellectual movement toward governance as an organizing concept for teaching and research is associated with the widespread impression that the focus of administrative practice has been shifting from the bureaucratic state and direct government to the "hollow state" (Milward 1994; Milward and Provan 1993; Rhodes 1994) and "third-party government" (Salamon 1981), and to the changing boundaries between state and society. In this view, public management increasingly relies on a variety of indirect relationships with dispersed and diverse entities, rather than on the supervision of civil servants who are organized by agency and governed by employment contracts (Frederickson 2005) mandating compliance with applicable laws and regulations.

As is the case with the terms administration and management, subtle differences in the definitions of "governance" abound. To Jon Pierre and Guy Peters (2000), governance means providing direction to society. In *The Transformation of Governance*, Donald Kettl (2002, 123) employs the idea of governance to confront the realities of administrative roles that require "capacities that lie far beyond the standard responses, structures, and processes that have gradually accumulated within American government." Richard Common (1998, 67) points out that "[t]he increasing use of the term 'governance' [by international organizations] indicates a shift in emphasis from economic to political management in affecting policy outcomes." Mark Bevir, R. A. W. Rhodes, and Patrick Weller (2003b, 13) use "governance" to encapsulate "the changing form and role of the state in advanced industrial societies," especially focusing on public sector reform and on "the changing boundary between state and civil society." Laurence Lynn, Carolyn Heinrich, and Carolyn Hill (2001, 7) define public sector governance as "regimes of laws, rules, judicial decisions, and administrative practices that constrain, prescribe, and enable the provision of publicly supported goods and services" through formal and informal relationships with agents in the public and private sectors.

To many scholars, the idea of governance is closely associated with the analytic concept of network and related ideas. According to Rhodes (1996, 660), for example, "governance refers to self-organizing, interorganizational networks." To Peters and Pierre (1998), the idea of governance encompasses the predominance of network relationships, deregulation, hybridization of public and private resources, and use of multiple instruments in policy implementation. Salamon (2002) proposes a paradigm that he calls the "new governance," which shifts the unit of analysis from programs and agencies to tools of action, and the focus of administration from hierarchy to network, from public-versus-private to public-plus-private, from command-and-control to negotiation and persuasion, from management skills to enablement skills. Bevir, Rhodes, and Weller (2003a, 192) argue that interpretivists (a term that includes ethnography, social constructivism, and hermeneutics) use the term governance "to refer to a pattern of rule characterized by networks that connect civil society and the state." And Werner Jann (2003) says that the latest tradition seems to be "the activating state," building on network theory, the cooperative state, and other concepts, and on fashionable ideas such as social capital and communitarianism. Governance, in his view, has come to refer to new forms of decentralized, self-organized steering.

These attempts at awarding a distinctive meaning to the concept of governance are not persuasively different from many of the broader definitions of administration and management. Recognizing this, Frederickson argues (2005, 293) that "[g]overnance theorists must be ready to explain not only what governance is, but also what it is not [and] be up-front about the biases in the concept and the implications of those biases." His proposed conceptualization of governance encompasses three parts: "(1) vertical and horizontal inter jurisdictional and inter-organizational cooperation; (2) extension of the state or jurisdiction by contracts or grants to third parties, including sub-governments; and (3) forms of public non-jurisdictional or nongovernmental policy making and implementation" (2005, 294). Governance, then, is "a kind of public administration" rather than a replacement for public administration" (2005, 295). Whether this becomes the definitive view remains to be seen.

PUBLIC MANAGEMENT OR PUBLIC *MANAGEMENT?*

The popularity of managerialism has reignited interest in one of the field's most enduring and fundamental questions: whether or not management is, or ought to be, any different in the public sector than in the private sector. As Johan Olsen noted (2003, 501, 522), New Public Management implies that "the public sector is not distinctive from the private sector," that its practitioners are "self-interested, utility maximizing administrators" in the manner of corporate executives. Still others fear managerialism's threat to the public service values that distinguish the public from the private sphere (Box 1998).

One's view on this issue has considerable practical importance. To the extent that public and private management involve similar temperaments, skills, and techniques, then the extensive body of ideas and practices relating to corporate success can be applied to the problems of public management, and the public sector can in principle draw on the large pool of private sector managers to meet its own managerial needs. To the extent that, from structural, craft, or institutional perspectives, the two sectors are different, then the public sector must have access to sources of knowledge, techniques, and skills suited to its unique character, a proposition that, unlike in the US, has long been accepted in Europe and elsewhere.

At the dawn of professional public administration in America, Frank J. Goodnow argued that "[i]n transacting its business [the government's] object is not usually the acquisition of gain but the furtherance of the welfare of the community. This is the great distinction between public and private business" (1893, 1902, 10). At a more subtle level, Goodnow argued that "the grant to the administration of . . . enormous discretionary powers" means that "[t]here has . . . been a continuous attempt on the part of the people to control the discretion of the administration in the exercise of the sovereign powers of the state" (1893, 1902, 10, 11). In 1926, Leonard D. White added that the principle of consistency – today, we would say equity – governs public administration to an extent not observed in business administration (White 1926). That same principle, "arising from the very root nature of the things with which [government] deals," had been cited by Englishman Josiah Stamp (1923, 168), who also noted that "[t]here is no possibility of a Government department experimenting, shall we say 'going off the deep end,' in anything requiring monetary expenditure, in the same way as the business can."

The matter of difference can be put even more succinctly: it is a matter of law. Public agencies and investor-owned corporations are governed by different bodies of law. In addition to the controlling influence of constitutional law, according to which public action must be reconciled to individual rights, the public sector is governed by administrative law. As Emmette Redford has pointed out, administrative law is directive in that it defines the purposes and methods which administrative organizations must pursue (Redford 1965), especially for activities that are quasi-legislative or quasi-judicial in nature. Corporate law, which governs the business sector, is, in contrast to public law, enabling rather than directive, in effect authorizing a firm's owners to pursue self-defined interests in ways largely left to their discretion, subject only to public laws which, while restrictive in various ways, never extinguish the default authority of owner discretion.

During the formative period of the administrative state in America, however, the industrial corporation was growing in economic power and in both political and cultural influence. As a consequence, business administration and the idea of management as a specialized function and skill were concurrently emerging as a focus for university-based teaching and research. In the efforts to combat what they saw as the pernicious consequences of the corrupt spoils system regimes, the reform-oriented founders of the American administrative state found it convenient to overlook the private sector's own tendencies toward corruption (including the corruption of public sector institutions) and advocate business-like management of the new and expanding regulatory and service agencies. Though it has ebbed and flowed, the idea of business-like government – hard-headed, efficient, competitive, results-oriented – has never lost its ideological appeal in the United States. In recent decades, that idea has attained world-wide popularity, as already noted, under the heading of New Public Management (discussed at length in Chapter 6).

Should the emphasis of scholarship and teaching, then, be placed on "public," and on the conceptual differences between a government or quasi-government entity and a private (for-profit or not-for-profit) enterprise? Or should it be placed on "management" and on its generic features: empirical similarities in the determinants and characteristics of managerial behavior and practice across sectors? This is both a normative and an empirical question.

The normative argument that public and private management are fundamentally unalike in all important respects (Allison 1983) has several elements. First, the public interest, as Goodnow argued, differs from private interests. Second, public officials, because they exercise the sovereign power of the state, are necessarily accountable to democratic, public service values above any particular private, material interest. Third, constrictions require equal treatment of persons and rule out the kind of selectivity that is essential to sustaining the profitability of a business. Les Metcalfe and Sue Richards (1993, 115) argue that "[w]hat distinguishes public management is explicit acknowledgment of responsibility for dealing with structural problems at the level of the system as a whole."

The empirical argument insists that the question be addressed on the basis of gathering evidence concerning actual similarities and differences in managerial values and behavior. The results of doing so, not surprisingly, are somewhat ambiguous. Hal Rainey and Young Han Chun (2005, 90) argue that "[u]ltimately, both sides in the continuing controversy over whether public and private management differ get to be right in a sense." However, they continue,

> the evidence indicates that most public managers [and especially those at higher levels] will face conditions much more strongly influenced by the governmental institutions and processes designed to direct them and hold them accountable, and by the goals of producing public goods and services in the absence of profit indicators and incentives, than will most managers in business firms.

The evidence supports the conclusion that "management in many private firms generally does have advantages over public management, in achieving operating efficiencies, but not always" (2005, 91).

Some will argue nonetheless that an enumeration of differences is misleading because it obscures important existential similarities. All organizations are public, argues Barry Bozeman (1987), by which he means that all organizations, whether governmental, for-profit, or non-profit, are affected to at least some degree by political authority. Thus, he argues (1987, 146), "[p]ublic managers can be found in most every type of organization" because public managers are not limited to government employees but encompass "persons who manage publicness" in any sector. However, one might also argue the converse, that all organizations are "private" to the extent that they are responsible for tasks that are performed by experts who are governed by professional or technocratic authority rather than (strictly) by stakeholder interests. These tasks were first recognized by Frank Goodnow (1967 [1900], 85) as "the semi-scientific, quasi-judicial, and quasi-business or commercial" functions of administration, although, as Don Price later warned (1959, 492), "the expert may come to believe that his science justifies exceeding his authority," a pervasive danger in all organizations requiring specialized expertise.

Professional acknowledgment is widespread that constitutions, collective goods, and electoral institutions create distinctive contexts for management that justify a separate field (Lynn 2005). The distinction between public and private management, then, is arguably definitive. The two sectors are constituted to serve different kinds of societal interests, and distinctive kinds of skills and values are appropriate to serving these different interests. That the distinctions may be obscured or absent when analyzing particular managerial responsibilities, functions, and tasks in particular organizations does not vitiate this conclusion.

PLAN AND METHOD OF THE BOOK

The content and purpose of the first two chapters of the book were described above. This section describes the plan and method for Chapters 3 to 8.

"Old," or traditional, public management, covering the period from antiquity through the 1960s in Continental Europe (France and Germany in particular), Great Britain, and the United States is the subject of Chapters 3, 4, and 5. "New" public management, or managerialism, covering developments beginning in the 1970s through the early years of the twenty-first century, is the subject of Chapters 6 and 7. Chapter 8 elaborates on the insights to be gained by viewing contemporary public management from a historically elongated perspective.

Continental European traditions of public management are discussed in Chapter 2 against the background of pre-modern developments in administrative thought and practice and their foreshadowing of later developments in the self-conscious administration of nation states. It was on the Continent, subsequent to the Peace of Westphalia in 1648, that the modern administrative state began to emerge in the absolutist regimes of France and the German states, and with it the systematic study and practice of "administrative science." It was on the Continent, too, that the rule of law – *Rechtsstaat* – quelled popular fears of unfettered bureaucratic power, enabling the reconciliation of popular sovereignty with the emergent bureaucratic institutions that had become the instruments of state authority.

The evolution of British public management is the subject of Chapter 4. Emerging within a framework of common, rather than positive (Roman, Napoleonic), law and of parliamentary rather than executive preeminence, public management in Great Britain is distinguished by its unique constitutional traditions. The British model of public management exerted a substantial influence throughout the British Empire and Commonwealth, including pre- and post-colonial America. At the same time, this model constitutes the point of departure for fully understanding the nature of what is commonly known as American exceptionalism.

Itself unique in combining a common law legal tradition, a popularly elected president, and a constitutionally prescribed separation of powers, the American model of public management, discussed in Chapter 5, emerged in recognizable form a century after its sovereignty and democratic traditions were well established. The founders of the modern American administrative state were, therefore, in a position to balance the obligations of its constitutional institutions with selective adaptation of "best practices" from Continental and British experience, in the process producing institutional innovations which have found their way back to Europe.

Developments beginning with the emergence of a managerial emphasis in American graduate schools of public affairs and with governmental responses to the political, economic, and fiscal challenges of the 1970s and 1980s are the subject of Chapter 6. It becomes evident that "old" national public management traditions and institutions ensured differentiated responses to comparable pressures for reform and change and that, in addition, significant adaptations of national institutions were occurring in each country that had little or nothing to do with managerialism.

These same developments are reconsidered in Chapter 7 from the perspective of delegation and accountability using theoretical lenses commonly associated with the subjects of public choice, positive political economy, and the new institutional economics. While this choice of lenses is neither inevitable nor uncontroversial, it is insightful, perhaps surprisingly so, with respect to the central issue of this book: revealing the historical continuities and discontinuities that are foundational to the study and practice of public management.

Finally, Chapter 8 takes up the questions: What is new? What is not new? In what ways are the answers to these questions of interest? A variety of theoretical perspectives are invoked to argue that, while fundamental transformations, "punctuations" if you will, are facts of history, they cannot obscure the fundamental path dependence of national administrative development, a dependence that has ensured and will continue to ensure the differentiation of state experiences and undermine the forces of convergence or isomorphism.

Beyond reference to the three-dimensional view of public management mentioned earlier (and discussed at greater length in Chapter 2), no particular effort is made to "pot" each nation's stories in identical containers (for example, using phases of state institutional evolution (Page 1995) or an institutional/descriptive scheme for administrative systems such as that of Pollitt and Bouckaert (2004)). Rather, the national narratives emerge as one finds them in the relevant literatures. Thus, the Continental story is about the emergence of administrative states from a sequence of absolutist institutions and popular revolutions leading toward *Rechtsstaats*; the British story is about the gradual evolution of a unitary administrative state governed by a royally sanctioned democratic parliament; and the American story is about the creation of a responsible and competent administrative state within a durable, legislatively centered regime of formally separated and federated powers. That said, a guiding purpose of the book is to identify similarities and differences that emerge from these stories and that will be useful to drawing appropriate lessons for scholarship and practice concerning public management as both a national and an international, comparative field.[15]

A final note concerns the choice of individual countries to explore in some depth. The selection of the United States, the United Kingdom, France, and Germany (the same basic scheme used by John Barlow and colleagues (1996) and, excluding the US, by

Arthur Benz (1995)) includes two "civic cultures" or "public interest regimes" (the US and the UK) and two Continental heartland, *Rechtsstaat* regimes (France and Germany). Each pair is differentiated in revealing ways, however. In terms of basic legal framework, France is Napoleonic whereas Germany is, well, Germanic. Although the US and the UK are common law regimes, formal authority is separated in the former, unified in the latter.

Left out of this scheme are the Scandinavian countries and Southern and Eastern European states, and smaller and geographically peripheral European states (such as Belgium, the Netherlands, Austria, Switzerland) that might be variously described as consociational, consensus democracies, neo-corporatist states, or culturally fragmented states (Kickert and Hakvoort 2000), and, of course, the rest of the world in all of its permutations and combinations.[16] The inclusion of three major state traditions and the variations among them is, however, sufficient for the book's purpose: to establish the relevance of the past to the present and future of public management.

NOTES

1 The importance of public management to the survival of democracy was argued in 1861 by John Stuart Mill (see Chapter 4), in 1936 by US president Franklin Roosevelt and his Committee on Administrative Management (the Brownlow Committee) at a time when America confronted powerful fascist, communist and anti-democracy movements (discussed further in Chapter 5), and in 1949 by J. R. Simpson, at the time a British Treasury official, during the earliest stages of the Cold War (discussed later in this chapter).

2 The United States, where management has long been a term of art, if not dominant theme, within public administration, is an exception, as will be discussed more fully later.

3 No such discussion can fail to acknowledge Andrew Dunsire's magisterial *Administration: The Word and the Science* (1973).

4 The deep historical background of administration and management is discussed further in Chapter 3.

5 The word "managing" in German is "wirthschafften."

6 The reference is to Goodnow's 1893 *Comparative Administrative Law.*

7 In his 1926 textbook, White rebuked the notion that public law is the proper foundation of public administration, arguing that "[T]he study of administration should start from the base of management rather than the foundation of law. . . . Public administration is the management of men and materials in the accomplishment of the purposes of the state" (White 1926, vii, 2).

8 It was the idea of administration as encompassing the quotidian functional activities of government that was the point of departure for the American policy schools' idea of public management as strategic and political.

9 The Wharton School was founded at the University of Pennsylvania in 1881, business schools at the University of Chicago and the University of California at Berkeley in 1898. By 1911, thirty business schools were in operation (George 1972), although Oliver Sheldon was saying in 1924 that "our science of management is in the most infantile stage" and "[m]anagement is in its youth" (36).

17

10 At virtually the same time, John Pfiffner (1935), in his second-generation textbook, was referring to "the new public administration" (following Gaus's 1923–4 usage of a similar term) but offering endorsement of White's "new management" usage.

11 The early writings of Jeremy Bentham distinguished between "contract-management" and "trust-management," the latter being equivalent to "management by one holding an office or duty to do so" (quoted in Dunsire 1973, 62).

12 Because British thought placed more emphasis on psychology, American writer Mary Parker Follett was more popular in the UK than in the US. See Follett (1918).

13 It is interesting to note that Leonard White quotes Sheldon in an epigraph to the first chapter of his 1926 textbook.

14 Lyndall Urwick (1969 [1937]) uses the word "government" in place of the word "management" in this quotation. Urwick (1969 [1937], 120) quotes Henri Fayol: "Administration is only one of these functions, but the managers of big concerns spend so much of their time on it, that their jobs seem to consist solely of administration."

15 Historical and comparative scholarship often employs, both deductively and inductively, various theories and causal arguments or analytic frameworks, a practice discussed at greater length in Chapter 8 (see Page 1995; Lynn 2001a). Various methods are used for confirming their explanatory power (such as narratives or storytelling, analytic narratives, interpretive case studies, or multiple lenses such as "traditions" (see Bevir, Rhodes and Weller 2003b)). This book constructs narrative accounts of national administrative developments generally guided by the three-dimensional analytic framework described above but has no greater theoretical pretensions.

16 Peters (2000) identifies four major state traditions: Anglo-Saxon, Continental European/Germanic, Continental European/French, and Scandinavian (a mix of Anglo-Saxon and Germanic).

Chapter 2

History and contemporary public management

INTRODUCTION

To many Americans and Europeans associated with the field of public management, there is no "old" public management. Much as poet Philip Larkin once quipped that sex was invented in 1963, many have argued that public management and public sector managerialism were invented in 1979 by Margaret Thatcher's government in Great Britain, or, more generally, in the last twenty to thirty years as management eclipsed administration as an ideology of public service delivery. Even when there is acknowledged to be an "old" public management, as is the case in the United States, its influence is being obliterated, so a popular argument goes, by global, regional, and national forces for change. Why, those who hold this view wonder, remain besotted with the past?

As already noted in Chapter 1 and argued at greater length in Chapter 8, there now exists a relatively new field of teaching, research, and practice called public management, with a robust and growing public management literature – complete with its own *Oxford Handbook of Public Management* – which, among other things, both reflects and documents the accelerating pace of world-wide interest in the subject. There exists as well a new rhetoric of managerial reform, new ways of thinking and talking about public management, and a new "community of discourse," developments which are reflected in the declared managerial goals and policies of most countries and international organizations.

All of these developments do not, however, add up to an accumulating record of transformed managerial institutions and practices or to a robust body of evidence concerning operational results and performance improvements. The growing body of empirical evidence is, if anything, inconclusive concerning actual achievements of the new emphasis on managerialism, suggesting that the managerial reforms of recent decades may have shallow roots and are, with few exceptions, incremental, heterodox, and often ephemeral, far more adaptive to national political and administrative traditions and contemporary political environments than to a new global paradigm, and not at all convergent.

If the various forces for change can summon a new professional field into existence but produce only ambiguous evidence concerning institutional transformation and performance improvement, what can we learn about the dynamics of institutional change under what is clearly a configuration of circumstances that challenges the status quo? What accounts for the incrementalism and heterodoxy of actual managerial change in the face of global transformations of markets, technologies, and popular aspirations? How should the answer to this question affect thinking concerning the design of and prospects for further public management reform?

This chapter first discusses the concept of path dependence as a potential explanation for the differentiated, incremental character of managerial reform and as a justification for examining the trajectories of change in various countries. Next, a three-dimensional definition of public management incorporating structures, practices, and institutionalized values is described, a definition that enriches the substantive implications of path dependence by suggesting the basic dimensions of its inner dynamics.

In addition to this conceptual preparation for the chapters to follow, there are appended to this chapter brief summary descriptions of the basic structures, practices, and institutionalized values of contemporary public management in each of the four countries examined closely in this book. The purpose of these descriptions is to provide a point of orientation for considering both the historical evolution of present arrangements, and recent adaptations, changes, and reforms that might, or might not, be transforming them.

The table will then be set for the assessment of public management old and new that begins in Chapter 3.

PATHWAYS OF CHANGE

The issues that arise under the heading of public management and its reform are, in fact, not at all new. In the United States at least, as noted in Chapter 1, neither is the term public management.

Public administration has ancient origins in the Orient and the Occident (as will be discussed further in Chapter 3). It is a necessary if not sufficient condition for the survival and growth of a successful sovereignty, whether the sovereign is the emperor, the crown, or the people. Administration came into existence to enable the maintenance of standing armies, the collection and administration of the sovereign's revenues, and the maintenance of internal order. Sixteenth- and seventeenth-century managerialisms were, it is worth noting, the wellsprings of modern economic science. From absolutist origins, public administration later became an indispensable concomitant of constitutional democracy.

Can there be a sovereign state without public management, without executive agencies swollen with unelected officers endowed with considerable discretion to act in their own, as well as the sovereign's, interests? The unequivocal answer is yes. The first American Republic, under the Articles of Confederation, in effect had but one branch of government: the Congress. (The first president of the United States was Samuel Huntington, "The President of the United States in Congress Assembled.") All state business was conducted by members and committees of members of the Continental Congress, which comprised representatives from each state. To take another case, that of Great Britain, only in the latter part of the nineteenth century, when the Northcote–Trevelyan civil service reforms and the doctrine of ministerial responsibility began to take effect, did the Crown's governments have a reliable, institutionalized means of implementing their policies. Prior to that, British governments were seriously lacking in organized administration.

One can imagine, as do most libertarians, a Hayekian catallaxy, that is, a self-organizing system of voluntary cooperation in which the state consists of a parliament to define property rights and rules governing private exchanges, which are enforced by ordinary courts of law. To Friedrich von Hayek, the price mechanism serves to distribute and synchronize local and personal knowledge on behalf of achieving the diverse ends of society's members. Primary dependence on that mechanism would make for an altogether different kind of state, but would be hardly beyond the pale if a sovereign people were determined to have it.

The fact is, however, that sovereigns create administrative institutions to carry out their purposes and have done so since ancient times. In little more than a decade, the American Confederation gave way to the Constitutional union, with its Article II establishing an executive branch of government, and by Jacksonian times, public administration was becoming structured and institutionalized. In the case of Great Britain, by the early twentieth century, Ramsay Muir was proclaiming that John Stuart Mill's "free England" had become "bureaucratic England," and a unified and obedient civil service implemented the government's policies. Administrative institutions are created and evolve in comprehensible ways. They are virtually inevitable.

Many will argue nonetheless that the "old or new" question is a distraction from the serious business of governing. As noted at the beginning of this chapter, some argue that, yes, public administration has a charming history, but that history is irrelevant to understanding present circumstances that demand competent management of governmental operations. "Clean-slate" analyses of state modernization and reinvention, perhaps framed by public choice, organizational, or other appropriate theories, will provide serviceable knowledge for policy making and practice. The historical contexts of change may be useful for cautionary lessons, but historicism need not burden the field's search for solutions to the challenging management problems of the twenty-first century.

Others take an opposing perspective: nothing much is really new. That which is said to be new may represent no more than a linguistic shift, the substitution of one term of art for another (for example, of "public management" for "public administration"), or the adoption as a political convention of expedient coinages (such as "New Public Management"), or the refocusing of attention from one aspect of a well-established subject to another (for example, from "control" to "coordination"), or, finally, a recon-ceptualization of previously identified phenomena (for example, recasting the traditional problem of accountability as a "principal–agent" problem). If we look below the surface

21

of current public management discourse, according to these skeptics, we shall find an enduring intellectual and practical agenda related to the design, practice, and improvement of government administration. The "new" is epiphenomenal.

Still others argue that the "old or new" question is of considerable importance because it is about whether or not, and how, the past either enlightens or fetters our ability to understand the problems of contemporary, some would say post-modern or post-industrial, government. If, on the one hand, the issues associated with public management and its reform are in significant measure "old," then those interested in public management reform and state modernization can benefit from insights derived from the long history of efforts to create and sustain effectively functioning states and governing institutions. From this perspective, history reveals the fundamental dynamics of state building, the better to evaluate contemporary prospects for governmental reform and the adaptation of public institutions to new circumstances (Nash 1969, Gladden 1972a, 1972b; Kickert and Hakvoort 2000).

Against the hypothesis of global transformation and isomorphism, the cardinal "clean-slate" proposition of New Public Management, is another hypothesis: changes in the managerial structures, practices, and institutions in any country during any period are "path dependent." As Douglass North, the economist and theorist of the evolution of institutions, puts it (1990, 98), "[a]t every step along the way there [are] choices – political and economic – that [provide] real alternatives. Path dependence is a way to narrow conceptually the choice set and link decision making through time." Relations among political choices over time can, for example, be formally expressed as a hierarchical structural model that incorporates a complex lag structure, a structure which might even be recursive.[1]

In short, when it comes to managerial reform and change, countries are unlikely to wander very far from their paths, even when confronting revolutionary changes in their societies, so it is important to know what paths they are on. The present is influenced in systematic ways by prior choices and conventions. Thus, as we shall see, American public management reflects the Founders' choices concerning, among other things, the formal separation of powers; British public management reflects the evolution of parliamentary sovereignty and the diverse authorities of its uncodified constitution. French and German public management reflect the transformation of absolutist bureaucracies into democratic *Rechtsstaaten*, albeit in different ways. Without understanding these path dynamics, we cannot understand why, when it comes to public management reform, America is incoherent and incremental, Great Britain is, or can be, zealous, Germany is reluctant, and France is both reluctant and indirect.[2]

One's passion for or indifference toward history and the concept of path dependence may well depend on one's disciplinary or epistemological orientation. Most public choice theorists, for example, tend to emphasize the structural determinants of individual and collective choice in government agencies. Their question is: what consequences for governmental outcomes and performance will follow from changes in organizational structures and incentives? Approaches such as these relegate to the background, or treat only tangentially, the cultures and traditions that are the contexts for public management improvement.[3] Many contemporary institutionalists, too, tend to focus on existing administrative systems and to take an ahistorical, pragmatic view of the possibilities for public management reform.[4]

Interpretivists and historians are, in contrast, inclined to emphasize contexts of all kinds: organizational, professional, structural/legal, historical, and national/cultural/social. For them, the importance of national traditions is almost too obvious to require justification. Their question is: based on our understanding of national traditions, how might the future unfold in the event that certain changes in governmental arrangements are adopted? What are the prospects for far-reaching, fundamental change? Similarly, those with a conventional historical orientation are apt to take for granted that the present depends on the past in complex ways. They tend to be critical of ahistorical analysis and at least initially skeptical of all arguments to the effect that the future will be unlike the past. Their question is: if we are able to identify historical pathways of change, how might this knowledge influence our expectations and actions concerning the prospects for public management reform?

To this debate about the influence of the past on the present, one might well respond: "it's an empirical question." That assertion is the point of departure for this book. Gaining perspective on the importance of the past depends on attempting to understand, at least in a general sense, how history affects the comparative evolution of state and governmental institutions. In Elaine Swift and David Brady's view (1994, 83), "[b]ecause a longer time line confronts scholars with conditions of stability and instability, thereby challenging them to account for both, historically-informed theory is more likely to be dynamic, that is, better able to account for both continuity and change." More specifically, Kickert and Hakvoort (2000, 223) argue that "the institutionalized context of a particular state and administration is relevant for the form and content . . . reforms assume there, and for their success and failure."

A careful consideration of "public management old and new," then, is important to locating the subject of public management within the larger community of inquiry into the nature and evolution of organized societies and democratic governments. As Leonard White noted in his seminal American textbook (White 1926, 4): "[T]he natural history of administration connects its ancient and modern forms in an unbroken sequence of development."

As noted above, it will be useful to have a definition or view of public management that facilitates the depiction of pathways of change. Path dependence can be fully understood only if we broaden the definition of public management to recognize its multiple, interrelated dimensions. What exactly are we talking about when we talk about public management?[5]

PUBLIC MANAGEMENT: A THREE-DIMENSIONAL VIEW

To many American teachers and practitioners, public management is about managerial practice or craft or operational choice, that is, about what officials holding managerial positions in government *do* and about how they might go about both their extraordinary and quotidian tasks in the most effective and responsible way. To many Europeans, public management is about the operational aspects, the effective functioning, of public services: organization, control, performance, and accountability (Keeling 1972; Pollitt and Bouckaert 2004). Despite their differences of emphasis, both American and European perspectives view public management as concerned with managerial actions *within given policy and institutional settings* (Moore 1995; Toonen and Raadschelders 1997; Toonen 1998). Such definitions, as Pollitt and Bouckaert (2004) imply, seem especially appropriate to European *Rechtsstaat* regimes, but they are relevant to most hierarchical managerial arrangements, especially if the emphasis is on short-run performance.

Many other scholars, especially those associated with traditional public administration, believe that such a restrictive assumption unduly narrows the intellectual range and intrinsic importance of the subject of public management. To them, public management necessarily incorporates those structural, legal, and procedural arrangements that constrain and enable managerial practice in government and that give formal expression to the politically expressed values of state and society: a "welfare state," a "liberal state," an "activating state," a "nightwatch state." From the work of Stewart Ranson and John Stewart (1994), for example, Christopher Pollitt has derived a complex, multidimensional list of "specific issues" for public management that include cognizance of the socio-political system, public behavior, and societal change (Pollitt 2003).

Considerable misunderstanding and miscommunication can result from failure to distinguish the multiple dimensions of public management. The argument here is that the subject of public management, whether the object of managerial concern is a policy, an agency, a program, a function, or a territorial jurisdiction, necessarily includes three distinct but interrelated dimensions, expressed in shorthand as structure, craft, and institution.[6] That is to say, public management should be viewed broadly as encompassing the organizational structures, managerial practices, and institutionalized values by which officials enact the will of sovereign authority, whether that authority is prince, parliament, or the people. Use of this analytic framework both clarifies the axes of tension and miscommunication among the field's many participants and, more to the point of this book, assists in sorting out issues concerning that which is old and that which is new and why such a distinction might be important. It will be useful, then, to sketch this framework more fully.

Structure and process

As a matter of both administrative science and practical statecraft, formally mandated structures and processes have long been regarded as having a determinative influence on the conduct and accomplishments of public officials. Formal authority both enables and constrains officials' activities toward the ends of the polity or of the elites claiming to act in its name or represent its interests. Public administration's classic American literature understood management in a democracy to be the responsible and lawful exercise of discretion by public administrators (Davy 1962; Bertelli and Lynn 2003). In this view, public management is a *structure* of governance, that is, a formalization of managerial discretion intended to enable public officials to effect the will of the people or, better, to give effect to the balance of interests among them (Lynn 2003; Bertelli 2004). In remarkable point of fact, despite the proliferation of new forms and tools of public governance, such as networks and partnerships, the preferred form of formal organization has been and continues to be bureaucracy, and bureaucratic organizations remain the most common settings for public management (Meier and Hill 2005).

The importance of structures and processes – the organization and programmatic and regulatory responsibilities of departments or ministries, the requirements of an administrative procedure act or of civil service regulations, statutorily mandated evaluation, planning, budgeting, and reporting – to effective public management was memorably highlighted in the United States by the diagnosis of Vice President Al Gore early in the Clinton administration that the problem of government was "good people trapped in bad systems" (Gore 1993, 2). To Gore, as to British prime minister Margaret Thatcher, US president Ronald Reagan, Canadian prime minister Brian Mulroney and numerous other policy makers of recent years, "bad systems" meant, simply, "bureaucracy": public agencies and employees muffled in the red tape of "budget systems, personnel systems, procurement systems, financial management systems, information systems" (Gore 1993, 2) and lacking any motivation to improve the efficiency and quality of public service delivery.

The Clinton administration's argument about bad systems was sustained by the claim, popularized in the US and globally by David Osborne and Ted Gaebler's *Reinventing Government* (1992), that Weberian bureaucracy, once considered the most efficient form of organization, was rapidly yielding to more flexible, team-oriented, decentralized, virtual, and consociational – in short, democratic and networked – forms of resource allocation, coordination, and control. Owing to dramatically reduced costs of communication and information exchange and to growing employee demands for autonomy and flexibility, these forms were said to have become the most efficient and responsive means of delivering on public policy mandates. Citizens, now recast as consumers of public services, would reward leaders who could create a government that "works better and costs less" with the coin of popularity and trust.

That bureaucratic power, symbolized by red tape, is a threat to democracy is hardly a new issue, as subsequent chapters will show. Popular fears of executive and bureaucratic autonomy and power were central to the popular revolutions in America and on the European Continent and to the evolution of British political philosophy in the late eighteenth and nineteenth centuries. The issue preoccupied not only the founders of the

American Republic but, a century later, the reformers who began to design the American administrative state. The various structural and procedural solutions inspired by these popular movements – formal separation of powers, *Rechtsstaat*, parliamentary supremacy, a civil service of either neutral, liberally educated officials or technically trained experts acting in the interests of the state, doctrines of managerial responsibility, representative bureaucracy – remain pillars of administrative states to this day.

At the same time, public bureaucracies that are under proper democratic control have been extolled as a solution to the problem of ensuring that sovereign power – in democracies, "the people" – has the capacity to implement its policies. Hierarchical, bureaucratic organizations, Weber and many others argued, ensure not only administrative transparency and accountability to sovereign authority but also the institutionalization of the impartial expertise necessary to meet the complex, technical needs of the modern state. In late nineteenth-century Germany, Lorenz von Stein, following Hegel, expressed high esteem for bureaucrats, who represented unselfish service to the state against the opposing power of special interests. American Progressives viewed hierarchical departments staffed by a neutrally competent civil service as antidotes to the corruption and inefficiency of a spoils system based on the rotation-in-office of technically unqualified political hacks. British socialists likewise viewed bureaucracy as a means for accomplishing just and humane government. Bureaucratic power, summed up Guy Peters (1996, 8), "may simply be a prerequisite of effective government in contemporary society."

The term "structures and processes" is not restricted to the organization and operations of the departments, ministries, and agencies of government, however. Included as well are the great variety of formal (whether constitutional, statutory, or judicially enjoined) arrangements which enable and constrain the internal administration of the state. These arrangements include, for example, the existence, powers and subordination of different levels of government, rules governing elections and office holding, and provisions defining such matters as the separation of powers, levels of concentration or centralization within organizations or territorial jurisdictions, the allocation and management of public funds, and accounting and auditing systems. To an increasing extent in Europe, these arrangements include the structures and processes of the European Union and Commission.

From a structural perspective, public management history necessarily encompasses both "constitutional history," that is, the evolution of institutions of state sovereignty, and "administrative history," that is, evolution of the formal structures and processes of constitutional government. Subsequent chapters will show that the interrelationships between these two histories vary across countries. In France, for example, a constitutional event, the adoption of the Fifth Republic, had pervasive effects on subsequent administrative history. In the United Kingdom, in contrast, the managerial reforms of Margaret Thatcher and subsequent governments, vivid chapters of British administrative history, have, by the peculiar alchemy that is the "unwritten constitution" of the United Kingdom, had major implications for British constitutional history. Understanding these interrelationships is vital to understanding how history matters to the form and direction of public management reforms in various countries.

Craft

Beginning in the 1970s, scholars and teachers at America's new graduate schools of public policy (at Harvard University, Princeton University, the University of California, and elsewhere) began to advance a perspective on public management that was an intentional departure from what they perceived as traditional American public administration. This new perspective emphasized what Roscoe C. Martin had earlier termed "the nature of the craft" (Martin 1965, 8), that is, a concern for decisions, action, and outcomes, and for the personal skills needed to perform effectively in specific managerial roles. "[S]trategic political thinking sets off the public manager who is able to *move* an agency from one who plays a custodial role," argued Donald Stokes (1986, 55). "[T]he strategic manager sees the small openings presented by the agency's routine to induce change toward an identified goal, step-by-step." In Mark Moore's view, the gist of public management is "conceiving and implementing public policies that realize the potential *of a given political and institutional setting*" (1984, 3, italics added), potential he later termed "creating public value" (Moore 1995).

In Europe, managerialism was viewed as officials "acting differently from traditional civil servants and also in different ways from leaders of private organizations" (Eliassen and Kooiman 1993, 16). An actor-focused literature began to appear in which European scholars began to focus on public managers and their practices (Kooiman and Eliassen 1993a; Barlow *et al.* 1996). John Barlow and his colleagues (1996, 24) observed that "personnel working in the public sector are increasingly required to be more flexible in the ways that they work and the work that they do." Christopher Pollitt's 2003 *The Essential Public Manager* emulates the American craft literature using cases and examples to motivate learning.

The new appreciation for craft was hardly unprecedented. E. N. Gladden (1972a, 239) noted that "the senior administrator of the eleventh century A.D. was facing daily tasks that differed little from those of his successor in succeeding ages. . . . The early officials were generalists, but nevertheless one cannot avoid being impressed by the broad functional scope of their activities." The craft perspective was present in traditional American literature (Bertelli and Lynn 2005). For example, in *Bureaucracy: A Challenge to Better Management: A Constructive Analysis of Management Effectiveness in the Federal Government*, Joseph Juran (1944, 136) argued that, although not yet not trusted, the managers of public bureaucracies confront the need to take action "which through professional pride will resist management uncleanliness, and which in the passing years will build up a lasting tradition of good management." Drawing on personal observation and experience, Donald Stone (1945, 212) argued that the executive's job is to "maximize his influence" throughout the organization rather than relying exclusively upon his formal authority and power of command, overcoming strong centrifugal forces in the process.

27

Numerous other authors attempted to articulate what public managers actually do and the lessons that could be derived from their experience.

The "reinvented" craft perspective on public management grew out of the increasing academic interest in the subject of public policy implementation in American public policy schools (Lynn 1996).[7] This perspective soon became closely identified with the case method of teaching long popular in American business schools, thereby reinforcing the impression in some quarters that the craft perspective reflected a managerial ideology rather than a political orientation. In recent years, this perspective has become virtually synonymous with what is termed "best practices" or "smart practices" (Overman and Boyd 1994; Lynn 1996; Bardach 1998).

The craft dimension of public management encompasses the operational and pragmatic concerns of public officials who have managerial responsibilities and are motivated to apply proven, actionable ideas to the problems they face or, alternatively, to fashion solutions appropriate to their specific circumstances. A much lower priority is placed by this perspective on the manager's role in developing institutional capacity and in adhering to durable democratic values that legitimize their role (although the subject of "managerial ethics" is given some attention). In America, although not in Europe, there tends to be less emphasis, as well, on management at middle and lower levels of administration. The popularity of the craft perspective in professional education in part reflects the fact that it brings drama, resonance, and verisimilitude to a subject matter, governmental administration, often regarded by students and their teachers as uninspiring.

Unlike many American innovations in public management research and teaching, the craft perspective has enjoyed limited popularity in Europe and elsewhere (although a European, Giandomenico Majone, was a leading creator of the perspective; see Majone 1980, 1989). There are exceptions, however, including Desmond Keeling's *Management in Government* (1972), which reflects the intellectual influence of Simon's *Administrative Behavior* (1947), and Pollitt's *The Essential Public Manager* (2003), which uses case-like examples to motivate student learning and reflects on managerial values, ethics, and motivation. Both works are, however, more oriented toward "management" than toward "managers" or "managing" within given institutional frameworks. Clearly within this perspective, however, is Mirko Noordegraaf's *Attention! Work and Behavior of Public Managers amidst Ambiguity* (2000), which sets out to answer the question, "What do public managers do?" based on the author's having observed twelve public managers at work.

The formality of America's separation of powers combined with its common law jurisprudence (discussed in Chapter 5) is primarily responsible for the popularity of the craft perspective there.[8] These institutions tend to highlight the importance accorded to public managers as individuals in their own right rather than as the embodiment of the state as an instrument of the popular will. Further, these institutions reinforce the importance of the individual case and its precedential value (for example, as a "best practice" or "success story" or as evidence in a so-called "class action" (or institutional reform) lawsuit) more than the deductive formality of *Rechtsstaat* regimes (discussed in

28

Chapter 3) or the unifying conventions of Westminster regimes (discussed in Chapter 4) that ensure the sovereignty of parliament. An emphasis on craft is, moreover, congruent with America's relatively pragmatic, experiential approach to professional education and practice, with its emphasis on cases, examples, inductive reasoning, and expedient, or "second best," solutions to specific and immediate (rather than systemic or institutional) problems.

Institutionalized values

Accumulating evidence that demonstrable and enduring improvements in public management and governmental performance are exceptionally difficult to achieve has brought into the foreground of public management reform discussion yet a third dimension of public management: the values that infuse the organizations and practices of public management, values that often seem beyond the reach of formal structural controls or of managerial craftsmanship. The sources of these values are diverse and include beliefs within the wider society, professional standards, informal norms of practice, ethical precepts, institutional memory, and shared experience.

Historically, controversies that have arisen over the role of bureaucracy in national governance have reflected concerns not only for the structural power of bureaucracies but for what are often held to be the anti-democratic values of empowered bureaucrats. Bureaucratic values have always been much more suspect in America than in Europe, however. In a European *Rechtsstaat* such as France or Germany, "service to the state" by those trained in the impartial application of the legal framework has been a generally accepted legitimizing value. In Great Britain, officials' taken-for-granted commitment to serving the Crown and its governments has performed a similar legitimizing function. Ensuring that American public servants' values will faithfully reflect democratic ideals and policy mandates has proven more elusive, and the legitimacy of "unelected bureaucrats" is a hot-button issue in American politics. European solutions to legitimacy having long been regarded as politically unacceptable, American administrative reformers have been reduced to exhorting public officials to be "responsible" or "professional" or "democratic." There is, however, no consensus and considerable controversy concerning what such terms might mean in practice.

In recent years, issues associated with institutionalized values have become especially prominent in both Europe and America. This dimension of public management is reflected, for example, in the controversies associated with public management reforms such as "reinventing government" or New Public Management (discussed at greater length in Chapter 6). The neo-liberal critique of government in Great Britain, the United States, and elsewhere was in fact intended to be an indictment of traditional, and undemocratic, public service values. In their turn, the traditionalists' critique of these reforms indicted the emphasis placed on consumerism and efficiency narrowly construed.

In renouncing bureaucracy, policy makers' primary means of effecting the public will, Ezra Suleiman (2003), for example, argues that neo-liberal politicians are undermining their own legitimacy and that of the democratic state. Paul du Gay is concerned by the way the differences between public and private sectors have been eroded by a mistaken belief that the public sector, and its staff, are somehow incomplete versions of their private sector counterparts (du Gay 1996, 2000; du Gay and Salaman 1992). "Entrepreneurial governance" has, he says, come to be "the dominant form of management" (du Gay 2000, 6, quoted by Dingwall and Strangleman 2005, 483). He continues:

> If . . . "entrepreneurial governance" has one overarching target – that which it most explicitly defines itself in opposition to – then it is the impersonal, procedural, hierarchical and technical organization of the Weberian bureau. Put simply, bureaucratic government is represented as the "paradigm that failed".

Christopher Pollitt (2003) gives extended consideration to the question, are public service ethics being undermined by the new public management? There can be, he insists, no clear-cut answer.

The relative popularity of the terms "administration" and "management" in a public sector context is itself believed to have implicit value implications. Marshall Dimock (in Thomas 1978, xvi) once asserted that "[m]ost Americans feel that the term 'management' is preferable to 'administration'" because it sounds dynamic rather than wooden, whereas the British are apt to see administration as implying principled respect for others and management as manipulative and self-aggrandizing.[9] More recently, Peter Aucoin has argued (1990, 118) that "[t]he very term 'management' is one that derives from private sector experience, denoting as it does a concern for the use of resources to achieve results in contrast to the presumed focus of 'administration' as the adherence to formalized processes and procedures." In a similar vein, David Rosenbloom (1998, 16) argues that "[t]hose who define public administration in managerial terms tend to minimize the distinctions between public and private administration." The term "administration," in this view, conveys respect for the constitutional and political foundations of governance, whereas the term "management" implies respect for, even deference to, the organizations, methods, and values of the business sector.[10]

The elusiveness of public management values has invited normative exhortation, especially in America, where the separation of powers creates a vacuum of legitimizing values. In a popular early view, Leonard White argued that the objective of administration is efficient use of resources. It is also, however, "the most expeditious, economical, and complete achievement of public programs" (1926, 4). Not only that, other objectives of the state include the protection of private rights, the development of civic capacity and sense of civic responsibility, the due recognition of the manifold phases of public opinion, the maintenance of order, and the provision of a national minimum of welfare.

In another representative American view, Fritz Morstein Marx (1949, 1127) insisted that "[t]he highest task of public administration is . . . to serve as an effective instrument in attaining the purposes of the political order." Administrators "must act as

30

the conscious agents of a democratic community [and] . . . seeking ways of stimulating civic participation in public management is a corollary of the ethical derivative . . . that administrative officials are bound by duty to promote the healthy growth of a free society" (1949, 1128, 1131). More simply, he said, reminiscent of the cameralists, the "mission of public management" is to seek "the common good." Morstein Marx (1949, 1137) cautioned, however, that

> [h]owever deep-felt their concern with the common good, government officials are constitutionally out of order in undertaking to serve as a continuing corrective in the political process. . . . There is no basis in administrative ethics for the official's right to overrule democracy if it is in favor of democracy as it ought to be.

Although the legitimacy of administration has long been accepted in Europe, Europeans, too, have felt the urge to identify or prescribe the meta-values of administrators. Christopher Hood's three sets of core values in public management, for example, include parsimony and economy; honesty and fairness; and reliability, survivability, and adaptive capacity (Hood 1991). Christopher Pollitt (2003) cites various categories of values identified in a 1996 Canadian Report of the Task Force on Public Service Values and Ethics: democratic values (accountability, lawfulness, fidelity to the common good), professional values (merit, impartiality, service), general ethical values (integrity, equity, probity), and people values (civility, respect for differences). Such enumerations lead Pollitt to the view that governing values, while durable in many respects, vary across contexts and over time.

The significance of institutionalized values has arisen as well in specific organizational contexts. The controversial crash of the American space shuttle *Columbia*, for example, over a decade after the space shuttle *Challenger* suffered a similar fate for similar reasons, focused attention on the renitent organizational culture of the National Aeronautics and Space Administration and, in particular, its ingrained approach to safety-of-flight issues. The controversies that have surrounded the activities of the American Federal Bureau of Investigation, Central Intelligence Agency, and Internal Revenue Service have raised questions about the deeply ingrained values that infuse the managers and line employees of these agencies, values that seem defiant of national policies and democratic precepts. Similar issues have arisen concerning failures of the National Health Service and of other organizations in the United Kingdom (Dingwall and Strangleman 2005).

Issues associated with organizational culture were popularized by a number of publications in the early 1980s such as Thomas Peters and Robert Waterman's *In Search of Excellence* (1982) and Terrence Deal and Allan Kennedy's *Corporate Cultures: The Rites and Rituals of Corporate Life* (1982; see also Ouchi and Wilkins 1985). "Culture," argues Susan Wright, "has turned from being something an organization *is* into something an organization *has*, and from being a process embedded in context to an objectified tool of management control. The use of the term culture itself becomes ideological" (in S. Wright 1994, 4, quoted by Dingwall and Strangleman 2005, 474). The idea of

31

managing or manipulating culture is now an accepted aspect of managerial craftsmanship (Khademian 2002).

Throughout this book, the significance of these three dimensions, individually and jointly, will be a leitmotif of the analysis. In Chapter 8, it will become clear how distinguishing among them assists in interpreting the significance of whatever changes have occurred in the era of managerialism.

PUBLIC MANAGEMENT IN FRANCE, GERMANY, THE UNITED KINGDOM, AND THE UNITED STATES: OVERVIEWS

To serve as points of orientation for subsequent chapters, there follow brief descriptions of contemporary public management in France, Germany, the United Kingdom and the United States. As noted earlier, "old" public management will account for the historical emergence of these arrangements; "new" public management will analyze how these arrangements appear to be evolving under contemporary forces for change.

France

France is a democratic republic deriving its sovereignty from the people but, in the Napoleonic tradition, relying on the direct imposition of central state authority over its citizens more than Germany, the UK, or the US (Peters 2000). The current constitution was adopted on 28 September 1958 but formally recognizes the authority of the 1789 Declaration of the Rights of Man. The state is divided into twenty-two regions which are subdivided into ninety-six departments. There is a strong central presence at regional and local levels through the office of the *préfet* and many local units of central ministries (Pollitt and Bouckaert 2004), although decentralization of state authority has gradually been taking place.

The chief of state is the president, who is elected by popular vote for a five-year term. The head of government is the prime minister, who is nominated by the National Assembly majority and appointed by the president. The prime minister is not, however, in a powerful position *vis-à-vis* the president. France is generally regarded as having a strong central government and a strong administrative tradition in the Napoleonic/ Gaullist tradition and, since 1958, a strong executive, especially when the president's political party forms the government.

France's legislative branch is a bicameral parliament consisting of the Senate, or *Sénat*, and the National Assembly, or *Assemblée Nationale*. The Senate has 321 seats, 296 of which are for metropolitan France, 13 for overseas departments, and 12 for French nationals abroad. Members are indirectly elected by an electoral college to serve nine-year terms.

The National Assembly has 577 seats, its members elected by popular vote through a single-member majoritarian system to serve five-year terms.

The state is the protector of *la volonté générale*, its civil servants, the *haute fonctionnaire publique*, educated at one of the *hautes écoles* and members of one of the *grands corps*, such as the *Conseil d'État* or the *Cours des Comptes*. Many top politicians are graduates of the *École Nationale d'Administration* (ENA) (and are called *Enarques*) and, via the *pantouflage* (civil servants assuming executive roles in companies formerly under their jurisdiction), experienced in the management of the large state corporations or the private sector or even politics. Up to 1993, eight of the previous eleven prime ministers had been civil servants (Pollitt and Bouckaert 2004).

France has a civil law system and judicial review of administrative but not legislative acts. There are three distinct courts within the judicial branch. The Supreme Court of Appeals, or *Cour de Cassation*, is made up of judges appointed by the president from nominations of the High Council of the Judiciary. The Constitutional Council, or *Conseil Constitutionnel*, consists of three members appointed by the president, three members appointed by the president of the National Assembly, and three appointed by the president of the Senate. Finally, the Council of State, or *Conseil d'État*, which performs both judicial and administrative functions and is a "supreme court" for administration, is composed of senior jurists, whose head is regarded as the foremost civil servant in France. France is a *Rechtsstaat* in that the administrative system "is regulated by legal rules which conceive the state administration as inhabiting an autonomous domain apart from civil society" (Pollitt and Bouckaert 2004, 249).

Germany

Germany is a constitutional, federal republic. The 1949 constitution (extended to a unified Germany in 1990) is known as the Basic Law, or *Grundgesetz*. It was designed to preclude the emergence of either another fragmented and ineffective Weimar Republic or another authoritarian Nazi-type regime. The Basic Law regulates both federal administration and the implementation of federal laws, and guarantees the principles on which public administration is based (Badura 2001). The three main principles are the separation of powers, federalism, and local government. Accordingly, the republic comprises 16 *Länder*, or states (including three city states: Berlin, Bremen, and Hamburg), nearly 330 counties and well over 14,000 non-county municipalities (Pollitt and Bouckaert 2004).

The largely symbolic chief of state is the president, who is elected for a five-year term by a federal convention that includes all members of the Federal Assembly and an equal number of delegates elected by the state parliaments. The head of government is the chancellor, who is elected by an absolute majority of the Federal Assembly for a four-year term. The chancellor "sets the political course" and determines the number and responsibilities of ministers, whom he or she appoints. The federal ministers are, like the chancellor, independent constitutional entities, each with his or her own duties and

33

powers (Badura 2001). Ministers are both members of the government and heads of their departments. Unlike those in Westminster systems, however, German ministers are not assumed to be accountable to parliament. Due to the high level of independence enjoyed by federal ministers, coordination problems between ministries arise.

Germany's legislative branch is a bicameral parliament which consists of the Federal Assembly, or *Bundestag*, and the Federal Council, or *Bundesrat*. The Federal Assembly has 603 seats, and representatives are elected for four-year terms by popular vote utilizing a system combining direct and proportional representation. The Federal Council has a total of 69 votes, which directly represent the state governments. Each state government has three to six votes depending on population and is required to vote as a block. There are no elections for the Federal Council, because its composition is determined by the composition of the state governments, meaning the composition of the Federal Council has the potential to change any time once of the sixteen *Länder* holds an election. Implementation of federal legislation (and of European Union law) is the responsibility of the *Länder*, which are organizationally autonomous, with their own constitutions and administrations. Most federal ministries also exist at the *Land* level, but the central government plays a limited role in direct service delivery.

Unlike the US, Germany has a single, unified civil service. The state is viewed as a transcendental entity, and its citizens are members of an organic society; civil servants, or *Beamte*, are "personifications of the power and centrality of the state" and have a firm legal and moral status (Peters 2000). The Federation determines the legal status, pay, and pensions of all civil servants. Civil servants are distinct from state employees, who are governed by private sector labor law. The Basic Law reserves to civil servants "the right to act on behalf of the state," thus affirming the concept of a permanent civil service loyal to the constitution. In general, civil servants have a lifetime occupation and appropriate salary, and are impartial and politically neutral, moderate and dedicated to public service. The upper levels of the civil service, however, are highly politicized, and high-level civil servants may leave their posts or take leave with a change in administration (Pollitt and Bouckaert 2004).

Germany is a classic *Rechtsstaat*, with a highly juridified Weberian bureaucracy. Germany has a civil law system and a Federal Constitutional Court. Half of the judges are elected by the Federal Assembly and half are elected by the Federal Council. The sole function of the Federal Constitutional Court, the *Bundes Verfassungsgericht*, is judicial review, and it has the power to declare as unconstitutional acts of all three branches of government. Unlike the US Supreme Court, however, the Federal Constitutional Court does not serve as a regular court of appeals from lower courts. Issues may be brought directly to the court by persons, regular courts, political institutions, or federal institutions, and the court is constitutionally mandated to review the validity of statutes immediately after they are passed upon the petition of one-third of parliament's members. It is a reticent body (Kickert and Hakvoort 2000); there are no "activist judges," as in the US.

United Kingdom

The United Kingdom is both a constitutional monarchy and a parliamentary democracy governed by an "unwritten constitution," which John Rohr (2002) prefers to call an uncodified constitution with substantial written elements. The British constitution consists of several kinds of elements: acts of parliament; principles of common law; major scholarly treatises concerning matters of law and its interpretation; the body of law that relates to the status and operation of parliament and its members; and, finally, unwritten "conventions" or accepted ways of conducting public affairs, which are numerous and significant. There is no formal separation of powers.

The UK comprises Great Britain (England and Wales – a single legal jurisdiction – and Scotland) and Northern Ireland. England is subdivided into nearly fifty boroughs, three dozen counties, nearly thirty London boroughs, a dozen cities and boroughs, ten districts, a dozen cities, and three royal boroughs. The other components of the UK are similarly subdivided into local jurisdictions. The national government is the only level of government with permanent legal status. While this fact hardly means that local government is unimportant, it does mean that sub-national levels of government can be reformed at the will of the national government. In England, excluding greater London and eight regions of relatively minor importance, local government exhibits one of two patterns: unitary authorities, where an elected district council is responsible for all services, and non-unitary authorities, where responsibility for services is divided between elected county councils and district councils.

The chief of state is the reigning head of the royal family: the Crown. The formal prerogatives of the Crown include the power to approve all acts of parliament (not exercised since the reign of Queen Anne early in the eighteenth century), to make treaties (exercised on the advice of the foreign secretary), to grant pardons (exercised on the advice of the home secretary), to dissolve parliament (exercised on the advice of the prime minister), and to wage war (exercised on behalf of the Sovereign by the prime minister). By convention, these prerogatives are delegated, and the monarch plays a largely ceremonial role.

The head of government is the prime minister, who is usually the leader of the majority party or coalition in parliament and comes to power following parliamentary elections. The executive branch also has a cabinet of ministers whose members are appointed by the prime minister. By relatively recent convention, its key members must come from the House of Commons. General government ministers, about 120 in total, are appointed from within either house of parliament. Because members of parliament run the risk of losing ministerial office if they vote against the government, the government in power has important leverage ("payroll voting") over parliament. Primary legislation often delegates to ministers the power to implement the legislation by the making of Orders and Regulations, termed "delegated legislation," which must be approved "en bloc" by a resolution of parliament and which may be reviewed by the courts. The Crown's prerogative power to create and abolish offices affords the British

35

government considerable flexibility, including, for example, the power to create, abolish, and reorganize ministries at will.

The British legislature consists of the Sovereign and a bicameral parliament: the House of Commons and the House of Lords. The House of Lords consists of 500 life peers, 92 hereditary peers, and 26 clergy. The House of Commons has 659 seats, and members are elected by popular vote within their districts to serve five-year terms unless the house is dissolved earlier.

The formal authority for the civil service is an order-in-council rather than an act of parliament. Civil servants are considered to be servants of the Crown subject to the authority of ministers appointed by the Crown.

The United Kingdom has a common law tradition. Judicial review is the responsibility of an Administrative Court, a component of the Queen's Bench Division of the High Court, whose judges hear cases in which a citizen wishes to challenge the legality of action or inaction by a minister, government department, or other public authority. Actions may be declared "*ultra vires*" (or beyond the power granted by) the enabling legislation or incompatible with the European Convention on Human Rights and quashed, but the court may not substitute its own view of the best course of action for that of the department.

United States of America

The United States of America is, like Germany, a constitutional, federal republic. Its powers are derived from the people as expressed in their Declaration of Independence in 1776. The Constitution was drafted in 1787 and became effective upon ratification by the states in 1789. It creates a formal separation of powers among the legislative, executive, and judicial branches of government, and extensive checks and balances on the power of each. Though it is possible to amend the US Constitution, the process for doing so is politically onerous; as a result, it has been amended only twenty-eight times.

The USA is divided into fifty states and one district (the District of Columbia). According to the Tenth Amendment, adopted in 1791, "The powers not delegated to the United States by the Constitution, nor prohibited by it to the States, are reserved to the States respectively, or to the people." Thus while the powers of the federal government are considerable, they are, at least in principle, enumerated, whereas the powers of the states are reserved. The states are organizationally autonomous, each having its own constitution and administration. Most federal agencies maintain regional and local offices in the states, but they have no formal power over state or local administration. Local governments are creatures of state governments. As of June 2002, there were 87,849 units of local governments: 38,971 are general purpose local governments, 3,034 county governments, and 35,937 subcounty governments, including 19,431 municipal governments and 16,506 township governments. The remainder, which comprise over one-half of the total, are special purpose local governments, including 13,522 school district governments and 35,356 special district governments.

The president is the chief of state and head of government and is elected to a maximum of two four-year terms by a college of representatives ("electors") who in turn are elected directly by voters in each state in numbers equal to the state's number of representatives in both houses of the US Congress. A candidate may receive a majority of the national popular vote but not a majority of the electoral vote. The executive branch cabinet is appointed by the president following advice and consent by the Senate. The president appoints members to the cabinet (comprising somewhat over fourteen positions) and numerous sub-cabinet positions, to regulatory commissions, and to other offices that are subject to the advice and consent of the US Senate. In general, legislative approval is necessary for the creation and reorganization of cabinet-level agencies. The cabinet has no formal powers and performs only those functions designated by the president.

The US legislative branch is a bicameral Congress made up of the Senate and House of Representatives. The Senate has 100 members, two from each state, who are elected by popular vote to serve six-year terms. The House of Representatives has 435 seats, and members are elected by popular vote by districts to serve two-year terms. The extensive powers of Congress are enumerated in Article I of the Constitution. All bills for raising revenue, for example, shall originate in the House of Representatives. In general, legislatures authorize and monitor public administration.

The federal civil service includes all appointive positions in the executive, judicial, and legislative branches of the federal government, except positions in the uniformed services, and consists of the competitive service, the excepted service, and the senior executive service (SES), which differ in terms of appointment procedures and job protections. In the competitive service, appointment procedures, merit promotion requirements, and qualification requirements are prescribed by law or by the Office of Personnel Management and apply to all agencies. In the excepted service, only basic requirements are prescribed by law or regulation, and each agency develops specific requirements and procedures for its own jobs. The general merit system principles of the competitive service apply to the SES; appointment procedures and qualification requirements are determined by individual agencies, based on minimum requirements prescribed by law and the Office of Personnel Management. Provisions for compensation, performance evaluation, and removal from the SES are significantly different from those governing the other systems. Civil servants other than political appointees are by law non-political.

The US legal system is based on English common law traditions. The Constitution provides for judicial review of legislative acts to determine their constitutionality and of administrative acts to determine both their constitutionality and their compliance with statutes. In general, the courts have the power to say finally what the law is. A body of administrative law, inscribed in statutes and judicial rulings, ensures that public administration does not exceed or abuse its authority. The federal judicial branch comprises the Supreme Court, the highest-level appellate court, which chooses to hear only cases that raise constitutional issues, the United States Courts of Appeal, or lower appellate courts, and US federal district courts, where lawsuits are initially tried. Each state has its own common law legal system and procedures for judicial review. State court determinations can be appealed to the federal appellate level.

NOTES

1 By recursive is meant that choices are characterized by processes which can be indefinitely and repeatedly applied to their own output, such as algorithms which create branching and subdivision. Specifically, contemporary public management might be viewed as a stage in a stochastic process whose asymptotic distribution (that is, the structures, practices, and institutionalized values that we can observe) evolves as a consequence of the history of that process, that is, it is non-ergodic, or path dependent. In short, a path-dependent process or time series is one whose asymptotic distribution – the outcomes toward which it is tending – evolves as a consequence of the history of the process.

2 In Chapter 8, the concept of "punctuated equilibrium" will be introduced to accommodate the reality of discontinuous change in an otherwise path-dependent process.

3 Alternatively, the restraints of cultures and traditions, to the extent that they are acknowledged, tend to be regarded as weakening under the relentless pressures associated with the technology-driven internationalization and globalization of economies and the interdependence of public policies.

4 Important exceptions are economist Douglass North and the historical institutionalists in political science, for example, Theda Skocpol.

5 Ideas in this section were first developed in Lynn (2003, 2005). A contrasting view in a similar spirit is that of Pollitt and Bouckaert (2004), who say that public management may be used in three senses: "the *activity* of public servants and politicians" (13); "the *structures and processes* of executive government" (13), although they associate this with the use of specific tools such as TQM and performance budgeting; and "the *systematic study* of either activities or structures and processes" (13).

6 In a similar spirit, Aberbach and Rockman (1988) designate the three analytic building blocks of comparative administrative study as structures (organizations), actors (executives and various species of bureaucratic officialdom), and actions (behaviors), noting the numerous confounding sources of variation among them.

7 For an overview of public policy implementation and its intellectual development, see Hill and Hupe (2002).

8 In common law legal systems, private law is inductively derived and, if appropriate, amended, on a case-by-case basis from precedents established by earlier rulings by the courts. In civil law legal systems, which include most of those on the Continent of Europe as well as many others around the world, law comprises an exhaustive system of *a priori* rules from which appropriate rulings in particular cases are deduced by the courts.

9 Marshall Dimock (in Thomas 1978) notes that the early American preference for the term administration reflected the fact that Woodrow Wilson, when a young academic, and W. F. Willoughby were influenced by English experience, and that Frank J. Goodnow used the term administrative law, and, naturally, administration, because it was well established in Germany and France, where he studied. The relationship between American and European thought is discussed at length in Chapter 4.

10 Ronald Moe (1990) credits the influence of Richard Neustadt's classic *Presidential Power* (1970) for the abandonment of public and organizational principles. "The message was for scholars and practitioners to study the techniques of influence and persuasion rather than public law and organizational management if they wanted to understand how decisions are really made. . . . Scholars could now forsake the rigorous study of laws and institutions and feel no guilt" (Moe 1990, 131).

Chapter 3

Old public management: Continental traditions

INTRODUCTION

Public management, broadly defined as systematic administrative effort on behalf of the interests of the sovereign and subjects of a state, is, as noted in earlier chapters, hardly new. Tracing its origins, however, is a lot like tracing the origins of the game of baseball, serious business in America. Was baseball invented in Hoboken, New Jersey in 1846, or was it Cooperstown, New York in 1839? Wait: are a bat and a ball on that ancient Greek vase? What makes a game "baseball" anyway? Is it a "bat" and a "ball" or a game governed by an infield fly rule and rules concerning a "balk"? Such issues are deep and difficult.

Its ambiguities notwithstanding, the field of public management can trace its lineage at least as far back as the seventeenth century and the rise of the absolutist states of Continental Europe following the Peace of Westphalia in 1648. To these states can be credited the establishment of centralized organizations for administration, professionalism in public service management, and the emergence of an academic community engaged in teaching and research to support effective managerial performance. The foundations laid by the absolutist state builders of the seventeenth and eighteenth centuries would adapt to and survive the revolutions, wars, and social and economic transformations of the nineteenth and twentieth centuries to provide stability and continuity to modern democratic governments. Thus, although both Fifth Republic France and reunified Germany have been through numerous political transformations in the last two centuries, the stability of their public administrations is remarkable.

Post-Westphalian developments nonetheless reflect prior innovations in statecraft in the sense that there was at least some awareness among absolutist reformers of the statecraft of ancient and pre-modern civilizations. The path of influence of pre-modern public administration passed through Continental Europe.

PRE-WESTPHALIAN PUBLIC ADMINISTRATION

The existence of organized bureaucracies and systematic administration in Egyptian, Chinese, Greek, Roman, and other early civilizations and in feudal Europe has been well documented. Although Albert Lepawsky (1949, 82) found only limited evidence in early civilizations for "the rise and the development of administration as an art, of organization as a science, or of management as a technique," that there is any evidence at all is notable (Lynn 2005).

The field of public management might plausibly be said to have originated in recognizable form in ancient China. Confucius (551–479 BCE) held that the conductor of a government should "hold the mean," that is, "approach a problem by seeking the widest differences of opinions and by making the most careful study of the facts in the spirit of absolute impartiality and unselfishness, and then to solve it moderately, practicably, and logically, in accordance with the best ethical rules," a precept on which it is hard to improve (Confucius, quoted by Lepawsky (1949, 83) from Hsü (1975 [1932]), 121–2).[1] H. G. Creel makes the strongest (albeit controversial) claim for the existence of Chinese doctrines of administration that were influential in later times. By the second century BCE, Creel (1964, 155–6) says that

> an increasing number of [administrative] officials was selected by civil service examinations. . . . An increasing proportion of officeholders were educated in an imperial university that was expressly founded, in 124 B.C., for the purpose of inculcating in future officials the values and attitudes desired by the government. Many of them were career bureaucrats from an early age.

Creel finds further support for his claim not in Confucianism, which had little to say about statecraft, but in the career of Shen Pu-hai (d. 337 BCE), who was chancellor of a small state in north-central China. A book attributed to his authorship was widely read and influential as late as the reign of Emperor Hsüan (74–48 BCE). Not a Confucian, Shen Pu-hai was "concerned, with almost mathematical rigor, to describe the way in which a ruler can maintain his position and cause his state to prosper by means of administrative technique and applied psychology" (Creel 1964, 160).

Chinese influence on the subsequent history of public administration and management is proverbial, and not just because the widespread use of examinations for entry into public service probably originated in China. As late as the seventeenth century, there may have been knowledge of the doctrines of Shen Pu-hai, according to Creel, and Shen's book was extant as late as the early eighteenth century.[2] Creel and other scholars find Chinese influence specifically in the regimes of the Kingdom of Lower Italy and Sicily under Roger II (1101–1154) and Frederick II (1208–1250), whose statutes, promulgated at Melfi in 1231, have been characterized by Ernst Kantorowicz (1931) as "the birth certificate of modern bureaucracy" (quoted by Creel 1974, 58).[3] Whatever their provenance, reforms recognizable to modern students of public administration and management were, as we shall see shortly, adopted in several medieval regimes (Rosenberg 1958).

The Greek and Roman civilizations provided their own contributions to the field. According to Albert Lepawsky (1949, 88), "[t]hose scholars who advocate the recentness of administration as an art, science, or systematic technique, have not adequately analyzed

41

the accounts furnished by the ancient Greek civilization." Socrates offered a generic concept of competent management (Lepawsky 1949).[4] Further, notes John Gaus (1936, 27), "[f]rom the Roman republic came the idea, founded upon actual institutions and practices of the simpler city-state, that political responsibility to the people of the republic was enjoined upon the administrator." Roman law (the *Corpus Juris Civilis*, first promulgated in 529), perfected during the reign of Emperor Justinian I from 527 to 565, was to spread to Germany, where, despite being a "foreign" idea, it was embraced as a "cultural Rome-idea" that comported with the universalist tendencies of the Middle Ages (Wylie 1948).[5] The main legacies of Roman law and administration, according to Farrel Heady (2001), are the principle that the head of state receives his powers from the people, the distinction between the private and public personalities of the head of state, the hierarchical nature of administrative structures, and the division of government into major constituent parts.

By the end of the eleventh century, argues E. N. Gladden (1972a, 238), "all the basic means for effective office work and record-keeping had become available." He continues:

> With the gradual emergence of administration as a specialized governmental activity, of an organization specifically to deal with the transmission of instructions and regulations, the handling of information from agents, and of ordinary correspondence as well as the keeping of records and inventories of all kinds, public administration had already assumed its basic form.

There is little evidence, however, of bureaucratic hierarchy at that point, says Gladden. "[I]t is more realistic to regard the public service of most of the early governments as a plurality of officialdoms of varying status rather than a broadly conceived hierarchy under the leader" (1972a, 251). A high degree of complexity and a high level of competence characterized the larger state systems: Egyptian, Achaemenian (Persian), Imperial Roman, Byzantine, and Chinese. Wherever large administrative services developed, complicated spheres of personnel management were called into being, although there is little evidence that bureaucracies had a degree of permanence or were, in effect, a constitutional form of government. Indeed, S. E. Finer (1997, 1616) emphasizes the "endemic corruption of the pre-industrial state." "[G]overnment's role," Finer argues, "was architectonic, that is, its role was to provide the most basic of frameworks for an ocean of *spone acta* and self-regarding activities" (1618).

Feudal regimes in England and France saw the institutionalization of impersonal government in an office equivalent to "deputy king" (under monarchs who were absent from the realm for long periods), of functionally differentiated financial and judicial administration, and of networks of royal field agents that "strongly contributed to the weakening of feudalism" (Fesler 1982, 11).[6] Richard Fitzneale, Treasurer of England and Bishop of London, wrote in 1179 as follows: "For not in its reckonings, but in its manifold judgments, does the superior [or greater] *science of the exchequer* consist" (1912, 32, emphasis added; source cited by Lepawsky 1949).[7] Jos Raadschelders and Mark

Rutgers point out that the papacy in the eleventh and twelfth centuries evolved into "the first 'government' departments [a chancery, exchequer, court] in a modern sense" (1996, 72).[8] They cite the monk Gratian's *Concordance of Discordant Canons*, which dealt in part with the functioning and position of those in clerical office. "A formal, legal bureaucratic structure was created by the church" (1996, 72), a point also noted by Gaus (1936), who interpreted the papacy as "the means whereby the responsibility of the ruler for the exercise of his powers might be enforced."

Of particular interest is the emergence of a concept of "public trust" in numerous Continental towns, "established as legal associations under a corporate authority and vested with varying rights of self-government" that "adumbrated some of the modern ideas of public need and public service" (Rosenberg 1958, 6, 8). During the fourteenth and fifteenth centuries, these towns discharged the kinds of governmental powers we now associate with national governments, including maintenance of military forces (Goodnow 1906).[9] Gaus (1936, 28) notes that eventually the nation state was to afford an opportunity for political expression of "the rising middle class of the towns" that neither the papacy nor feudal institutions could provide.

What we know of the history of organized administration across time and civilizations suggests, therefore, that common forms of self-awareness and codification concerning the structures, practices, and values of public management accompanied the emergence of organized societies (Waldo 1984 [1948]). "One may wonder," said Gerald D. Nash (1969, 3),

> whether there ever was an organized society that did not develop administrative tools and concepts that were as vital to its existence as scientific discoveries. The attributes of civilization – the accretion of scientific knowledge, a money economy, political and legal institutions, social and military organizations, the development of ideals, or value systems – seem impossible to maintain, without the concomitant development of administrative institutions and techniques to ensure their proper functioning.

Broadly construed, precursor forms of public management have been a concomitant of the earliest quests for security, order, wealth, and civilization. "[P]ublic administration in the West did begin [in early civilizations] and confronted the problems that are still with us," argues James Fesler (1982, 15). He continues: "Functional differentiation, bureaucratization, contracting out, financial accountability, records keeping, judicialized administration, field administration, and a body of professional public servants continuing under successive 'Administrations' were then and are now among the resources and challenges of public administration."

ABSOLUTISM AND THE MODERN STATE

Questioning the significance of early non-European precedents, Hans Rosenberg declares that "[t]he modern bureaucratic state is a social invention of Western Europe" (1958, 2;

see also Friedrich and Cole 1932). Moreover, as Rosenberg notes, while learning was important for the permanent, trained professionals of feudal regimes, who enjoyed a good deal of discretion, their purpose was feudal: "the personal enrichment and dynastic advantage" of their prince (Rosenberg 1958, 5). The fifteenth and sixteenth centuries nonetheless saw an increasing formalization of secular administration and increasing recognition of the monarch as an instrument to provide for the public welfare. Gradually personal and state households became more separated. "The separation of public and private can be seen as a prerequisite for the creation of a civil service in the modern sense," argue Raadschelders and Rutgers (1996, 74–5). Only under absolutism did administration establish itself as a type, a prerequisite both for a standing army and for the very implementation of absolutism (Ellwein 2001).

The emergence of modern forms of public management depended on two historic developments: the rise of absolutism in Europe following the Peace of Westphalia in 1648, which created a political environment conducive to the emergence of a field of "administrative science," and the revolutionary idea of "popular sovereignty" institutionalized in France and other Continental sovereignties after 1789 (Barker 1944; Merkle 1980).

Sovereignty and administration

The Peace of Westphalia established a European community of sovereign states (Riggs 2002). All members of this community had come to recognize each other as having equal legal standing, and they agreed to guarantee each other's independence and to recognize their internal legal treaties as binding. In defining the principles of sovereignty and equality in numerous sub-contracts, the treaty became the constitution of the new system of European states. "In the post-Westphalian world, royal sovereignty was extended, generally, from kings to their kingdoms at the expense of the sacred and secular authority of popes and emperor at the imperial level and of feudal lords, dukes, and counts at lower levels" (Riggs 2002, 4; see also Merkle 1980).

Major social and political transformations were associated with these post-Westphalian developments. Traditions associated with the Renaissance, territorial expansion, the Reformation, and the Enlightenment produced a secularization of governance and created societal systems based on individualism, capitalism, rationalism, urbanism, and democracy that took centuries to unfold (Toonen and Raadschelders 1997). Martin Luther, for example, advocated a separation of office and official. The separation of church and state led to the transfer of health care, poor care, and education from the church to local government and private associations (Toonen and Raadschelders 1997). Thus "privatization" in this sense is a deeply rooted tradition in many Continental state systems. The church retracted from being a political actor and became "conceived as invisible, apolitical, alegal" while the state became the vehicle for a "secularization of law and the emergence of a positive theory of law" (Berman 1983, 29). Von Seckendorff's *Teutscher Fürstenstat*, first published in 1756, "sometimes regarded as the first book on public administration" (Raadschelders and Rutgers 1996, 75), addressed itself to the tasks of household and civil servant.

The reign of Louis XIV in France represented absolutism in its paradigmatic form. The break with the past was in the growth of large bureaus of officials and a new system of financial administration under the powerful *contrôleur général* (finance minister), Jean Baptiste Colbert. Revolutionary change occurred at the local level with the institution of the *intendant*, a permanent administrator answerable to the king and his ministers, especially in matters of finance, and the *intendants*, too, required staffs. Against the background of the scientific spirit created by Bacon, Galileo, and Descartes, scholars such as Vauban and Jonchère began addressing the needs of absolutist institutions (Deane 1989; Merkle 1980). Such scientific thinking (in contrast to descriptive or philosophical thought) "drove the mysticism from statecraft" (Merkle 1980, 141; Raadschelders and Rutgers 1999).

The main story concerning modern public management arguably occurred in the German states, however. Beginning in 1640, a succession of Hohenzollern kings – Frederick William of Brandenburg (the Great Elector) (1640–88), his grandson Frederick William I (1713–40), and Frederick the Great (1740–86) – created an absolutist state. Sovereign power was under the sole control of the ruler, thus breaking with medieval tradition by instituting public administration by trained and competent civil servants answerable to the ruler. However, these officials acted on behalf of a "public interest" rather than (solely) out of narrow dynastic concerns (albeit on behalf of Hohenzollern and Hapsburg political interests as against powerful rivals; see Morstein Marx 1935).

In 1640, Frederick William, the "Great Elector," took the reins of government in Brandenburg (after 1701 the Kingdom of Prussia). He established a body of officials throughout his dominion chosen by himself. By 1688, he had established public service as a duty to the people (rather than to the feudal nobility), a principle extended to the army and the revenue, postal, and education systems (Morstein Marx 1935). "Prussian absolutism . . . was the rule of a categorical imperative of duty rather than of a personal will; but the obedience exacted was obedience not to the moral law of practical reason, but to the political law of 'reason of state'" (Barker 1944, 18).

The Great Elector's grandson, King Frederick William I, "coined the definite features of the Prussian civil service" (Morstein Marx 1935, 171). He erected a method of finance and a system of administration to correspond to its needs, initiated the training of officials, and established two university chairs in administrative subjects in the 1720s; by the end of the eighteenth century there were twenty-three such chairs (Wagner n/d). These studies were not scientific in the modern, positivist sense; they were instead descriptive and oriented toward best practices (Dunsire 1973). But they were concerned with administrative studies or administrative sciences, and they were rooted in an economic rather than a legal mode of thinking. The great merits of the system were that it recruited the nobility to useful service to the state, and it gradually trained, with the participation of Prussian universities, a class of professional administrators devoted to Prussia (with the assistance, incidentally, of officials imported from France). The only

45

unity in the fragmented, evolving Prussian state was that of a common administration and the philosophy of a transcendent state.

The administrative achievements of Frederick the Great included examinations and a civil service commission. The consequence of these developments was the emergence of a field of study and practice termed "cameralism" (the word refers to the room or place (*kammer*) from whence the domain is ruled), perhaps the most conspicuous precursor of the contemporary field of public management. "The rise of this academic discipline," noted Carl Friedrich (1939, 131), "is clearly born of the training-needs of the expanding administrative machine of modern governments." He continued (1939, 137): "It is very important to keep it in mind that cameralism as an academic discipline thus owes its inception to the conscious decision of an absolute ruler anxious to provide himself with officials who possessed technical knowledge of a very definite kind." Similar patterns of centralization and training were adopted in Austria, France, the Low Countries and Scandinavia (Dunsire 1973).

Unlike in England (see Chapter 4), because judges were not subject to their power or removal, the prince in Germany (as well as the Crown in France) did not permit the development of wide judicial control over administrative action. Instead, special administrative tribunals were created (Goodnow 1905). As a result of administrative independence of judicial interference, especially after the time of Napoleon, "a much more efficient administrative system than England could develop under her régime of judicial control, and the study of administration and administrative methods assumed a place on the continent which it never reached in England" (Goodnow 1905, 32).

Not all absolutist regimes were alike, however. The highly professionalized Prussian administration was distinctly different from the French *ancien régime*, in which offices were bought or gifted by the Crown or were inherited. The origin of the highly qualified and esteemed French administration lies in the period of Napoleon Bonaparte's reign, first as consul, then as emperor. The public administration of Imperial France under Napoleon was transformed into a highly qualified bureaucracy, with the rise of sectoral professional organizations, the *grand corps*. The *haute fonction publique* gained high public esteem, and France became an administrative state run by an elite of high officials (Kickert and Hakvoort 2000). In general, however, the so-called New Monarchy initiated "disengaging public prerogatives from the law of private property, from vested family interests, and from the grip of the possessors of legal, social, and political privilege" (Rosenberg 1958, 15).

These developments in the structures and responsibilities of the state were, as already noted, assisted and sustained by the emergence of a so-called science of administration.

Administrative science

The seventeenth century was a scientific age. Bacon, Galileo and Descartes devised new approaches to scientific discovery. "Bacon's most enduring and significant contribution to the scientific revolution was . . . a bold, open-minded, free-ranging attitude of enquiry" (Deane 1989, 17). Descartes emphasized mathematical precision and simple analogies to mechanical systems such as the clock. "It was against [the] disturbed backcloth of political problems, events and upheavals, and within a new framework of religious, philosophical, and scientific ideas," says Phyllis Deane, "that seventeenth-century thinkers began to formulate rational explanations of the way the market economy worked, or ought to work" (1989, 12).[10]

Louis XIV, argues Judith Merkle (1980, 139), was "at once the philosophical predecessor of the international Scientific Management movement and its diametric opposite." During his reign, Vauban (Sebastien Le Prestre, Seigneur de Vauban (1633–1707)), "drove the mysticism from statecraft" (141), by proposing the statistical apparatus of the modern state as a means of routinizing the exercise of power and promoting economic growth. His use of mathematical argument and practical documentation "shaped the terms of debate about reform for generations to come" (141). Merkle argues (1980, 142, 143):

> The classical configuration of elite-sponsored, centralized, bureaucratic, and scientific reforms came to form the basis of French utopianism as well as the direction of government evolution. . . . It is the pattern of public accountability of previously "invisible" organizational functions which strengthens at one time the formal organization, those specialists who monopolize the accounting process itself, and the leader(s) of the organization.

These developments were the basis for the embrace of Scientific Management in France in the twentieth century.

It was cameralism, however, which reflected the scientific spirit of pre-revolutionary Europe. Cameralism, said Albion Small (1909, 591), "was an administrative technology . . . a theory of managing natural resources and human capacities so that they would be most lucrative for the prince in whose interest the management was conducted" (see also Lepawsky 1949).[11] According to Johann von Justi (1760), one of its most eminent scholars and practitioners, the aim of cameralism, or *Staatswissenschaften*, was to achieve the common happiness of the ruler and his subjects (an early version of the concept of "public will" or "public interest") through rules that amount to applications of benefit–cost economics toward the end of efficiency in resource allocation. The first rule of wise expenditure, according to von Justi, was that no outlay must be undertaken without the most thorough previous consideration, and estimate of the involved cost, and of the income likely to accrue from the same to the state (1760 II, 476, cited by Small 1909; cf. Lindenfeld 1997). The second rule was that the outlay should never exceed the income (1760 II, 478). Von Justi referred to a "science of government," saying (in 1759) that "[t]he common happiness of the whole society is accordingly the ultimate end of the civil constitution" (quoted by Tribe 1984, 275). Cameralism, according to Carl Friedrich (1939, 130–1), "was the academic counterpart of modern bureaucratic administration and, hence, in its essence was administrative science."

47

Cameralists were often successful practitioners. Joseph Schumpeter (1994 [1954], 143–208) described them as "Consultant Administrators." In contrast to modern deductive science, "[t]he cameralists proceeded much more by the statement and elaboration of practical maxims than through the construction and logical manipulation of analytical models" (Wagner n/d, 7). Administrators participated at a high level in literary discussions of cameralistic topics and produced a "massive German literature" that addressed general problems and issues of public management (Tribe 1984, 273; Morstein Marx 1935).

As a professional field, cameralism reflected what would today be called a managerialist ideology. Aristotelian political philosophy and administrative science were intimately intertwined, and both were bent toward the practical task of training governmental officials (Friedrich 1939). Cameralists advocated meritocracy rather than noble birth, administrative science rather than feudal law, standardized principles rather than local particularity, and formalism and professionalism rather than traditionalism (Hood and Jackson 1991b). The best interests of the prince and the people lay in economic development, which, in turn, required active management by administrators who were trained by, examined by, evaluated by, and held loyal to a strongly led state. Its central tenets were sufficiently modern, as was the emphasis on political economy, that Christopher Hood and Michael Jackson refer to the late twentieth-century New Public Management as a "new cameralism" (Hood and Jackson 1991b, 182).

STATE, BUREAUCRACY, AND *RECHTSSTAAT*

The latter part of the eighteenth century saw the second great development leading toward the modern administrative state: the beginnings of intellectual and political developments that were to culminate in fundamental structural change – national sovereignty, the *Code Napoléon*, *Rechtsstaat*, the bureaucracies that were to be idealized by Max Weber, and law as the basis for training officials – and undermine the preeminence of administrative sciences (other than economics) as the intellectual foundation for public management. In other words, with state building largely accomplished on the Continent by the late eighteenth century, "the struggle for legalizing or constitutionalizing these great administrative mechanisms" began (Friedrich 1939, 132).

The period 1780–1850 saw the emergence of the constitutional state. Royal servants were to become state servants (for example, in Prussia's Legal Code of 1794), state servants were to become public officials, government by officials became synonymous with bureaucracy, and bureaucracy became both inordinately powerful and sufficiently controversial to arouse concerns for democratic control. The process was accelerated after the popular revolutions of 1848, "when most European monarchs feared for their future and hence consented to more democratic constitutions" (Kickert and Hakvoort 2000) and, in particular, political democracy and *Rechtsstaat*: a political system and a constitutional/legal system. After that, liberal democracy began to prevail and governments confined their tasks to legislation and execution, in which, it was believed, mainly juridical expertise was needed. Following the territorial consolidations among German states, the completion of the process of transformation in Germany awaited Bismarck's creation of the first German Reich in 1870, after which it took until 1900 for legal codes to be unified in the *Bürgterliches Gesetzbuch*: "deep, exact and abstract" (Kickert and Hakvoort 2000).

The imperial bureaucracy

The "age of reason" had proclaimed the supremacy of law as early as the seventeenth century, and Holland and England (the latter led by Sir Edward Coke and prominent English lawyers) had embraced the idea of law as right reason. The motive for abandoning *Staatswissenschaften* on the Continent, however, was widespread dissatisfaction with what was coming to be known as "bureaucracy." A pejorative expression attributed to M. De Gournay, a French Physiocrat who died in 1759, the term "rapidly became part of an international vocabulary of politics" (Albrow 1970, 17), accepted in the Dictionary of the French Academy, according to Albrow, as "power, influence of the heads and staff of government bureaux." The French *bourgeoisie* finally rebelled against the taxation needed to support their kings' propensities to wage war. "A new conception of the state now appeared in the doctrine of 'national sovereignty'," according to Ernest Barker (1944, 13).

Far from displacing the role of administrators, however, "France retained the administrative machine of the past, but gave it a new motive power" (Barker 1944, 13). The revolution "did not destroy, but consolidated the administrative organization of the old regime by sweeping away its feudal inconsistencies and uncovering its logical structure" (Merkle 1980, 144). The result was that "the Revolution left its new theory of democracy curiously united with the old practice of bureaucracy" based on the scientific utopianism of Saint-Simon (Barker 1944, 13–14).

L'état was, following the revolution, the collective people, not the person of the king. Napoleon was, as Barker puts it, the successor to both Louis XIV and Colbert, and he organized a new administration around a *conseil d'état* and the system of *préfets* nominated and controlled by the central government. Because judicial authorities of the *ancien régime* were suspected of counterrevolutionary sympathies, they were prohibited explicitly from interfering in administrative acts, and a separate system of administrative law and jurisdiction was created. Napoleon used the already existing *conseil d'état* for that purpose; its members were officials appointed by the state. The French model was to become influential in the rest of Europe.

The Napoleonic model of government borrowed from the *ancien régime* and combined ancient and medieval practices (uniform territorial division, experts, hierarchy, records), ideas from the Middle Ages and Renaissance (separation of office and officeholder) and ideas from the early modern period (unity of command, separation of politics and administration, use of statistics) (Raadschelders 1995, 264). Moreover, the Napoleonic

49

model "was profoundly marked by the Revolution, and developed in a haphazard way during the Consulate and Empire" (Wright 1995, 4). Its principles included a powerful, impartial state; hierarchy; uniformity in structures and service delivery; separation of politics from administration, with legislatures subordinate to the executive; technical expertise; strong control mechanisms; and administration endowed with prestige and privilege.

Rationality as the centralization of authority subject to popular sovereignty was to take legal and bureaucratic form in the *Code Napoléon*, under which state administration "was to learn to govern France without ever losing continuity through successive periods of revolution" (Merkle 1980, 144). The French civil service became the "indestructible backbone of government" (Merkle 1980, 136). The contributions of the self-aware French public administration have arguably been seminal (Martin 1987).[12] Administrative principles that were later to be embraced in America and elsewhere included:

- a politics–administration dichotomy, articulated both by Charles-Jean Bonnin in 1812 and by Alexandre François Auguste Vivien in 1859 – administration was associated with the administrative code, which was independent of traditional political and judicial laws. The French understood that "administrators actually made policy all the time" (Martin 1987, 298), but the dichotomy served the normative purpose of precluding excessive intermingling.
- the idea that scientific study of administration leads to discovery of principles of administration – more than half of Bonnin's (1812) sixty-eight administrative principles "were rules by which administration could operate more efficiently and responsibly than they could without a principle-based code" (Martin 1987, 299).[13]
- the belief that administration can be taught to practitioners in schools – rigorous courses of study of three to four years' duration, surprisingly similar to contemporary curricula, were common, with a heavy emphasis on statistics to be used in needs measurement.
- functional administration, of which POSDCORB (Planning, Organizing, Staffing, Directing, Coordinating, Reporting, Budgeting) was a latter-day version.

However, "[b]y 1859," according to Martin (1987, 301), "the French had reached a dead end. Their structural studies were comparable to the best [later] produced in the U.S., but they had no behavioral revolution." The vitality of the field awaited "the rebirth of French public administration schools and journals in 1948."

Following its defeat by Napoleon at Jena in 1806, the Prussian state, too, was quickly revolutionized. The pre-modern state was only as efficient as its locally grown elements, with administration experienced subjectively (Ellwein 2001). Prior to 1806, administrative theory was dominated by the idea of the *collegium*, collective responsibility for advising the ruler. Following Napoleonic logic, after 1806 and the advent of a representative parliament, the *collegium* was replaced by the *Buro-* or *Einheitssystem*, in which, in the interests of efficiency, responsibility was clearly vested in an individual at each level of authority up to a minister. Sinecures were abolished, rank and pay structures introduced, nepotism, patronage, emoluments, and the like controlled. "By the first half of the nineteenth century, the Prussians had achieved a synthesis of merit and patronage in the construction of the aristocratically-based state bureaucracy that was necessary to maintain military effectiveness in a relatively poor state" (Merkle 1980, 174).

The nineteenth-century administrative state was separated strictly from the judiciary and designed according to relatively strict rational principles largely by the higher-ranking civil servants themselves, with their legal training (Ellwein 2001). Any administrative act involving the citizen was regarded as an application of law. As the notion of the constitutional state was associated with that of the application of laws and of the realization of legal principles, the civil service did not perceive itself as being part of politics, which made its relationship with its political masters all the easier. Each civil servant had a clearly defined function, often associated with the sciences of the state. The legal branch of administrative science guaranteed uniformity of legal interpretation.

German administration enjoyed an especially high reputation. According to Thomas Ellwein (2001, 38),

[i]n an age of "civil-service" ministries few people were interested in pondering the relationship between politics and administration, the manageability of public administration, the value of the law as the guiding principle of administration, or the matter of public participation. The general public could no longer imagine a state which knowingly committed an injustice.

Only after 1918, under the Weimar Republic, did the question of public participation in administrative affairs arise in earnest, although to no avail.

A key figure in the Germanic transition to a modern public administration was Freiherr vom Stein, head of the Prussian civil service, who was like the Great Elector in spirit and who had already transferred official allegiance from the person of the king to the head of state (Morstein Marx 1935). Vom Stein referred to post-1806 Prussian government as rule by "buralists" (Albrow 1970). Against the rigidity that had developed in the Prussian system and the displacement of ordinary middle-class civil servants by the nobility under Frederick the Great, vom Stein sought a closer relationship between the people and the organs of government in order to strengthen the state against Napoleonic dominance. He was a genuine liberal in his faith in the political education of the masses. Vom Stein revitalized local government by creating the legal forms for the cooperation of the citizenry in the vast field of administration of the interior, and his legacy is the German people's desire for a responsive bureaucracy.

By the middle of the nineteenth century, argues Robert Miewald (1984, 18), German *Verwaltungslehre* (administrative theory) "was a coherent body of thought." However, a concern for administrative science was beginning to be replaced by a highly structured approach to administrative law that, in its celebration of an ideal state with a strong administrative component, was in essence Hegelian. The bureaucracy was "the carrier

51

and guardian of the general interest of all against the structured clash of particular interests within 'civil society'" (Miewald 1984, 18).[14]

Continental bureaucracies were widely admired. Lorenz von Stein, following Hegel, expressed high esteem for bureaucrats, who represented unselfish service to the state against the opposing power of special interests. The state, as an organic personality, including its administration, was regarded as independent of the larger society (Miewald 1984). Russian, Austrian, and other European writers regarded the bureaucracy as indispensable to reform and good government (the "aristocracy of capacity" (Anderson and Anderson 1967, 175)). Bureaucrats regarded the people as incapable of self-government and themselves as guarantors of their well-being.

At the same time, the increasingly powerful and indispensable bureaucracy was also seen as a problem. "As the economic and social transformation associated with industrialism advanced, the bureaucracy refused to alter its leisurely pace, and even more irksome, to diminish its paternalism" (Anderson and Anderson 1967, 178). Balzac's best-selling novel *Les Employés*, published in 1838, imprinted contempt for bureaucracy on popular consciousness. Von Mohl's definitive analyses tended to fuse the term bureaucracy with the system of state administration that was inherently unresponsive to public concerns (Albrow 1970). For Frederick Le Play, bureaucracy "meant the dissemination of authority among minor officials, absorbed in details, intent upon complicating business, and suppressing initiative in others" (Albrow 1970, 30). Otto Hintze cited the weaknesses of bureaucracy as "corruption and laziness, excessive ambition, servility toward superiors, brutality toward inferiors, conceitedness, and narrowmindedness" (Anderson and Anderson 1967, 183). Austrian scholar Josef Redlich said, "The combination of parliament and a traditionally authoritarian bureaucracy evoked the worst qualities of each body" (quoted by Anderson and Anderson 1967, 184).

With the introduction of parliamentary government and confronting articulate criticism, bureaucracy "learned to protect itself and to guard its power" (Anderson and Anderson 1967, 181). Political struggles over the control of these bureaucracies "partly fed upon arousing popular indignation against the bureaucracy itself, although nobody who in this fashion attacked the hierarchies has ever been known to suggest any substitute for them" (Friedrich and Cole 1932, 3). By the end of the nineteenth century, the idea that bureaucracy and democracy are incompatible had become popular with the critics of "imperial bureaucracy" (Friedrich and Cole 1932), an idea that has been given new life in post-modern democratic theory.

Rechtsstaat

The term *Rechtsstaat* had begun to enter the discourse, referring generally to law as the foundation for public administration.[15] Frederick William I and Frederick the Great had been avowed enemies of the lawyers, seeing them as "troublesome and irritating formalists who inclined to split hairs where common sense gave an obvious indication of what was substantive 'justice'" (Friedrich 1939, 143). Professors of the sciences of the state "generally held liberal views, such as beliefs in the rule of law, a limited degree of popular representation, a free press, and a vital public opinion" (Lindenfeld 1997, 91). Under *Rechtsstaat*, these academics believed, a strong, positive government could be reconciled with individual and social autonomy.

In practice, however, the emphasis was placed on law, not on *Staatswissenschaften*. "[T]he rising emphasis upon law as the necessary form of all governmental action . . . engendered a considerable shift in the concept of what was necessary for the training of governmental officials" (Friedrich 1939, 133): law, not the administrative sciences. Despite an emancipated peasantry and liberated townsfolk in a new system of municipal administration, Prussian absolutism, in Friedrich's account, endured, as did the power of the administrative class, university-trained and office-experienced. Over time, the Prussian bureaucracy was to become iconic. The sciences of the state, though not bureaucracy itself, were also undermined by the growing influence of Adam Smith's *The Wealth of Nations* and the emergence of the field of economic analysis, which shifted the focus of thinking away from the state as the engine of wealth creation toward individuals and entrepreneurs operating in free markets.

Thus law – "legal reasoning" – along with economics eclipsed completely the older administrative sciences in intellectual discourse and the training of officials. The change was completed in the reign of Francis II of Austria before 1809, "when in all admin-istrative branches legal training was required by law for officials in the higher-rank groups" (Friedrich 1939, 135). It was completed somewhat later in Prussia, after the reforms of Baron vom Stein. Throughout the nineteenth century, administrative adjudication was expanded, which further justified legal preparation for administrative officials. Gradually the prestige of judicial officials rose at the expense of administrative officials such that the training of the latter tended to approximate the training of the former.

In the classical tradition of *Rechtsstaat*, the state was autonomous and stood above society (Jann 2003). One belonged to one sphere or the other. The state had a legal personality of its own. When the monarch passed from the picture (Jann 2003, 98),

> only the civil service as a class of its own – responsible for the public good – remained. Pluralism, interest groups, parties and even parliaments were seen as dangerous because they undermined state unity and autonomy. Only the state, represented by its loyal parties, was above parties, interest groups and private interests. . . .
>
> The great achievement of this tradition is the construction of the state as a purely legal entity, the victory of administrative law over policy and politics. Whatever the state does (starting in the nineteenth century) was looked upon as the implementation of laws. Thus there was no room for politics and policy[;] Germany does not even have a word for policy.

This tradition still influences German thinking, owing to the continued supremacy of the legal profession in the public service.

53

Rechtsstaat, too, came under criticism, however. Earlier in the century, tension became apparent between the idea of a *Rechtsstaat* and the idea of a welfare state responsible for the well-being and happiness of its inhabitants and concerned with protecting civilians against the state (Raadschelders and Rutgers 1999). "One of the last to attempt to develop a generic study of public administration in Europe was Lorenz von Stein. He was also the first to describe the modern state as an administrative state (*Verwaltungsstaat*)" (Raadschelders and Rutgers 1996, 84). Ellwein notes, however, that, in Germany, "administration" means a social caste which, around 1800, comprised so-called "higher" civil servants, university-educated members of the bourgeoisie. The administrative state appears above all as "the continuity of a ruling class" (Ellwein 2001, 37), a statement applicable to France as well. Later, Stein argued that *Rechtsstaat* "left no room for a proper conceptualization of administration" (Lindenfeld 1997, 201). In Stein's view, according to Lindenfeld (1997, 201), "administration was the wave of the future," a view that found its way to the heart of Goodnow's seminal American treatises. Later, Gustav Schmoller attempted a revival of the sciences of the state in the form of social science, and despite the opposition of many law professors, a doctorate in the sciences of the state was established in 1880 (Lindenfeld 1997).

During a century marked by revolutions in the name of popular sovereignty, therefore, the primary institution of public administration became bureaucracy, albeit within a *trias publica* (Lindseth 2004, 1343). A dominant intellectual "memory" of the era is Max Weber's positive analysis of legal/rational bureaucracy, which had become so common that it was regarded by Weber as natural (although the power of Weber's work has obscured the intellectual ferment that preceded it). In Weber's ideal bureaucracy (Bendix 1977), official business is conducted on a continuous basis in accordance with stipulated rules by an administrative agency in which personnel have defined duties, authority to carry them out, strictly defined powers, and appropriate supervision. They have no property rights in the resources at their disposal or in their offices. Official business is conducted in writing. Without these features, "there cannot be a system of legal domination in which the exercise of authority consists in the implementation of enacted norms" (Bendix 1977, 424).

The dominant administrative idea became the ideological separation of policy and management, the former the responsibility of parliaments, the latter governed by *Rechtsstaat*. Issues relating to management of hierarchies (what are now called "techniques of management") came to the fore: the content of the education and training of officials at different levels; the use of entrance examinations and apprenticeships; the use of performance standards and evaluations; discipline; reassignment; promotion; salary structures; retirement benefits; status and rights of workers in state enterprises; and retention of personnel (Anderson and Anderson 1967).

By the end of the nineteenth century, the field of public administration had become preoccupied with the *de facto* separation of policy and administration and the resulting tensions between an institution, bureaucracy, which exhibited imperialistic proclivities, and the revolutionary idea of popular sovereignty, with its expectation of democratic accountability. Theo Toonen and Jos Raadschelders argue that "[t]he advent of labor unions and political parties in the second half of the [nineteenth] century, as well as the extension of the suffrage in the 1880–1940 period, are testimony to the degree to which representativeness and participation became considered as the capstone of the development toward democracy" (Toonen and Raadschelders 1997, 5–9). But the bureaucratic state had held its own against republican ideals – and would continue to do so.

SURVIVAL, RECONSTRUCTION, AND THE WELFARE STATE

The history of Europe's Weberian bureaucracies during most of the twentieth century has largely been overshadowed by momentous events such as the Bolshevik revolution in Russia and its aftermath, the rise of Fascism, two world wars and associated dislocations and constitutional transformations, a world-wide economic depression, the nationalization of basic industries and financial institutions, and the demands of post-World War II reconstruction and then of a Cold War. The size, scope, and structure of national administrations naturally adapted to developments that exceeded even nineteenth-century political conflict in their disruptive effects on politics and civic life.

This period in the history of European public management is nonetheless of great importance to our understanding of the "new" public management. Although the public administrations of France and Germany had already established themselves as bulwarks of a transcendent state and instruments of national continuity, especially during the Napoleonic era and the mid-nineteenth-century revolutions, their importance to national survival was proven beyond doubt under the most extraordinary of circumstances during the twentieth century. The capacity of these institutions to perform this role was greatly enhanced by "extreme delegations" of power by ineffectual parliaments to dominant executives (Lindseth 2004, 1348).

The interregnum

The aggrandizement of executive power in Europe was especially evident in Germany between the wars. "The First World War," says Hans Mommsen (1991, 80), "had reinforced the belief that in critical situations the bureaucracy was the one stabilizing force which could guarantee the continuity of the state." The prestige of the pre-war civil service as representing the interests of the state survived undiminished, and new governments refused to interfere in the structures and composition of the bureaucracy. During the interwar period, anti-Republican elements saw to the expansion of bureaucratic autonomy at the expense of legislative influence in both the Reich and the *Länder*, a process reinforced by the rapid turnover of cabinet ministers and by executive use of emergency decrees. Bureaucracy gained a decisive influence, even a *carte blanche*, in political affairs (Mommsen 1991).

55

The French bureaucracy, too, not only survived but appeared to grow in influence during the interwar period. Preoccupied with the concept of Greater France as a bulwark against national insecurity, Republican France nonetheless was itself in crisis (Wilder 2001). That the National Assembly was proving incapable of effectively governing during the economic crises that arose in the 1920s and 1930s only enhanced the prestige and importance of the central administration.

During World War I, "the emphasis on reorganization for the war effort rooted both Taylorism and Fayolism firmly in French . . . governmental organization" (Merkle 1980, 161). The rise of an American science of administration "had considerable influence in the Europe of the 1920s and 1930s," notes Andrew Dunsire (1973, 86), and the flow of ideas from Europe to America (discussed in Chapter 5) was reversed (Merkle 1980, 137).

> The French heritage of rational reformation fused with Taylorism to produce a vision broader than any created by Taylor himself. In the pattern of centuries-old tradition, the rationalists planned to capture the state and convert it into a center of rational planning; from the center, they would impose order on a nation.

Following the war, a movement for "municipal Taylorism" emerged (Payre 2002a). The companion movement, Fayolism, reached back through the *Code Napoléon* to pre-revolutionary administrative thought.[16]

In general, economic and political crises in France and Weimar Germany drove a process of extreme delegation as parliaments abandoned their constitutional function as the representatives of the people. As Peter Lindseth puts it (2004, 1347–8):

> By the third and fourth decades of the twentieth century, the notion of parliamentary supremacy paradoxically provided the foundation, through its support for extreme delegations, for the degeneration of the parliamentary system into dictatorship . . . [creating] an increasing gap between the constitutional ideal of parliamentary democracy inherited from the nineteenth century and the socio-institutional reality of executive and administrative power in the early twentieth.

The legacy of a world shadowed by depression and the prospect of war was the growth and consolidation of executive power.

Reconstruction and social welfare

Between post-World War II reconstruction and the beginnings of the era of man-agerialism some three decades later, a new episode in the public management story unfolded in Continental Europe, although it is seldom recorded as such. Sustained by the strengthened powers of the executive inherited from the interwar period – the increased use of subordinate legislation, expanded regulatory authority, and judicial concern with procedural regularity in the exercise of delegated powers (Lindseth 2004, 1344) – the post-war period saw the rapid expansion of the welfare state (on both sides of the Atlantic), which brought about "an interdependence between government and society the likes of which have not been seen in history" (Raadschelders and Toonen 1999, 39). Changes of this magnitude required extensive adaptation of public administration structures and processes, practices, and institutional values in the light of the new demands of government–civil society relationships.

These adaptations were of various kinds (Raadschelders and Toonen 1999). Post-war reconstruction required substantial expansion of technical and legal expertise and of administrative systems for processing and monitoring claims and clients. Welfare state expansion required the reorganizing of government departments, the restructuring of territorial boundaries of local government and reorganization of central–local financial relations, administrative professionalization, and a mastering of techniques and procedures for administrative decision making and control. Reforms were often focused on one organization (the government department), one level (municipal amalgamations, regionalization), or one aspect of central–local relations (from block to specific grants, decentralization). The distributional and regulatory dimensions of strongly expanding government programs in the 1970s required planning and budgeting expertise, often of American provenance: Planning–Programming–Budgeting System (PPBS), Management by Objectives (MBO), Zero-Based Budgeting (ZBB), and new forms of policy analysis and program evaluation.[17] The quality of the public service was enhanced through a proliferation of pre-service and in-service training opportunities (Toonen and Raadschelders 1997, 3–6).

These kinds of developments encouraged a revival of the study of public administration as separate from that of law (Rutgers 2001). The modern study of public administration on the Continent, however, retained its pre-twentieth-century emphasis on "multidisciplinarity, an optimistic outlook on the ability to improve and steer society, an abstract and theoretical orientation, and the aim for systematic and coherent thought" (Rutgers 2001, 228–9). As will be discussed further in Chapter 6, not until the 1970s and 1980s did the intellectual field of public management exhibit any of the vigor that had characterized the administrative sciences prior to the advent of *Rechtsstaat*.

These administrative and intellectual developments had important political consequences. The new welfare state agencies and programs tended to be oriented more toward clientele, provider, and professional interests and values than toward universal public service values and democratic accountability in a classical sense. "Political officeholders increasingly have been forced to show that they could keep the ever-growing bureaucracy in check" (Toonen and Raadschelders 1997, 5–1). Ambitious efforts occurred in several countries to democratize the administrative system in the 1960s and 1970s, searching for more citizen participation, openness, and other efforts to involve the public and "bring public administration closer to the people" (Toonen and Raadschelders 1997, 6–5).

57

Under the increasing international economic pressures of the 1980s, however, the existing institutional structures and interrelationships began "to keep functional systems in a mutual embrace of immobility" (Toonen and Raadschelders 1997, 6–10) while losing their legitimacy and thereby creating the dynamics for change. After World War II, many countries reversed themselves and substituted block grant systems for specific, categorical grant systems in the belief that it would better promote service delivery. In the governmental decentralizations of the 1970s, for example, specific grants were abolished in favor of block grants to emphasize the importance of local self-government. But it was increasingly recognized in the fiscally pressured 1980s that intergovernmental grants were useful instruments for achieving budget cut-backs, central government downsizing, and the imposition of unfunded mandates.

Old public management on the Continent, then, saw significant changes and adaptations – indeed, the restructuring of government–society relations – on the secure foundation of entrenched Weberian governance and traditions of public service. The tendency in Germany was "to revert to many of the bureaucratic patterns which had been altered temporarily by the political turmoil earlier in the century" (Jann 1997, 207; cf. Heady 2001). Civil service reforms in post-war France broadened the recruitment base, brought more uniformity into the selection process, promoted educational reforms (the most significant of which was the creation in 1945 (by Charles de Gaulle) of the *École Nationale d'Administration* (ENA)), and established a civil service directorate and a uniform code concerning the rights and responsibilities of civil servants. Bureaucracies necessarily bent, but they did not break.[18] In summary, the aftermath of World War II established in France and in Germany "a system of governance that could sustain the welfare state bureaucracy while also remaining true to the ideal of parliamentary democracy and developing notions of human rights" (Lindseth 2004, 1341).

CONTINENTAL LEGACIES

The history of public management in France and Germany is arguably more an administrative history than a constitutional one. John Rohr (2002, 18) notes that the constitution of the Fifth French Republic "presupposes an elaborate administrative structure already established. . . . In France, constitutions come and go, but administrative institutions remain."[19] Thomas Ellwein (2001) notes the extent to which self-aware administration was able to influence reconstruction of society in the German states after the breakdowns of order of the French Revolution and the Napoleonic wars. Moreover, whereas both world wars were watersheds in constitutional history, "the core structures of administration remained practically intact" (Ellwein 2001, 36).

The Continental legacy for public management is its distinctive nexus of state, bureaucracy, and *Rechtsstaat*.[20] Continental administrators are called *state* administrators, not *public* administrators (Stillman 1999). Their main task is "to deduce rules from state principles and apply state law" (Stillman 1999, 256). In Mark Rutgers's (2001, 226, 227, 228) useful summary,

> [p]ublic administration is regarded as an exponent of the state, with its own legitimate sphere of action. . . . [B]y means of law and constitution, the state regulates social interaction and at the same time limits its intrusion into the life of the individual. . . . Consistency and coherence are stressed; strict definition, categorizing, system building, and grand theory are preferred. . . . As an essential part of the state, administration cannot be reduced to an instrument for politics. Consequently, public administrators can be regarded as legitimate guardians of the public interest.

State administrators thus become "guarantors of the public good . . . expected to act to some degree as a counterweight to the changeable and volatile political executive" (Goetz 1999, 158).

Yet one can overstate the legitimizing power of Continental public administration. In the post-World War II period, nineteenth-century *trias publica* "reasserted itself, albeit in a modified form that took cognizance of the demands of governance in the welfare state" (Lindseth 2004, 1414). As Peter Lindseth puts it (2004, 1414): "By necessity, the normative output of the administrative state still needed to be channeled through political and judicial bodies that were understood to possess a constitutional legitimacy in some historically recognizable sense; negotiation among executive politicians, administrative officials, and corporatist interests was not enough."

Administration has long been the object of systematic study, reflected in cameralism in German-speaking countries and policy sciences in France until both were largely eclipsed by legal training during the nineteenth century. Thereafter, as Luc Rouban (1997, 142) notes, traditional concepts of public administration "have never had in France the force that they may have in Britain or in the United States. French public administration has been historically built around administrative law. . . . Public management was culturally unknown, did not meet [*grands corps* higher civil servants'] intellectual sensitivity and appealed only to economists." In general, *Rechtsstaat* imposes limits on managerialism. "In France, for example, personnel management is constrained by special laws regulating the civil service, and public money is handled according to complex legalistic controls" (Barlow *et al.* 1996, 14; Rouban 1997). The high degree of internal differentiation of administration in Germany, Klaus Goetz (1999) notes, requires strong integrative institutions, a function which, at both intellectual and practical levels, *Rechtsstaat* fulfills.

The interpenetration of politics and administration at elite levels on the Continent also inhibits managerialism, unlike in Great Britain and the United States, where a sharper separation exists. British civil servants are servants of the Crown, and American civil servants are employees of government agencies, although ideally motivated by public service values (Bertelli and Lynn 2006). German civil servants are the "bearers of state sovereignty" and French civil servants perform "acts of public authority" (Barlow *et al.* 1996, 18).

Although, as Chapters 4 and 5 will show, these traditional French and German bureaucracies have long been held in contempt by public intellectuals in Great Britain and the United States, their histories provide convincing evidence of how well they have served to stabilize and provide continuity to the state through upheavals that are unexampled in the Anglophone world. They impart to public management a respect for law and a rectitude that, while inhibiting certain kinds of administrative experimentation and reform, justify the regard in which Weber and others have held them.

NOTES

1 According to Leonard Hsü, Confucius's "principles of administration" also included public spirit, avoidance of partisanship and keeping busy.
2 "I do not agree," says John Louton (1979, 446) "with Prof. Creel's view of the range of Shen Pu-hai's influence, the magnitude of his importance, nor with each of his interpretations of Shen's relation to some other schools of thought."
3 According to Ernst Kantorowicz, "What the world . . . seized upon, and what each of the European states sooner or later, directly or indirectly, adopted was the technique of statecraft which Frederick had deduced from his metaphysics: the administrative body of jurists; the bureaucracy of paid officials; the financial and economic policy. . . . The measures by which Frederick II extended one unified system of administration throughout his whole kingdom, ultimately throughout the whole of Italy, making Sicily in very truth the 'pattern of states,' . . . brought in their train a most admirable simplification of the whole machinery of government. . . . This imperial administration was the first that had ever achieved *uniformitas* over an area so large." (1931, 271, 281).
4 Lepawsky cites Plato and Xenophon: *Socratic Discourses*, Book III, Chapter 4. Translated by J. S. Watson, edited by Ernest Rhys. New York: E. P. Dutton, Everyman's Library, 1927.
5 Wylie's work is a review and commentary on Paul Koschaker's *Die Krise des römischen Rechts und die romanistische Rechtswissenschaft*, published in 1938.
6 Fairlie (1935) refers to the Norman creation of a common law in England (during the reign of Henry II in 1154–89) as the beginning of a "modern administrative system" (4).
7 It is revealing that the distinction between the exercise of judgment or discretion and the performance of routine operations was clearly understood, and its significance recognized, in pre-modern England.
8 Schuyler Wallace (1941) also recognized the Roman Catholic Church as a hierarchy of power and thus germane to the history of the field.
9 During the seventeenth and eighteenth centuries, the cities were reduced to a position of complete subordination to the governments of the states within which they were situated. As commercialization and industrialization progressed, there was no particular advantage to the cities' remaining independent.
10 Scientific influences on the emerging public sphere were manifest in the thought and work of, for example, Sir William Petty and John Locke. "Petty was a forerunner of the modern breed of government economic adviser. . . . [H]e set out to formulate and justify his policy prescriptions in terms of the national interest as a whole, rather than

from the point of view of a particular section or class of society" (Deane 1989, 22–3). Petty and his followers developed "political arithmetic" or "the art of reasoning upon things related to government," "the beginnings of an objective discipline of applied economics" (Deane 1989, 23). "His policy advice was supported by a logical reasoning process within a framework of theoretical concepts which he did not invent but which he defined and deployed consistently and imaginatively" (24). The royal domain was the central object of economic analysis.

11 The word "managing" in German is "wirthschafften." George Zincke, perhaps the foremost cameralist academic scholar, said: "[A] prince needs genuine and skillful cameralists. By this name we mean those who possess fundamental and special knowledge about all or some particular part of those things which are necessary in order that they may assist the prince in maintaining good management in the state" (quoted by Lepawsky 1949, 99 and Small 1909, 253).

12 *Revue administrative*, a journal devoted exclusively to public administration, was published from 1839 to 1848.

13 According to Daniel Martin (1987), the French did not think that principles could be effectively adopted in the United States because of legislative dominance of administration.

14 Note the sharp contrast between this view and that of the American John Dickinson, who argued (1930, 295, 304) that "[e]very representative is a potential mediator for the interest which has the strongest control over him in the face of other interests; and in this way opportunity is given for bringing interests into touch and convincing each of the advantage of accommodating itself to the others with which it has to live. . . . Government . . . is bound to be in the long run far more a reflection of the balance of interests in the community than an agency capable of making the community reflect the independent will and purposes of the governors."

15 Toonen and Raadschelders (1997) note that there are in fact two *Rechtsstaat* traditions: the institutional type (France), where the legislator emphasizes the importance of a legal basis for public institutions and focuses on establishing a system of political and administrative bodies; and the policy type (Germany), where the legislator provides for those policy areas of collective importance through concrete and detailed measures.

16 "French bureaucrats during the interwar period did not see economics as a policy relevant field of knowledge and consequently, economists were not able to enter the state and have their ideas influence policy" (Saint-Martin 1998, 324).

17 France, for example, attempted an adaptation of the American Planning–Programming–Budgeting System (PPBS), termed *Rationalisation des choix budgétaires*.

18 Of ENA, Theo Toonen (1998) notes, however, that its success is attributable more to its serving as gatekeeper for the best jobs in government than to the quality of its curriculum.

19 John Rohr argues, however, that the Constitution of the Fifth Republic introduced significant changes in French governance, including the enumeration of the powers of parliament and the creation of a Constitutional Council with the power to declare acts of parliament unconstitutional.

20 According to Goetz (1999, 157), "In the German constitutional order democracy as representation is complemented by the notions of the constitutional state under the rule of law, subsidiarity, inclusivity and transparency. Accordingly, democratic public administration is also fully subject to the Constitution and to the substantive and procedural requirements of the *Rechtsstaat*."

61

Chapter 4

Old public management: British traditions

INTRODUCTION

An island nation, like Great Britain, or a former colony isolated in an aboriginal hemisphere, like America, face different state-building tasks than Continental European nations such as France and Germany, where protection of territorial integrity and enforcement of unity historically are of paramount importance (Barker 1944). The differences widen when the influence of democratic institutions and the nature of legal systems are taken into account. Unlike in Continental Europe, democracy in Great Britain and America was built on a system of common law and of legislative and judicial institutions that preceded and governed the creation of their administrative states. As Klaus König (1997, 217), puts it:

> While bureaucracy in the classical administrative systems may be said to be older than democracy, the development of public bureaucracies in civic culture administration countries such as Great Britain and the United States was governed from the outset by the political régime, the historic continuity of which has been maintained up to the present day.

The Continental ideas of "the state" as independent of the political regime and of officials as "servants of the state" are, as König observes (1997, 217), "still not understood easily in the Anglo-American administrative culture." Likewise, the ideas of popular sovereignty and of the accountability of officials, fundaments of Anglo-American political discourse, are not as easily understood on the Continent (Peters 1997). König (1997, 217) puts it well again:

> The permanent dominance of politics over the public bureaucracies is in compliance with the concept of social values in a civic culture; continental Europeans, on the other hand, have had to learn by experience that, in certain historical situations, people may expect certain things from the administration which cannot be provided by the political sector such as, for instance, certain basic supplies in times of political confusion.

62

The field of public management has nonetheless evolved in quite different ways in Great Britain and the United States despite their common political and legal heritage. The reasons lie in the differences between the two nations' constitutions and political institutions, which, in turn, reflect their specific histories.

In sharp contrast to the Continent, where administrative state-building was clearly under way in the seventeenth century, the structures and institutions of an administrative state would not begin to emerge in Great Britain until the nineteenth century, and a self-aware, scientifically oriented field of public administration would not emerge there until a century after that. British public management is governed by its unwritten constitution, notably the conventions associated with parliamentary sovereignty in a unitary state (discussed further below). The field of public management in the US, and the intellectual and practical challenge of conceptualizing managerial responsibility there, directly reflect constitutional tensions between executive, legislative, and judicial branches of government in a federal state with a strong tradition of states' rights. The implications of these constitutional differences between Great Britain and the US did not become apparent, however, until the emergence of the American administrative state in the late nineteenth and early twentieth centuries (discussed in Chapter 5).

To those from nations with an enacted, written constitution – most of the world's nations[1] – the idea of an "unwritten constitution" is difficult to grasp, all the more so in the case of Great Britain because of its long, always actively evolving constitutional story. The British constitution consists of several elements: acts of parliament (including Magna Carta and all basic statutes enacted over the course of English history); principles of common law (including many principles often included in written "bills of rights" as well as administrative regulations pursuant to acts of parliament); major scholarly treatises concerning matters of law and its interpretation (such as Blackstone's Commentaries; one of the very few American parallels is *The Federalist*, often cited in Supreme Court decisions); the body of law that relates to the status and operation of parliament and its members; and, finally, unwritten "conventions" or accepted ways that things are done (for example, that parliament shall meet annually, or the principle of ministerial responsibility), which are numerous and significant (Rohr 2002).[2]

In the absence of an organic civil service statute – the formal authority for the British civil service has been and is an order-in-council rather than an act of parliament – public officials are servants of the Crown, and the organization of the civil service is subject to the authority of ministers appointed by the Crown. Because these various elements are continuously changing, so, too, is the UK constitution, often inconspicuously amended and augmented, unlike the American and Continental constitutions.

The history of public management in Great Britain, therefore, is necessarily, perhaps even primarily, a constitutional history, whereas in France, Germany, and the United States, the history of public management is for the most part an administrative history, although one often invested with constitutional significance and influenced by constitutional developments resulting from periodic revision and judicial review.

63

AN UNWRITTEN CONSTITUTION

At the same time that the states of Continental Europe were creating the absolutist states within which the systematic study and practice of public administration emerged, a short distance across the English Channel England was engaged in virtually the opposite process. "[T]he theory of the English State [after 1660 and 1688] is a theory not of the administrative absolutism of a king, but of the legislative omnipotence of a parliament" (Barker 1944, 31) and of the power of justices of the peace and municipal councils as against royal administrators or prefects.

The pre-modern history of English government is especially important to understanding the emergence of British public management traditions. According to Geoffrey Elton (1953, cited by Fry 1997), the first two of three administrative revolutions in English history occurred prior to the seventeenth century. The first was the Anglo-Norman creation of a centralized feudal state governed by the king in his household. After the Battle of Hastings in 1066, William I centralized the judiciary system and unified the law, and Henry II created an inductively derived "common law" for all England. The second was the Tudor revolution of the 1530s, in which, under the leadership of Thomas Cromwell, reliance on the household was replaced by reliance on bureaucratic departments and officers of state.[3] In place of inefficient and illogical feudal government, Cromwell favored trained professionals operating outside of the royal household.

It was during the violent struggles between the Crown and the nobility of the seventeenth century (the "Great Rebellion" of 1640–60 and the "Glorious Revolution" of 1688) that the British constitution began to assume its modern form. After the Commonwealth and the violence of parliamentary power, the Glorious Revolution established a monarchy with curtailed powers. The Bill of Rights of 1689 restricted the use of royal and prerogative rights and required parliamentary consent and appropriation for royal maintenance of a standing army as well as for the maintenance of the monarchy itself. The Settlement Act of 1701 required parliamentary consent for war, subjected ministerial appointments to parliamentary approval, and located the power to impeach judges in parliament, placing them beyond royal punishment and enabling judicial control of public administration. The Mutiny Act of 1765 required that parliament be prorogued on an annual basis to approve the armed forces.

The origin of the contemporary appellate function of the House of Lords can also be traced back to medieval times, when the king was the supreme law-giver and judge. The appellate function was later delegated to the King's Council, which, from the thirteenth century on, sat with the Lords to form the *magnum concilium in parliamento* (the Great Council in parliament). (In Victorian times there arose the convention that all appeals from rulings of inferior courts are referred to the Judicial Committee of the House of Lords, the so-called "Law Lords": life peers who have held high judicial office. This Committee decides the case although in form it is the decision of the whole House of Lords.) The present structure is a recognizable legacy of medieval reforms.

During the eighteenth century, the origins and principles of British constitutional government were subjected to sharp debate. Because of the diverse views on these issues, H. T. Dickinson (2002, 3) has said that "[i]t is difficult to trace the shifting balance between crown and parliament that occurred almost imperceptibly throughout the whole eighteenth century or to state with precision what the constitution was at any particular date in that century." Nevertheless, the prescriptive and organic nature of the British constitution, as Fry (1997) puts it, was being firmly established as the French revolution inaugurated the second era of public administration on the Continent.

Despite constituting a complex system of checks and balances, the emerging British constitution did not prescribe a strict separation of powers. The three institutions of Crown, Lords, and Commons constituted the sovereign legislature (Fry 1997). Judges were appointed by the Crown but sat in the House of Lords and could be dismissed only by a vote of both houses of parliament. With the subsequent erosion of the Crown's political influence, the unitary nature of British government became even more pronounced, although subject, as will be discussed later, to limitations enforced by the courts. The basic principles of British constitutional government had become clear: the supremacy of parliament and the English version of the rule of law. In his 1765–9 *Commentaries on the Laws of England*, William Blackstone declared that parliament was sovereign and absolute and could change the constitution itself (Fry 1997).

This view was challenged by Whigs and radicals, who opposed excessive power in the hands of either Crown or parliament and argued for a more inviolable constitution. What the debates revealed, Fry (1997) suggests, was that parliamentary sovereignty, as Burke argued, was contingent on there being due regard for the consent of the people and for the protection of their liberties. Nonetheless, while all parliamentary laws continue to this day to be subject to Royal Assent (approval by the Crown) as a matter of constitutional prerogative, assent has not been withheld since very early in the eighteenth century.[4] Nor, in principle, can an act of parliament be declared unconstitutional by any other British governmental body.[5]

Also, by the end of the eighteenth century, the majority of the English political elite believed that British subjects were entitled to liberty in matters of conscience and expression (although not in the franchise), to equal access to justice, and to an inalienable right to their property. "It was accepted by all that every subject had the right to enjoy freedom from oppression and that each individual was free to do some things without interference" (Fry 1997, 10).

It is of considerable interest to note the extent to which British constitutional government depended on "political customs and practices which were nowhere embodied in formal acts of parliament" (Fry 1997, 12). Thus an exclusive elite of Crown-appointed political officials constituting an "inner or efficient cabinet" (Fry 1997, 13) would formulate decisions, secure royal support for them, and then present them to parliament for approval. Governments had come to have a leading, or prime, minister, usually the head of the Treasury, although the cabinet was appointed by the monarch. The prime minister and his colleagues "had three major political tasks to perform in order to retain royal favor and support: to maintain domestic peace, to avoid unsuccessful wars abroad, and to find the financial resources . . . to achieve these objectives" (Fry 1997, 13). At the time, therefore, Crown patronage ensured a powerful influence of the executive in parliament (similar to the way "payroll voting" reflects the influence of the British government today).

Owing in significant measure to these evolving unwritten conventions, there had begun to form what Walter Bagehot would later call "the efficient parts" of British government (Bagehot 1949 [1867]), by which he referred to "the nearly complete fusion . . . of the executive and legislative powers whose connecting link is the Cabinet" (1949 [1867], 9). "The prime minister," he continued, had become "the head of the efficient part" of the constitution (1949 [1867], 10). The Crown was the head of what Bagehot termed "the dignified parts" of British government, whose purpose is to "excite and preserve the reverence of the population" (1949 [1867], 4).

Concerning the rule of law, at the end of the eighteenth century, English administration was subjected to the control of the courts, in contrast to France, where, as discussed in Chapter 3, administration was free of the control of an independent judiciary (Goodnow 1905). Goodnow's argument is interesting. Prior to the Settlement Act of 1701, both judges and administrative officers were subject to the disciplinary power of the Crown and thus were part of the same administrative system. The jurisdiction of the courts was wide, however, because the Crown possessed ultimate control over judges. The Settlement Act severely limited the removal power of the Crown, thus in effect establishing independent judicial control over administration, a power which went unchallenged because of popular confidence in the courts.

This overstates the case, however. The administrative contours of British government had become clarified by convention. Parliament was the supreme authority; there was no separation of powers, and legislative and executive authority were in effect unified. No parliament could bind its successor, however, making it difficult for laws to become sacrosanct. The monarch's principal ministers (the cabinet), with the prime minister acting as first among equals, were collectively responsible to parliament (although technically to the Queen-in-Parliament) for the conduct of the government. Individual ministers who lost the confidence of the House of Commons had to resign. According to Barlow et al. (1996, 14), in Britain (in sharp contrast to Germany and most Continental countries), "comparatively little of the routine work of civil servants is regulated by law."

The ultimate sovereignty of the Crown was, however, to constitute a potential limit on the abuse of power by the government. Civil servants, judges, and the armed services were regarded as owing their allegiance to the monarch, not to the government in power, accounting for the ethos – the civic spirit – of the increasingly professionalized public service in Great Britain.

CREATING ADMINISTRATIVE CAPACITY

On the Continent, the revolutionary move toward popular sovereignty and the empowering of the middle class was dramatically changing the context but not the fundamental organization of public administration. A contrary development was taking place in Great Britain. With popular sovereignty long established, a century of reforms that began in the latter eighteenth century transformed the organization of public administration toward the objective of ensuring sufficient administrative capacity to implement Crown policies. "As the monarchy rose above party [during the period from 1760 to 1830], so the civil service settled below party. Constitutional bureaucracy was the counterpart of constitutional monarchy" (Parris 1969, 49; quoted by Rohr 2002, 27). Constitutional and administrative histories began to converge.

Intellectual preparations

Great Britain possessed little formal bureaucratic capacity prior to the nineteenth century. The "mercantilist state" denounced by Adam Smith was chimerical because there was no civil service able to administer one (Fry 1997). Prior to the reforms set in motion by the Northcote–Trevelyan Report of 1853, to serve the state in a public function was considered one of the duties of the gentry, and the gentry tended to resist reforms.

Edmund Burke and Jeremy Bentham began to lead the way toward civil service modernization with their leadership of the Economic Reform Movement of the 1780s, which, according to Fry (1997, 1–2),

> began the rationalization of the machinery of British central government, partly to assist Parliament's control over public expenditure and to push the Crown to one side, and partly to regularize staffing, which, at the time, was based on patronage appointments and the use of contractors. The conditions of service of officials were gradually changed, so that salaries replaced fees, and there was provision for pensions. By the mid-1850s, what had been a collection of largely separate offices had been brought at least into a working relationship with the Treasury (headed by Trevelyan).

Bentham's 1843 *Constitutional Code* was at least half devoted to "administration," and although not scientific in a contemporary sense, it resembled administrative science as it was known at the time on the Continent and was cameralistic in that he espoused specialized training and examinations for public officials and for single-headed administrative structures (Dunsire 1973). In Bentham's view, the civil service had to be an efficient one to conform to the kind of regulatory state foreseen by the classical economists.[6]

Whereas the French hoped to overcome the intractability of human nature by imposing order, the British relied on liberty and free choice to produce rational action.

67

Judith Merkle (1980) gives a lucid summary of British administration in contrast to that of the French. "[A]lthough there had been traditional connections between the British systematizers and the French rationalists," she argues (1980, 210), "their work differed greatly. For the British amalgamated the high rationality of the French with their own brand of common sense, practical discussion, and regard for the intractable nature of the human material." The English discourse, then, was carried on not by academics but by philosophers and public intellectuals, and concentrated on the structure of the administrative sector of government, on individual management and board management, on centralization and decentralization, and on the character and control of bureaucratic behavior (Dunsire 1973).

A modern civil service – and bureaucracy

The reform process under way since the 1760s produced no crystallization of civil service traditions or of the idea of administrative capacity before the 1850s (Finer 1942). American Schuyler Wallace (1941, 8), drawing on characterizations in Namier (1929), describes the British administrative class of the latter eighteenth century as "a huge aggregation of jobs, jobbing, sinecures, pensions, parliamentary politics, and public plunder." Dorman Eaton (1880) decried the British spoils system of that period, wherein a person's skill or ability to perform a job was not taken into consideration if they could provide political favors for the king or a member of parliament, rendering administration costly, feeble, and corrupt.

The spirit of reform began to infect the reign of George III following America's successful rebellion, which was motivated in significant part by abuses of administrative power. Legislation against bribery and office brokerage was enacted. With revolutionary tendencies growing in Europe, various reforms began to establish common patterns of education for officials modeled on classical instruction. But "practical technology and organization were considered beneath the attention of a gentleman" (Merkle 1980, 209). The Poor Law Amendment Act of 1834 has been said to have "constituted a virtual administrative revolution" in that it established a central commission, independent of both parliament and ministries, to professionalize local government (WEH 2004). The Municipal Corporations Act of 1835 required that local public officials be accountable to the public. Other acts sought to professionalize administration of prisons, education, mental health and public health.

The turning point occurred in 1853, when open competition for appointment to the civil service in India was approved by parliament. In the same year, having been commissioned by the chancellor of the exchequer, Sir Stafford Northcote and Sir Charles Trevelyan issued their famous "Report on the Organisation of the Permanent Civil Service" (the authors were two Treasury officials). Ostensibly a reaction to the patronage crisis that accompanied the extension of the franchise beginning in the 1830s (Hood and Jackson 1991b), this report advanced a specific administrative doctrine: "recruitment by competitive examination, promotion on merit, a separation of 'intellectual' and 'mechanical' work and a central classified pay scheme common to all departments" (Hood and Jackson 1991b, 135). It was, according to Kevin Brennan (2004), "the death throes of the aristocratic constitution."

Two years after the Northcote–Trevelyan report, Prime Minister William Gladstone overrode parliamentary objections to engineer the order-in-council of 1855 – Northcote and Trevelyan had recommended an act of parliament, which has never occurred – creating a Board of Public Administration (to become the Civil Service Commission in 1870) and requiring a minimum of competence among public officers (White 1935a, 1). Though the report had stirred up a political maelstrom and brought down a government, it acquired international significance.[7] The report became a landmark document in the development of European bureaucracy, and succeeded in "setting the agenda for UK public management for 70 years" (Hood and Jackson 1991b, 135).

The Northcote–Trevelyan report was not to achieve its full effect before 1920, however. After creation of the Board of Public Administration, there followed the Superannuation Act of 1859, the Civil Service Order in Council of 1870, which established open competition for all civil service appointments (and created the Civil Service Commission), and the MacDonnell Royal Commission of 1914, whose review led to all ministerial departments being brought into a uniform regulatory framework. After World War I, the Treasury established the familiar Administrative Class–Executive Class–Clerical Class distinction on the generalist side of the service.

The emergence of a professional civil service was significant to British public management traditions in several respects. First, owing to the flexibility of the British constitution, the civil service became an institution which provided protection against ministerial abuse of power (Thomas 1978). British civil servants were early freed from temptations toward partisan corruption and embraced the doctrine of neutrality of service and personal anonymity. Second, and of considerable importance, "the convention of ministerial responsibility was only universally accepted after the Northcote–Trevelyan reforms came to be slowly implemented" (Fry 1997, 2–2). Spurred by technological change and its complex demands, ministers recognized not only the growing need for professionalism among those serving government but also that their neutrality made political responsibility for government actions feasible (Dunsire 1990). Third, it became practical for the state to play "a more ambitious role in the economy and in social provision" (Fry 1997, 1–1). Although the reforms were intended to create a career civil service that served a classically liberal regulatory state, it enabled instead what became following World War II the Keynesian welfare state (Fry 1997). Finally, the reforms of the civil service, particularly that of 1870, brought Great Britain closer to, rather than further from, the Continental tradition of a public service bureaucracy (Albrow 1970).

None of these developments, which have come to be regarded as the "Westminister model" of parliamentary democracy, implied overt English acquiescence in bureaucratic government, however. English intellectuals compared the bureaucratized Continent with "free England" (Dunsire 1973). The term bureaucracy came into use in English in

69

the first half of the nineteenth century (Dunsire says 1830) mainly to distinguish English from Continental governance (Albrow 1970). In his *Principles of Political Economy* (1909 [1848], v. 2, 528), John Stuart Mill opposed "concentrating in a dominant bureaucracy all the skill and experience in the management of large interests, and all the power of organized action, existing in the community" (quoted by Albrow 1970, 22) as characteristic of "the over-governed countries of the continent." In *Considerations on Representative Government* (1861), Mill acknowledged that a bureaucratic government "accumulates experience, acquires well-tried and well-considered traditional maxims, and makes provision for appropriate practical knowledge in those who have the actual conduct of affairs" (quoted by Albrow 1970, 23). Mill was nonetheless influential in highlighting the antinomy between bureaucracy and democracy, an issue which, as we saw in Chapter 3, had also arisen on the Continent.

Mill was hardly the only English critic of bureaucracy. In *The English Constitution* (1867), Bagehot "warned against any undue admiration for the Prussian state system that might be occasioned by its recent military successes" (quoted by Albrow 1970, 23). In Bagehot's view, "The truth is that a skilled bureaucracy – a bureaucracy trained from early life to its special avocation – is, though it boasts the appearance of science, quite inconsistent with the true principles of the art of business" (quoted by Albrow (1970, 23) from Bagehot's *The English Constitution*), although he was also critical of the casual and unsystematic arrangement of public offices in England. Herbert Spencer and others began complaining about the increasing power of the growing British administrative organization. "An employed bureaucracy regularly became a governing bureaucracy, inflexible, fond of power, but enslaved by routine" (quoted by Albrow 1970, 25).

"As late as 1914, it could still be argued that bureaucracy was an intrusion from abroad, not yet deeply rooted in British government" (Albrow 1970, 26). In the broad perspective of English writers, "all European countries were of the same type: places where officials ruled" (Albrow 1970, 26). French and German critics of the rigid Prussian system envied what they regarded as English self-government. Even though amateurism was giving way to professionalism, "not only had England avoided bureaucracy, it had also avoided schools for public servants; and with them, administrative science textbooks" because there was no incentive to produce them (Dunsire 1973, 57). While creating the capacity for self-government and engaging in the study of administrative law, England remained unengaged in the academic study of administrative science until the twentieth century (some would say late in the twentieth century (Hood 1999)).

This view was contested, however. Ramsay Muir could argue by 1910 that bureaucracy was becoming a reality in England (Albrow 1970, 26). In Muir's cynical view (1910, 14),

[i]t is no exaggeration to say that, so far as concerns the carrying on of daily administration and the enforcement of existing laws, which is nine-tenths of the business of government, this country is governed by a pure bureaucracy, which is tempered

only by the fact that each group of bureaucrats has to convince a distracted and ill-informed politician, seldom interested in any subject that is not a matter of party warfare; and has also to satisfy the lively but quite haphazard and spasmodic curiosity of the House of Commons.

Muir continued (1910, 21–2):

Our bureaucracy directs, practically without control, nine-tenths of the work of administration; it is mainly responsible for the character and the growing amount of our national expenditure; it directly wields immense legislative powers under the terms of statutes, and is indirectly responsible for a large proportion of the parliamentary legislative output.

From this perspective, "free England" had already become "Weberian England" (Dunsire 1990).

All things considered, the British civil service had begun to enjoy high prestige for integrity, capacity, and intelligence, especially in an America engrossed in designing its own solutions to the emerging problems of public administration. Of the nineteenth-century British reforms, American Dorman Eaton (1880, 358) celebrated the change in the "justice and moral tone of a nation's politics" and the growing importance of "a principle of duty and responsibility in official life." Of the education of British civil servants, White (1935a, 24) noted that "[t]he emphasis is everywhere on developing capacity to make decisions, to take responsibility, and to think in large terms about the public service and public problems." The British civil service became a model, and in many respects a caricature (as was the Prussian bureaucracy), of such an institution.

Over time, however, not everyone remained so captivated. As Judith Merkle put it (1980, 209),

[r]eforms in the civil service, drawing on [the English] educational tradition, and derived from the examples of the new colonial service organized to govern India as well as from the Chinese examination system for civil service entrance, froze this attitude of "gentlemanliness," by the late nineteenth century, into a type of neo-mandarinism which saw government of every type the fit province of the generalist and the classicist.

Herman Finer (1942) summarizes H. E. Dale's view that "a great number of 'yes men' [populate the civil service]."[8] Dale talks of the quietist attitude which many in the civil service take and, as well, of the convention of neutrality. These three things seem to be tied up with his characterization of the mind and temper of the service as one of "stoical realism" (quoted by Finer 1942, 264). The gist of the prevailing creed, in Dale's words is: "They are doctrines of moderation and prudence, qualities abhorrent to enthusiasm or at least not easily reconciled with it" (quoted by Finer 1942, 264).

71

Great stability has been attributed to this institution. According to Peter Hennessy (1989), the archetype of the British civil service remained almost unchanged for some 130 years, surviving the 1918 Haldane Report,[9] two world wars, and the 1968 Fulton Committee, which intended to put an end to the gentleman-amateur-type civil servant. This, too, is a contested view, however. "The period between 1919 and 1943," according to Fry (1997, 3–2), was "the only period when Britain could be said to have had a unified Civil Service." Neither open competition nor promotion based on merit were ever universally in effect. Moreover, as we shall see below, important developments in thought and practice were arguably taking place.

The rule of (common) law

Unlike on the Continent (and to an extent not even true of the US), common law institutions governed British public administration. Rudolf Schlesinger *et al.* (1998, 276) argue that "the common law courts asserted, and through centuries of political and indeed military struggles successfully preserved, their power to curb abusive official action" (quoted by Bertelli 2005). Thus, the common law courts retained jurisdiction over all disputes, public and private. A. V. Dicey famously claimed that England had no administrative law like the *droit administratif* of France. Moreover, "Dicey condemned the *Conseil d'État* for its origins in the *ancien régime* and for its revival by the despot Napoleon" (Allison 1996, 19, quoted by Bertelli 2005). The Diceyan influence, argues Bertelli (2005), limited British (and Commonwealth) administrative law significantly until the 1980s (Schlesinger *et al.* 1998, 277).

Discretionary administrative power was nonetheless to grow. "By 1915," according to John Rohr (2002, 45), Dicey

> was well aware of the significant role played by administrative institutions in England, but he continued to insist that British officials had not succumbed to the blandishments of *droit administratif* because they could still be required to answer for their misdeeds before the ordinary courts of the realm.

In 1915, a landmark ruling of the House of Lords, *Local Government Board v. Arlidge*, held that an administrative body "in the exercise of statutory functions of a judicial character need not follow the procedure of a court of law, but could employ rules which appeared reasonable and fair for the conduct of its business." But English officials would still have to answer for their misdeeds before ordinary courts, and so Dicey was satisfied.

British judges have, however, created and aggressively used two fundamental principles of administrative law: *ultra vires* and natural justice. *Ultra vires* means that "public authority may not act outside its powers" (Rohr 2002, 47). Courts have held that parliament never intends to authorize abuses and thus that safeguards against abuse are implied. "This practice has had the happy effect of marrying the rule of law to parliamentary sovereignty" (Rohr 2002, 47). Natural justice, that is, acting fairly, is the procedural side of *ultra vires*: before being penalized, a person should be given a fair hearing, which means that both sides of the issue must be heard (*audi alteram partem*). According to Rohr (2002, 50), both France and Britain "share the common trait of solidly integrating administrative practices into [constitutional] traditions."

WAR AND WELFARE

While a certain stability could be claimed for British administrative institutions as world war, depression, and cold war preoccupied twentieth-century policy makers, subtle but important developments in administrative thought and practice were modifying the administrative system. There began to emerge not only the British welfare state but also, as noted in Chapter 1, a British philosophy of management.

Strengthening governance

As the twentieth century unfolded, an "Age of Anxiety" and "obsessive concern about government" were provoked by "a growing working class electorate, a fear of economic decline, a deterioration in industrial relations, a crisis of funding in the existing welfare system, and a crisis of confidence in international relations" (Turner 1988, 203). Public intellectuals, in particular Fabian socialists such as Sidney and Beatrice Webb and Harold Laski, began to study the details of government and to advocate both efficient administration to meet the demands of working-class constituencies and the participation in governance of outside experts and interests.

The specific issues raised by these developments were addressed by the MacDonnell Commission, or the Royal Commission on the Civil Service, active from 1912 to 1915 (Turner 1988). Among them were the arrival in the highest ranks of the civil service of the first merit system officials, increasing demands on the state by Liberals and Social Democrats, and increasing reliance by civil servants on professional organizations, trade associations, large commercial concerns, and trade unions. A spate of legislation between 1906 and 1914 was stimulated by new Liberal ministries and reflected tightened links and the creative tension between bureaucrats, outside experts, and interests (Turner 1988, 204). For example, the National Insurance Act of 1911 "created the political lobby which eventually secured the Ministry of Health" (Turner 1988, 217). Such precedents set the stage for developments between the wars, when state responsibility expanded through reliance on non-governmental entities, and for the "full flowering" of the interface between civil servants and citizens following World War II (Dunsire 1990, 262). These developments, as will be discussed presently, were to have a significant influence on British administrative values (Dunsire 1990).

An attempt to codify the emergent administrative model was the 1918 "Report of the Machinery of Government Committee," commonly referred to as the Haldane Report after its chair Richard Burdon, Viscount Haldane.[10] "Departments," said the report,

73

"appear to have been rapidly established without preliminary insistence on definition of function and precise assignment of responsibility" and, as a result, they failed to meet standards necessary for efficient action (Haldane 1918). The report also addressed the issue of the basis for allocating functions between departments. Though some have regarded the report as inconsequential, Richard Chapman (1997, 32) argues that it "set the tone for later thinking on central government administration in Britain," including the emphasis on vertical functional lines, partnership between ministers and civil servants (Foster 2001), and "canonization" (Beattie and Dunleavy 1995, 120) of the doctrine of ministerial responsibility.

Following World War II, the nationalization of basic industries, the accelerated growth of the British welfare state (including its icon, the National Health Service, founded in 1948), and the emergence of "quangos" (quasi-autonomous government organizations) as instruments of governance under the Labour government brought forth no new doctrines of government other than the implicit one of centralization (Dunsire 1990). Policy ideas for the welfare state were supplied by John Maynard Keynes and William Beveridge; organization models were the Central Electricity Board, created by the Baldwin government in the 1920s, and the wartime coalition government (Fry 1997).

The Fulton Report of 1968 recommended a managerial reform program similar in many respects to those advocated earlier in the century by the Socialists.[11] To encourage additional technical training, the government revised the criteria for promotion, eradicated long-standing divisions between administrators, professionals, and specialists, and established a Civil Service Department and Civil Service College (Silver and Manning 2000b). The report also recommended the creation of what are today called "agencies" wherever possible (Dunsire 1990), an idea discussed further in Chapter 6.

As for local government in Great Britain, "[t]he nineteenth century settlement of multipurpose local authorities collegiately controlled endured into the second half of the twentieth century remarkably without basic change" (Dunsire 1990, 268). In 1974, however, the number of "top-tier" and "second-tier" authorities was reduced dramatically, and other changes ensued (discussed further in Chapter 6).

Science and ethics

As in the US, where administrative reforms stimulated intellectual developments both to promote and to rationalize them in the first half of the twentieth century (discussed in Chapter 5), administrative change in Great Britain led to further articulation of a British philosophy of management, albeit different in emphasis from administrative thought both on the Continent and in the US.

"The real growth of the indigenous British management philosophy based on the study of the health and psychology of industrial workers," argues Judith Merkle (1980, 230), "dates from the First World War." Although scientific management – Taylorism – became popular on both sides of the Atlantic, "as a philosophy of organization [it] was rejected most strenuously by the British" (Merkle 1980, 223), although, Merkle notes, Lyndall

Urwick and John Child claimed the British invented it. Scientific management lacked the sympathetic view of workers and their representative organizations that was important to Quaker employers. Whereas the American solution to class divisions was an emphasis on efficiency and individualism that would increase the dividend for everyone, the British emphasis came to be on socialist ideas that emphasized a redivision of the product of industrial society.

Public administration, as noted in Chapter 1, reflected the general British philosophy of administration and "combined science and ethics, to be approached in a philosophical style" rather than in standard social science formats (Hood 1999, 291). Unlike in America and on the Continent, moreover, "social administration" was separated from public administration and political science early in the century. Also unlike American and Continental European scholarship, British public administration assumed a fusion rather than a separation of politics and administration. The focus of public administration was on local government, the civil service, imperial administration, and law and administration. The field "was conceived more as a co-operative enterprise between 'reflective practitioners' and academics, than as a detached world of scholarship" (Hood 1991, 292).[12] The British model of public administration came to enjoy a kind of prestige similar to that enjoyed by the British model of a civil service.

In her *British Philosophy of Administration* (1978), Rosamund Thomas identifies key figures such as Haldane, Wallas, Beveridge, Sheldon, Urwick, and Stamp as developing distinctive doctrines of administration which sharply contrasted with the ruling American ideas of the period, namely, a social-psychological focus on non-economic incentives and needs, and the idea of applying military general staff principles to public and other civilian organizations. British philosophers saw politics and administration as inextricably fused in the process of government; administration was a combination of science and ethics to be approached in a philosophical, not a natural scientific, style.

In his introduction to Thomas's book, the American Marshall Dimock contrasts the then American school of thought, which he calls the *computer-behavioral* school, rule by experts, with the British *cultural-humanistic* school. British public servants, he said, "believed in first principles and derived them to a large extent from the moral philosophy tradition" (Thomas 1978, xiii). He continued: "The first characteristic of these administrators was responsibility: they had initiative as well as accountability. The second was hardheadedness. . . . Another characteristic was balance. . . . Another characteristic was planning. . . . Another universal characteristic was a belief in people" (xiv–xv). Viscount Haldane was thought to exemplify these characteristics (he was the first president of what became the Royal Institute of Public Administration).

The roots of the academic field of public administration in Great Britain are, in Hood's view, Fabian and, in particular, found in the work of Sidney and Beatrice Webb and their followers (Hood 1999).[13] The highly diverse body of work was largely descriptive, concerned with the details of government operations, and oriented to the perspectives of public servants rather than of the academic political science community. The field nonetheless acquired conventional academic trappings of chairs at Oxford and the

London School of Economics, degree programs, and, beginning in 1922, the Institute of Public Administration and its new journal *Public Administration*. The teaching of public administration was in rising demand through the mid-twentieth century.

BRITISH LEGACIES

If the evolution of public management on the Continent is primarily an administrative history, the evolution of public management in Great Britain is primarily a constitutional history. That is true not only because the British constitution can be said to date back a millennium but also because it is uncodified, comprising numerous elements which are in constant flux. The British constitution can be "amended" at any session of the House of Commons, whenever new judicial or authoritative opinions are published, or by executive orders-in-council. "Old" public management in Great Britain, then, is deeply indigenous, ascribable less to rulers and revolutions than to the long-running drama of how English democracy emerged and was institutionalized.

An often-claimed advantage of the British constitution is its very flexibility, a point that will reemerge with force in Chapter 6. Yet it has also been argued that "it has a fixity that is predetermined by decades, if not centuries, of accumulated experiences that bind the political actors of the country more solidly than the most elaborate constitution does in another country" (Bélanger 2001). But, as we shall see, whereas "old public management" on the Continent and in America created obstacles to the reforms associated with "new public management," quite the opposite was true in Great Britain. Constitutional government in Great Britain, and in Westminster-model countries in general, provided a context within which executive power could implement far-reaching management reforms by merely announcing the determination to do so (Rohr 2002).

Another advantage of the British constitution, according to Fry (1997), is that, by ensuring recognition of the interests represented by the monarchy, the aristocracy, and the people, represented respectively by the Crown, the House of Lords, and the House of Commons, an appropriate balance between liberty and authority could more easily be struck. Although the prerogatives of each entailed risks to the maintenance of that balance, the presence of a monarchy precluded disputes over legitimacy; the aristocracy provided an able elite of capable leaders; and democracy protected the liberty of ordinary people. Owing to the absence of a single constitutional text, no structures of formal authority – no doctrine of the supremacy of the constitution over other legislative or executive enactments, no constitutional court, no separation of powers – inhibit or stifle change.

Still another advantage claimed for British governance is its relatively unitary character. Don Price (quoted by Finer 1942, 263) noted that "the government's program is considered much more as a whole in Great Britain than in the United States," as true today as when Price wrote. A party may advance a doctrine and have it debated as such, but in the US, Price says (Finer 1942, 263), parties go at it piecemeal and put over special programs with the support of special groups of administrators who may even help them organize their pressure on Congress. In other words, we have had a pluralistic system of administration and of politics operating under a constitution and a chief executive; whereas in Great Britain you have had a more unified system of administration under a single governing body with collective responsibility.

The exceptional nature of British parliamentary democracy notwithstanding, the British civil service can also be said to be a classic Weberian one (Fry 1997, 1–1) in that it carries out the government's policies regardless of party and, itself, is a career service independent of party. That this is true had not been anticipated by the Fabian Socialists, Laski, or the British Labour Party early in the twentieth century, and it was not so recognized until Clement Attlee's post-World War II Labour government came to power (Fry 1997). At that point, owing to a (misplaced) lack of trust in the Westminster model, public corporations were created to run the nationalized industries, with separate staff of their own. Eventually, however, the Fulton Committee was set up to set in motion creation of a reformed civil service. As will be shown in Chapter 6, a similar lack of trust, this time by the Tory administration of Margaret Thatcher, was to once again "reform" public management as only a Westminster government can.

NOTES

1 Even in countries with a written constitutional document, there are, arguably, unwritten or uncodified elements. Countries with unwritten – perhaps, better, uncodified – constitutions include Israel and countries, such as Saudi Arabia, governed substantially by Islamic Sharia law.
2 Conventions are described by Philip Norton as "rules of behavior that are considered binding by and upon those responsible for making the Constitution work, but rules that are not enforced by the courts or by the presiding officers in either house of Parliament" (Norton 1994, 60, quoted by Rohr 2002, 28).
3 The third administrative revolution was the nineteenth-century creation of departments responsible to parliament over which the Crown for the first time ceased to have ultimate control.
4 The British Crown has impressive prerogative powers, the exercise of which has proven significant in British history. In addition to approving all acts of parliament, the Crown summons and dismisses parliament and appoints the prime minister. Over time, however, the Crown has ceased to be a consequential element in British constitutional government, the exercise of Crown prerogatives being governed by well-established conventions that reinforce the supremacy of parliament and the rule of law.
5 British membership in the European Union subjects British legislation (as well as the legislative acts of all EU members) to review by the European Court, however, thus introducing a significant judicial restraint on the British parliament. This issue will be discussed further in Chapter 6.

6 Bentham's distinctions prefigured later developments in public management theory: between directive, executive, and inspective functions, for example, or between contract management and trust management.

7 The chief opposition to the Northcote–Trevelyan proposals, according to E. N. Gladden (1972b), came from members of parliament and the public, who were simply wary of tampering with things the way they were.

8 Finer's article is a review of H. E. Dale's *The Higher Civil Service of Great Britain* (1941), presented as a dialogue between Finer, of the University of London, Leonard White, and Don Price. Dale was a retired British civil servant.

9 The Haldane Report envisioned an intimate working relationship between ministers and civil servants, the latter, who would be independent of political party, counted on for providing intelligent and thoughtful analysis and recommendations to ministers, who retained decision-making authority. Haldane reforms encouraged the recruitment of generalists capable of working in any of the new post-war ministries and departments and formalized the classification of civil servants (which occurred in the US in 1923).

10 The report of the Haldane Committee is often cited as exemplifying a British version of the American "principles movement" and as a precursor to the report of the Brownlow Committee discussed in Chapter 5 (Dunsire 1973; Thomas 1978). Andrew Dunsire (1973) notes that Walter Bagehot had a version of principles of administration ("mountaintops"). He quotes Sir Edward Bridges on "generalized skills" that are distinguished from "departmental skills" but derived from them. According to Dunsire (1973, 35), Bridges talks of those "who can see round corners and through brick walls."

11 In 1968, the Fulton Commission urged radical reform in the civil service, recommending the establishment of agencies through the subdivision of departments on a functional basis. Other Fulton Report recommendations included the establishment of a civil service college, improving in-service training practices, and increasing the role of specialists. All centered on improving the quality of management in the civil service, as a means to increased efficiency and economy. The principal civil service reforms implemented since the early 1980s arguably had their origins in the recommendations of the Fulton Report.

12 The British central government traditionally gave little encouragement to the academic study of public administration, however.

13 A contrasting view is that of Mark Rutgers (2001, 232): "No specific study of public administration arose in England before the 1960s, although there are (influential) individuals who wrote on the subject."

Chapter 5

Old public management: American traditions

INTRODUCTION

The American state "is like no other!" proclaims Richard Stillman (1999, 249). What might be regarded as a conceit, often expressed in the solipsistic phrase "American exceptionalism," is forgivable, however. If there is a Westminster model of governance or a model of the state known as a *Rechtsstaat*, there is no equivalent *category* of states that includes, among others, the United States of America.[1]

Assembling a workable, democratic sovereignty on the eastern seaboard of a vast and isolated continent encountered formidable difficulties, including unsettled borders patrolled by foreign powers allied with hostile aboriginal peoples, jurisdictional and cultural fragmentation, dependence on the doomed institution of slavery, deep-seated distrust of European models of governance, and the legacy of an English administrative system against which the Colonists, overcoming their differences, developed a rebellious sense of grievance. There can be little wonder that a system of democratic governance with unique characteristics began to emerge within the American territories.

Characterizing that uniqueness is a more difficult matter, in no small part because, as Stillman has pointed out, "segmented layers of administrative reform resulted in incredibly complex, yet subtle sources for American state development," a process which, he argues, eludes comprehension (Stillman 1999, 249). Both Hegel and de Tocqueville saw America as "essentially a stateless society, devoid of an occupationally-distinct administrative class or even a noticeable institutional separation between government and society" (Nelson 1982, 748). In the view of Joel Aberbach and Bert Rockman (1988), America is unique because its institutional pathways are so convoluted that its parts tend to dominate the whole. Even a cursory examination of the American administrative system (see the summary description in Chapter 2) reveals that, combining federal, state, and local levels, America comprises more units of government, by far, than any other nation. Sovereign Americans have generously delegated their power.

Despite this complexity, other scholars attribute America's uniqueness to the nature and authority of its constitution, which, in prescribing a formal separation of powers among legislative, executive, and judicial branches of government, enables legislative control of administration and independent judicial settlement of disputes over what the

79

law of the land is (Riggs 1997b). One can go too far in contrasting America's written constitution with that of Great Britain. As Don Price has emphasized, America has its own unwritten constitution in the form of the primary system and party nominating conventions, congressional rules and organization, and a long list of statutes from the Administrative Procedure Act to the Freedom of Information Act (Price 1985) which, in Great Britain, would be considered parts of the constitution.

These rather convoluted arrangements have powerful implications for an institution, public administration, which has no independent source of legitimacy in the constitution.[2] Public administration in America must continuously establish its legitimacy with the political branches of government and before the bar, all of which have historically been skeptical of delegating authority to unelected officials. Of necessity, American public management is intensely political and almost invariably on the defensive with respect to the kinds of criticism that is endemic to pluralist democracy.

Yet the history of American public management as an institution is less a constitutional than an administrative history. The American Constitution is infrequently amended. Its impositions on public administration only occur in response to the petitions of aggrieved parties. American public management is the resultant of political activity within and between all those layers of government. It was through such activity that the American administrative state distinguished itself from its European forebears.

REVOLUTIONARY PUBLIC ADMINISTRATION

"[King George] has erected a multitude of new offices," complained the authors of the American Declaration of Independence in 1776, "and sent hither swarms of officers to harass our people and eat out their substance." The American revolutionaries' indictment of British colonial rule primarily concerned the abuse of administrative powers (Wilson 1975; Nelson 1982). Collectively, however, the Founders were clearer about what they did not want than about what they wanted in their institutional arrangements. What they did not want was a European-style government. "[T]he revolt against the old administrative order planted the seeds of a new administrative order without very much conscious attempt to pattern after foreign systems" (Learned 1912, 55, quoted by Nelson 1982, 751).

Founding views

The first attempt at sovereign government following the Declaration of Independence was a confederation of thirteen colonial states called the United States of America. The Articles of Confederation, America's first constitution, were drafted by the same Continental Congress that made the Declaration, and the required unanimous ratification by the states occurred on 1 March 1781. The articles established a "league of friendship and a perpetual union" between and among the thirteen former colonies, now states, reflecting their wariness of a strong central government. The states retained their sovereignty, the president merely presided over a Congress comprising representatives from each state, and Congress was denied the power to collect taxes, draft troops, regulate interstate commerce, or enforce the laws.

America's "First Republic" proved short-lived. Congress lacked the power to enforce its laws or even defend the fledgling nation against internal rebellion, and securing voluntary cooperation or agreement among the diverse colonies proved generally impossible. As George Washington reputedly opined, the government thus created was "little more than the shadow without the substance," except, of course, in the matter of defeating the British.[3] Nonetheless, the eight-year confederation period (1781 to 1789) left its imprint on Americans' view of their government. Americans have never ceased to regard their government as "primarily an aggregate and only secondarily as a unit" (Small 1909, 586). Moreover, whereas European states "began with the nation-state and worked downward[, i]n the United States the progression was reversed" (Mosher 1975, 8).

The most important legacy of the period was the tempering of fears about a central government with real powers. The management and defense of national interests, enforcement of laws, and the conduct of foreign policy, for example, had come to be understood as requiring a capable central government. Yet the process of drafting the Constitution was contentious, its popularity among citizens questionable, and the outcome in doubt. Delegates to the Constitutional Convention had to work through numerous points of conflict between large and small states, northern and southern states, and a variety of political philosophies before submitting the document to the states for ratification. Then, only the promise of immediately appending a Bill of Rights in the form of the first ten amendments enabled the proponent federalists to overcome antifederalist opposition and secure ratification by the minimum nine states.

To an extent notably different from the United Kingdom and the states of Continental Europe, the American government was conceived at a particular moment of history: during the several contentious months of the Constitution's drafting in Philadelphia in the summer of 1787. In less than two years, during which *The Federalist* papers were published, the constitutional scheme that endures to this day was formally put into effect following ratification by the states, thus establishing America's "Second Republic" legitimized by what is now the world's "oldest" constitution.

As John Gaus (1936) put it, the US contribution to the idea of administrative responsibility, forged during that summer of 1787, was the requirement that executive officials submit regularly, either directly or indirectly, to popular vote. When the Constitution was drafted, the responsibility of European executives to the legislature had not yet been established,[4] so the Founders set out to prevent the emergence of a European state of dangerously unaccountable executive power (Stillman 1999; Waldo 1984 [1948]). Moreover, noted Lloyd Short, "the adoption of a system of single-headed executive departments was a step distinctly in advance of formal English [administrative] development" (Short 1923, 75, quoted by Nelson 1982, 751), although "the idea was that agencies were to be run in the same way as the law firms, small businesses, plantations, and military units that agency chieftains came from" (Nelson 1982, 756).

John Rohr (2002) has long maintained that the groundwork for the administrative state that has emerged in America was laid in Philadelphia. He quotes Publius (the *nom de plume* of the authors of *The Federalist*: Alexander Hamilton, John Jay, and James Madison) as insisting that government must be given "an unconfined authority as to all those objects which are intrusted to its management," for "the means ought to be proportional to the *end*." Thus, says Rohr (2002, 148), Publius takes a managerial view of the Constitution, arguing (in *The Federalist*, No. 23) that "the persons, from whose agency the attainment of any *end* is expected, ought to possess the *means* by which it is to be attained."

A primary example of managerial self-awareness, *The Federalist*, together with early debates over governance in the new republic and early experience with governing, has been distilled into distinct (if not distinctive) administrative traditions or heuristics (for example, Stillman 1982; Kettl 2002): a Hamiltonian tradition, which echoes cameralism (see Chapter 3) in emphasizing strength in the executive to promote national economic interests; a perhaps uniquely American Madisonian tradition, emphasizing the interplay of group interests; a Jeffersonian tradition reminiscent of the English tradition of local government; and, dominant throughout much of the nineteenth century, the vaguely medieval Jacksonian tradition of party control of all aspects of administration.

Pre-bureaucratic America

For all the sophistication of the Founders' ideas, public administration prior to the progressive era was largely (although not exclusively) pre-bureaucratic. Of the first half of the nineteenth century, James Hart (1925, 267) wrote that

> There were several . . . important reasons why little discretion, and especially little rule-making discretion, was left to the Executive alike in state and nation [between 1815 and the Civil War]. Thus, there was the tradition largely inherited from England that the Executive had no independent or constitutional authority — no authority aside from statutory delegations — of supplementing by ordinances the terms of statutory law dealing with private interests. Added to this was the legislative method, also inherited from the mother country, of enacting detailed statutes, with concrete and specific provisions, and with generalities often modified by limiting provisos. . . . The result was that in the English method it was the judiciary that interpreted and applied in particular cases such generalities as found their way into the statutes.

These practices harmonized with American needs. Hart continues (1925, 268):

> With the theory abroad in the land that the legislature should legislate as little as possible, it was entirely possible for it to debate and prescribe every minute detail and try to anticipate every contingency. And with problems before them of relative

simplicity and stability, the laymen who are chosen by popular elections could with less absurdity than today attempt to decide in detail for future events.

When discretion was necessary, legislators preferred to give it, as did Great Britain, to common law juries rather than to the executive.

Administrative officers, many of them elected, functioned independently of executive authority with funds appropriated directly to their offices (Lynn 2001b). According to Waldo, "the lack of a strong tradition of administrative action . . . contributed to . . . public servants acting more or less in their private capacities" (Waldo 1984 [1948], 11). A "spoils system" (to the victor belong the spoils or privileges of office) of rotation in office dominated nineteenth-century selection and control of administrators, and haphazard oversight of administration was exercised by legislators, political parties, and the courts (Lynn 2001b).[5]

That standard account is somewhat misleading, however. Though credited with creating the spoils system, President Andrew Jackson also inaugurated the beginnings of bureaucratic government in America (Crenson 1975; Fesler 1982; Nelson 1982). The key idea, argues Nelson, was Jackson's notion that federal jobs "admit of being made" so simple that any intelligent person could do them. A related impetus was the need to restrain corruption among these officeholders. The result was the creation of agencies with significant internal checks and balances to prevent thievery. To citizens, however, these checks and balances often looked like red tape.[6] As Nelson (1982, 763) notes, "agencies organized to avoid evil became that much less able to do good." But a political dynamic was being established. Because the establishment of democracy in the US preceded the creation of administrative institutions, nineteenth-century political parties had little incentive to curb bureaucratic power; their goal was to mobilize it on behalf of their own political interests. In consequence, bureaucrats had every incentive to develop political bases of support. "Jackson's Democrats fostered the process of bureaucratization in order to reap the harvest of spoils such organizational changes allowed" (Nelson 1982, 775).

As will become clear below, Jacksonian traditions (basically, those described by de Tocqueville) were more quintessentially American than what replaced them beginning late in the nineteenth century, which was much more European (or Hamiltonian) in flavor. As Daniel Carpenter (2001, 38) has argued, "For Tocqueville, administrative decentralization and debility most distinguished American state institutions from their European counterparts. Whereas other nations endowed administrative organizations with significant autonomy, and whereas their national political cultures bestowed status on administrative careers, in the United States political culture and institutions conspired to create a feeble bureaucratic state,"[7] which was "starved of a career structure that could prescribe standardized career ladders and foster predictability and similarity of experience among career state officials" (48).

In one of the earliest attempts to define the field of public administration and management, Leonard White (1935b, 418) observed:

So long as American administrative systems remained decentralized, disintegrated, and self-governmental and discharged only a minimum of responsibilities, the necessity of highly developed machinery for its control was unknown. Administration was weak and threatened no civil liberties; it was unorganized and possessed no power of resistance; it was elective and quickly responsive to the color and tone of local feeling.

The problems of delegation, control and accountability that preoccupy the field now were not acute in pre-bureaucratic America. Beginning in the latter nineteenth century, however, they would rapidly become so.

AN AMERICAN INVENTION

Modern American public management grew out of a reform movement that reflected "a fundamental optimism that mankind could direct and control its environment and destiny for the better" (Mosher 1975, 3; Davy 1962). Following the Civil War, industrialization, urbanization, and immigration began to transform American society. Promoted by academically affiliated activists, the emerging field reflected a number of currents in American thought: a progressive political agenda, the growing popularity of science and of the idea of management, the professional development of administrative law and a spirit of pragmatic empiricism.

The groundwork for change was laid at the federal level by the civil service reform movement, the milestone of which was the Pendleton Act of 1883. "With the legitimacy of the early American state under attack from all sides," Stephen Skowronek argued (1982, 165), "government officials finally made the pivotal turn down the bureaucratic road," a road which, as we have already seen, was being traveled in Great Britain and was something of a superhighway on the Continent. The federal government began an inexorable expansion, initially into regulating the private sector but ultimately, as in Europe, into the service and public works agencies of the welfare state.

According to Frederick Mosher, however (1975, 8), "the real origins of public administration lay in the cities, especially the big ones, not in theories of sovereignty or the state or the separation of powers." The goal of municipal reformers was to substitute rational, fact-based governance for boss rule. The council-manager form of local government is arguably the most successful reform in American public administration. From seeds sown in initially barren terrain at the federal level by the interest of Presidents Theodore Roosevelt and William Howard Taft in promoting efficient government, administrative reform next took firm root in the fertile soil of state government, where the goal was to strengthen executive control over the expanding range of state policies and programs. Administrative reform finally reached the federal level with the Budget and Accounting Act of 1921 and, later, with Roosevelt's New Deal reforms (Bertelli and Lynn 2006), especially creation of the Executive Office of the President, which laid the foundations for contemporary presidential power.

The result of these various transformations at local, state, and federal levels of government was dramatic, wrote Harold Laski in 1923 in the new British *Journal of Public Administration*. "A state built upon *laissez-faire* has been transformed into a positive state. Vast areas of social life are now definitely within the ambit of legislation; and a corresponding increase in the power of the executive has been the inevitable result" (1923, 92). In the same year, John Gaus (1923–4, 220) could say with prescience and conceptual coherence that

> [t]he new administration includes a wide share of policy formulation; it requires a large measure of discretion on the part of the civil servant; it claims wide exemption from judicial review of its findings of fact; in brief, we are seeing a development somewhat akin to the rise of the administration in the days when the Tudors and the great monarchs were welding together the modern national state.

E. N. Gladden (1972b, 388–9) concludes that "[i]t was . . . in the United States, with its expanding plurality of governmental institutions and great variety of non-governmental enterprise providing a rich experimental environment for the examination of institutions and organization, that a new phase in the growth of reasoned awareness of administration really took shape," with "the primary impact [being] practical rather than academic."

Although noting that American reformers often suggested that European "administrative technology" be imported and adapted, Dwight Waldo insisted that "no substantial, systematic, transfer was possible. European administrative technologies were intimately related to the social, economic, and governmental systems in which they had evolved, and could not be simply copied in America" (1984 [1948], xxxii), implicitly denigrating the value of studying European legacies. Yet the American field's founders were more Eurocentric than is now remembered.

European influence

The first responders to the challenges of creating a modern administrative state had deep European roots. The work of Henri Fayol, Harold Laski, Lorenz von Stein, Otto Hintze, Henri Berthélemy, and other Europeans was familiar to Americans, many of whom had studied in Germany and elsewhere in Europe. There were good reasons for this Eurocentrism. "Since higher education, particularly technical education, was far more advanced in Europe than in the United States until the end of the [nineteenth] century, Americans widely differing in class origin spent crucial episodes of their lives abroad" (Karl 1976, 493). Americans studied in Europe and, in any event, looked to Europe for ideas concerning construction of an American administrative state. Early American contributors to the field of public management – Woodrow Wilson, Frederick Cleveland, both W. F. and W. W. Willoughby, John Dickinson, Carl Friedrich, John Fairlie, John Pfiffner – were familiar with, and often wrote about, European and British precedents in both administrative law and public administration, and many advocated at least selective adaptation of these precedents to American needs. But, argues historian Barry Karl, "[t]he American adoption of systematic methods of management being developed in Great Britain and Germany had to take place in a political environment, the democratic rhetoric of which could always render the very concept of management suspect" (Karl 1976, 491).[8]

In his obsessively analyzed 1887 essay, Woodrow Wilson drew heavily on European experience, tending "both to minimize the political role of administration by giving it a privileged position above politics within the framework of the state, and yet to glorify the bureaucracy as a creative political force" (Miewald 1984, 21), thus explaining his temporary affinity for separating public management from politics.[9] Wilson also drew on British models in his writing. Although his *Congressional Government* (1885) is cited by Waldo (1984 [1948]) as comparing the American governmental system unfavorably to that of Great Britain, Robert Miewald (1984, 23) argues that "[h]is major published works [showed] their admiration of English constitutional forms and unabashed praise for philosophers such as Burke and Bagehot." In effect, Wilson argued that Americans might well import what John Child (1969) later termed "the technical functions" of administration or what Bagehot (1949 [1867]) called "the efficient parts" rather than the "dignified" or symbolic parts. Americans interpreted what might appear to be Wilson's support for importing European administrative principles and technique as principled support for a program of domestic political reform. And Wilson, like Dorman Eaton (1880), "might have been holding up to Americans some foreign models for their emulation" (Dunsire 1973, 89; Raadschelders and Rutgers 1996).

By far the more significant figure in channeling European thinking to America, however, was Frank J. Goodnow, most conspicuously in the field of administrative law, but in public administration as well.[10] In 1886, Goodnow noted that there was little authority for use of the term administrative law in the US, but he nonetheless favored using the term already in use by French and German lawyers. "For we have already adopted the word 'administrative' in describing analogous relations. Thus, *e.g.*, we speak of reform in our governmental system as 'administrative reform'" (Goodnow 1886, 535). A few years later (Goodnow 1893, 1902, v), he noted that

the work was begun by first studying with considerable care books on foreign administrative law. This was necessary, owing to the complete lack of any work in the English language on administrative law as a whole, and was possible and profitable owing to the richness of the literature of foreign administrative law. . . . For in the present stage of the study it is to foreign writers that we must look for all scientific presentations of the subject.

In general, Goodnow argued that America had copied in great part the English system of judicial control and "formed in the ordinary courts a special 'administrative jurisdiction'" (1886, 544), albeit in more limited form than in England. The federal courts were denied original jurisdiction to issue writs of *mandamus* and *certiorari* to compel or review action on the part of the officers of the United States government, although they could issue the injunction. Thus American administration was more independent of judicial control than that of England, a situation that was regarded as benign until serious issues of governance at the national level began to arise in the latter part of the nineteenth century.[11]

Many of America's most prominent early public management reformers and writers were essentially comparative in examining American problems and solutions in the light of European experience. For example, John Mabry Mathews (1917), who was active in state-level reform, cites a number of European sources; his definition of administration is from *Dictionnaire de l'Administration Française*. James Hart (1925) refers frequently to systems of law in other countries, especially European ones. He notes, for example, that whereas in Germany the administrative head may organize and regulate services, in the US states these are matters of constitutional or legislative determination. John Dickinson (1927, 95) argues that

> [t]he idea of applying an abstract law as a check on the action of government has had a much wider subsequent development in the United States than in England. The development there has been almost wholly in the direction of the other idea – control by a popular organ of government; and the powers of the House of Commons have expanded until they have absorbed practically all that the monarch once claimed an independent right to exercise.

W. F. Willoughby, another active reformer and writer and founder of the Institute for Governmental Research, also drew heavily on European, especially German, experience, albeit in a more cautionary way than Wilson or Goodnow. He noted (1919, 153) with reference to the German bureaucracy that "there are inherent in it certain disadvantages or dangers which go far toward justifying the deep-seated distrust that Americans have of it," but was equally disapproving of the aristocratic nature of the British civil service.[12]

Some see the British influence as dominant in American public administration. Unlike Germany, Great Britain had a "common core of belief in participatory democracy, public opinion, and leadership held responsible to judgment from outside the ruling government" (Karl 1976, 493). Continental political thought in the nineteenth century, argues Karl, "moved much more easily to positions which identified debate with partisan deadlock and sought various versions of single party certification of decisive administration as the new route to industrial democracy" (Karl 1976, 493–4). In Waldo's view, English local government is the model for American public administration, not European monarchical, hierarchical systems, driven as they were by security concerns (Waldo 1984 [1987]).

Yet the German influence might be regarded as an antidote or corrective to the British influence, Karl notes (1976, 494).

American progressives in the years prior to the outbreak of [World War I] saw the German administrative experience as a more efficient and successful approach to the problems of relating the need for democratic involvement in government to the demands of a technological-industrial society. The German experience emphasized specialized management.

John W. Burgess, widely regarded as the father of American political science and the first chair in American studies at the University of Berlin, "retained his commitment to Germany as the logical, historical ally of the United States in world affairs, not Great Britain" (Karl 1976, 494).

Some scholars have argued for the significance of French influence on American public administration. According to John Fairlie (1935, 5), "[t]he development of a distinct body of administrative law on the continent of Europe was promoted by the French interpretation of the doctrine of separation of powers, under which it was held that the judiciary should not interfere with the legislative or executive agencies." Daniel Martin (1987, 297) argues that "virtually every significant concept that existed in American public administration literature by 1937 . . . had already been published in France by 1859. Most had been published by 1812," although this French intellectual capital was not incorporated into American academic scholarship. To a surprising degree, "the French used the same terminology that is now used in the U.S. and . . . suggested the same hypotheses" (302).

While the influence in America of British and Continental public administration is demonstrable, what was to emerge from a century of administrative reforms nevertheless produced a model of public administration that was distinctively American.

A pragmatic response

The profession of public administration is an American invention, Frederick Mosher once declared (Mosher 1975), and most American students of the field are inclined by their training to believe that this is true. According to Anthony Bertelli and Laurence Lynn (2006, 17), that invention

> originated in the reform movements that began in the nation's large cities and spread within a generation to state and national governments. So-called orthodox ideas – "scientific" management, a politically neutral civil service, unity of command – far from being products of abstract theorizing, were elements of reform agendas intended to empower government to meet the challenges of a growing, industrializing, urbanizing, and diversifying society.

Ideas now (inaccurately) regarded in America as the rigid credos of an orthodoxy or a bureaucratic paradigm (Lynn 2001b) were in their time pragmatic responses to problems of governance arising at federal, state, and municipal levels of government, devised by men and women of affairs, advocates of administrative reform, and public officials, together with the reform-minded organizations they founded, led, or consulted.

These early developments, Laurence O'Toole (1984) has argued, are far from representing an effort to blend European and American ideas. They constituted, rather, a reaction against European formalism, which used abstractions, deductive systems of logic, and formal coherence as initial principles. "Anti-formalism proposed action and reform was the stance of the activist" (O'Toole 1984, 145). He continues (p. 149):

> Our administrative tradition was developed by individuals who were hostile to doctrine, who have banked on experience, who have exaggerated the defects of previously proposed solutions and the probable beneficial consequences of the currently fashionable ones, and who were simultaneously held in thrall by the imperatives of technique and the goal of democracy.

Although reforms at federal, state, and local levels were similar in many respects – Leonard White felt confident that administration was "a single process" that did not justify distinctive municipal, state, and national analyses (1926, vii) – each of the three streams of reformist thought and action had a distinctive emphasis (or, rather, various ideas had different salience at each level (Bertelli and Lynn 2006). At the municipal level, reform was oriented toward the efficiency and impartiality of the rapidly expanding administrative operations essential to business development and social stabilization. At the state level, the dominant theme was reorganization: of independent boards and commissions into a more coherent departmental format subject to rational oversight by legislators and elected governors. At the federal level, the theme came to be the strong executive, a theme that was to culminate in the concept of the president as chief administrative officer that inspired the work of President Roosevelt's Committee on Administrative Management (the Brownlow Committee) and, after World War II, of the Commission on the Organization of the Executive Branch of Government (the first Hoover Commission).

As early Progressive-era reforms were beginning to give shape to a positive state, Frank Goodnow stated the problem of American public management concisely (1967 [1900], 97–8):

> [D]etailed legislation and judicial control over its execution are not sufficient to produce harmony between the governmental body which expresses the will of the state, and the governmental authority which executes that will. . . . The executive officers may or may not enforce the law as it was intended by the legislature. Judicial officers, in exercising control over such executive officers, may or may not take the same view of the law as did the legislature. No provision is thus made in the governmental organization for securing harmony between the expression and the execution of the will of the state. The people, the ultimate sovereign in a popular government,

must . . . have a control over the officers who execute their will, as well as over those who express it.

Separation of powers, Goodnow recognized, creates a discontinuity in the constitutional scheme such that the people cannot be fully assured that their wishes will be carried out or enforced. The problem is one of coordination between law and implementation – the central, multi-branch relationship in American public management – without creating unaccountable power in executive agencies.

It was also recognized, however, that "[t]he traditional dogma of the separation of powers is an over-simplification of the governmental process as it actually takes place and as it is recognized by the courts" (Hart 1925, 38). The fact remains, argued John Fairlie (1920, quoted by Hart 1925, 120),

> that there is a broad twilight zone between the field of what is distinctly and exclusively legislative and what is necessarily executive in character; that courts have recognized that matters within this 'no man's land' may be expressly authorized by statute for administrative action; and if neither of these steps is taken such action has been, under some circumstances, assumed as an inherent executive or administrative power.

The reality, in other words, is that under America's constitutional separation of powers, a considerable amount of discretion is available to public managers.[13] The body of rights and duties, in Hart's words, "does not come from the legislature complete" (1925, 35). Government in action and constitutional law in the concrete are more varied than the opening sentences of the first three Articles of the Constitution would indicate. As John Comer (1927, 14) put it, "government by rule and law has become, in large part, government by the wish and discretion of administrative officers."

This is not to imply, however, that there was a shift from administration subject to judicial rule to discretionary administration (Freund 1915). The result of the new administrative power was, according to Ernst Freund (1915, 667–8),

> plainly the other way: it substitutes for the more or less arbitrary judicial action – arbitrary because delegated to a jury – a fixed and responsible rule. . . . The real significance of administrative ruling authority then does not lie in any diversion of genuine judicial power, but in relieving the judiciary from functions in their nature more or less legislative.

In effect, "[t]he development of political institutions in America emphasized and strengthened what may be called the irresponsible elements in government. . . . [L]egislatures gained an independence of executive guidance and initiative such as no other legislative bodies have ever had" (Freund 1915, 671). Public administration, in other words, "shares with judicial action the respect of precedent and the respect of expert opinion, habits of mind which distinguish both from the irresponsible action of popular bodies" (Freund 1915, 675).

These evolving ideas coalesced around a particular idea: the need for a strong elected executive. Frederick Cleveland argued (1919, 252), "[W]e have purposely deprived ourselves of responsible executive leadership for fear we shall not be able to control it." "From about 1912 on," says Jane Dahlberg (1966, 239), "the New York Bureau [of Municipal Research] almost continuously devoted its energy to the inculcating of the idea of executive responsibility into our governing institutions, evolving a philosophy of executive responsibility." She continues: "In summary, it might be said that the essence of the Bureau's contributions was in the blocking out of a field of public administration" that implemented Goodnow's theory of the separation of politics and administration in a non-partisan, objective way.[14]

Support for aggrandized executive power in national government was strengthened by the lessons of World War I. "[M]aking due allowance for the lack of cooperation between the President and Congress due to personal reasons," argued Charles Fenwick in 1920, "it remains true that the constitutional separation of the legislative and executive departments resulted in constant friction, in needless delay in the passage of the necessary legislation, and in duplication of the activities and extravagance of expenditure which under more critical circumstances might have proved disastrous to the country" (Fenwick 1920, 576).[15]

The enactment by Congress of the Budget and Accounting Act of 1921 was a milestone in the development of American public management. Supporters saw the measure as enabling the president to be a strong executive leader, assisted by the staff of the newly created Bureau of the Budget (White 1933). The executive budget would become both an instrument of accountability of the president to the Congress and the public and an instrument of administrative control over the bueaucracy. The Budget Bureau was foreseen (by W. F. Willoughby, among others) as a general bureau of administration, a pacemaker of sound management, an extension of the chief executive, strengthening the forces of fiscal order, administrative consistency, and managerial responsibility. Thus it would serve as a bulwark against a rejection by the people of the constitutional system as corrupt and inefficient (Morstein Marx 1945).

The aggrandizement of executive power affected public administration in subtle but significant ways. "[S]ubordinate officials," said James Hart, "must be placed upon a permanent and relatively effective basis" (Hart 1925, 273). In 1931, John Gaus noted "the increasing role of the public servant in the determination of policy, through either the preparation of legislation or the making of rules under which general legislative policy is given meaning and application" (Gaus 1931, 123). Thus, he said, we can look forward with greater complacency upon delegations to these new departments. As we shall see below, however, such complacency is inconsistent with America's separation of powers.

91

Scientific management

In arguing for a science of administration, Woodrow Wilson had observed in 1887 that one already existed but that it was wholly European, originating in France and Germany. To be of use in America, he argued, such a science would have to be Americanized, a task made inherently difficult when the sovereign is popular opinion rather than a monarch (Dunsire 1973). "Scientific management" was to flourish during Wilson's presidency (from 1913 to 1921), but it reached the field of public administration via developments in the industrial sector.

Concurrently with the emergence of "the new administration," a contemporaneously identified "management movement" (Person 1977 [1926]) had been gathering strength in the industrial sector, reflecting primarily the thinking of engineers such as Henry R. Towne, Henry Metcalfe, and Frederick W. Taylor (George 1972; Person 1977 [1926]). Taylor was an engineer and his principal forums were in the engineering profession. The focus of what became known as "the scientific management movement" was on efficient use of labor and on costs and cost systems. From concerns with efficient use of labor and wage/cost systems there arose a more general concern for organization and coordination. Taylor's immensely influential book *The Principles of Scientific Management* was published in 1911.

Under the banner of Scientific Management, the generic concept of "management" (Church 1914) was to gain a following among those invested in the reform of public administration. Most famously expressed by Leonard White (1926, viii): "[T]he study of administration should start from the base of management rather than the foundation of law." However, argues Andrew Dunsire (1973, 93), "[t]his movement meant by 'science' something more than the eighteenth- and nineteenth-century writers on 'administrative science' (or indeed 'economic science' or 'political science') had meant by the word – something like 'disciplined study'." Taylor aimed to replace hunch with observation and measurement, traditional practices with calculation and "rational methods."

Taylor himself seemed to recognize that managing was a principal–agent problem (discussed further in Chapter 7); workers kept employers ignorant of how fast work can be done (Crainer 2000). The solution was the elimination of the information asymmetry between employers and workers through measurement, leading to the maxim "what gets measured, gets done." Taylor fervently believed that scientific management was humane, good for society, and likely to promote friendship between worker and employer. Writing in 1914, Hamilton Church (1914, iv) captured the excitement of the idea:

> The question of formulating some approach to a true science of management has been in the air for some time. The first and most forceful stirring of the subject is unquestionably due to Mr. Frederick W. Taylor, whose paper on "Shop Management," issued in 1903, opened most persons' eyes to the fact that administration was ceasing

to be . . . a kind of trade secret, known only to a few men . . . and that it was entering a stage where things could be reasoned about instead of being guessed at.

The rest is history. "[M]uch of modern American business and public administration," argues Judith Merkle (1980, 294), "is, for various historical reasons, the heir to the Scientific Management movement."

The appropriation of Scientific Management by the creators of "the new admin-istration" (or what Leonard White termed "the new management") exemplifies the pragmatic spirit of the emergent American field. "Scientific Management," both as a method and as a body of principles, was embraced because, owing to its business origins, it promised legitimacy for administration in the face of congenial American skepticism of the kind of bureaucratic power associated with European étatism. Judith Merkle (1980, 289) delineated the techniques and values of Scientific Management as follows:

1. "Democracy" means the satisfaction of the common man's material needs, not a "debating society" theory of government.
2. Elective democracy caters to the lower instincts of the masses at the expense of expertise.
3. "Authority" of the traditional governmental type is an ineffective, personalized, coercive attempt at control and must remain so until the introduction of scientific measures of performance.
4. . . . [G]overnment which is more efficient at encouraging high productivity and arranging fair distribution of goods is best (as well as "most democratic").
5. State power is therefore properly exercised by a technical elite through a process of scientific planning of the production and distribution of goods for the benefit of the entire population.

The ideas most widely attributed to early American administrative thought, of a dichotomy between politics and administration and of scientific principles as the basis for management, "were the foundation stones of the City Management movement (White 1927), of a similar reform movement in State government (Lipson [1968] 1939), of the municipal research bureau movement (Beard 1926; Waldo [1984] 1948, 33), and in the employment of professors of public administration as consultants to government" (Dunsire 1973, 94). In a more practical vein, Leonard White (1926) argued that the growing importance of science and scientific knowledge made the spoils system obsolescent.

It is notable that the popularity of the idea of scientific management preceded Taylor, whose pathbreaking book was published in 1911. "A scientific organization of depart-ments," according to Frank Prichard (1892, 22), "will, to a very large extent, increase the morality as well as the efficiency of the employee." The New York Bureau of Municipal Research, a seminal force in "the new administration," exemplified the scientific spirit. The idea of the Bureau, according to Henry Bruère, its first director, was "applying

93

the test of fact to the analysis of municipal problems and the application of scientific method to governmental procedure" (Dahlberg 1966, 16). As William Allen, Secretary of the New York Bureau of Municipal Research, put it in 1908: "Government is a matter of conditions, methods, acts and results, not a mere matter of theories. Conditions are objective; they can be seen, analyzed, understood, directed, changed [which] requires knowledge of their component parts and interrelations" (Allen 1908, 606). The "college man," said Allen (p. 606), must learn:

> (1) how to study community needs; (2) how to study official acts; (3) how to devise and manage the governmental machinery that is necessary to give effect to the wishes of the community; and (4) how to frame official reports that shall make this machinery intelligible and show in what measure the desired results are being attained.

The establishment of the Institute for Government Research in 1916, according to its first director, W. F. Willoughby, "represents the conviction on the part of its founders that the work of administration is, if not a science, a subject to the study of which the scientific method should be rigidly applied" (1918, 49). The Institute's goal would be scientific analysis to identify the principles that ought to govern in the interest of economy and efficiency of the national government, as the municipal research bureaus have done for local government. In a public statement at its founding, it was described as "an association of citizens for cooperating with public officials in the scientific study of business methods with a view to promoting efficiency in government and advancing the science of administration" (Willoughby 1918, 58).

Unfortunately, according to Church (1914, iv), "[t]he phrases 'scientific management' and 'efficiency' became the stock-in-trade of numberless amateurs and pretenders, the value of the movement was magnified beyond all reason, and the public were led to believe that some wonderful new and potent instrument for getting rich quickly had been discovered." In reality, "[s]cientific management was built on a lack of trust, a lack of respect for the worth, wit, and intelligence of individuals. In Taylor's mind, management was an ascetic science rather than a humane one" (Church 1914, 15). The psycho-physical connection between qualified professional work and imagination, fantasy, and initiative was to be replaced with automatic and mechanical attitudes. Moreover, people did not need to know what was happening elsewhere in the organization; coordination occurred by rigid, measured specialization.

The spirit of science has continued to infuse American public management. There emerged within political science serious interest in measuring "objectively the results of the administrative reorganization code movement" and, in general, the accomplishments of state government (Graves 1938, 508), to enable comparisons across states and before and after reorganization. Graves lists sixteen criteria for state effectiveness; although aggregated and imprecise, the criteria are comprehensive and clearly in the spirit of contemporary balanced scorecards. The spirit of scientific management continued to be influential through the work of Herbert Simon and the Carnegie School (which featured the behavioral study of organizations and decision making), the policy analysis movement, and neoclassical managerialism. Those aspects include strengthening the public executive in setting priorities and in making and enforcing policies and employing analytic methods to vet the efficiency and other consequences of alternative policies.

But the version of scientific management that originated with Taylor and the principles movement was to achieve an apogee within the traditional field during President Franklin Roosevelt's Depression-inspired New Deal.[16]

The New Deal

Beginning in 1933, the administration of Franklin D. Roosevelt, supported by large Democratic majorities in Congress, sponsored a heretofore unimaginable expansion of federal authority and programs, the essentials of which were held to be constitutional in a series of decisions by a cautious Supreme Court. Ranging from the Federal Emergency Relief Act and the National Industrial Recovery Act to the Social Security Act and the creation of the Tennessee Valley Authority, the administration's overall goal was social and economic recovery and stabilization. In the process, state and local governments were co-opted into the emergent American welfare state in a vast network of what became known as "intergovernmental relations" (D. Wright 1987; Milakovich and Gordon 2001), fueled in part by federal grants-in-aid, many with matching require-ments, and other financial coordination arrangements. But the question arose: did the presidency have the capacity to administer the rapidly expanding scope and reach of the federal government?

The 1937 Report of the President's Committee on Administrative Management (the Brownlow Report) became "a landmark statement of 'managerialism' in public administration and is closely associated with the alliance between Progressivism and the scientific management movement" (Hood and Jackson 1991b, 135; Dunsire 1973; Merkle 1980).[17] Fulfilling W. F. Willoughby's original aims, the Brownlow Report (PCAM 1937) brought scientific management to bear on problems at the federal level of American government. "The President needs help," proclaimed the Committee before presenting its solution.

The solution to weak presidential control over a bureaucracy burgeoning with Franklin Roosevelt's New Deal programs "is couched in terms of a more centralized top-down reporting structure based on a private business management analogy, with a large general staff apparatus around the chief executive" (Hood and Jackson 1991b, 136). The president should be in a position "to coordinate and manage the departments and activities [of the government] in accordance with the laws enacted by the Congress" (PCAM 1937, iv), achievement of which would require an expanded White House staff, stronger management agencies, a strengthened and expanded civil service system, a subordination of independent agencies, administrations, authorities, boards, and commissions to major executive departments, and an independent post-audit of the

95

fiscal transactions of an Executive with complete responsibility for accounts and current transactions (Bertelli and Lynn 2006). "There is nothing [in this program]," Roosevelt insisted, "which is revolutionary, as every element is drawn from our own experience either in government or large-scale business" (PCAM 1937, iv).

Like the Northcote–Trevelyan report (see Chapter 4), the Brownlow Report ran into immediate political trouble. However, like its British predecessor, it had an "agenda-setting" effect in the longer term and "has acquired unquestionably 'classic' status. . . . It appeals to the march of history and the laws of administrative science to back up its assertions" (Hood and Jackson 1991b, 136–7), although it "no more demonstrates the validity of the measures it advocates than does the Northcote–Trevelyan Report" (Hood and Jackson 1991b, 142).

The involvement of Luther Gulick and other scholars in the work of the Brownlow Committee, note Gary Wamsley and Larkin Dudley (1998), was the first involvement of scholars in publicly appointed committees or commissions concerned with administration since Willoughby was involved with President William Howard Taft's 1910–1912 Commission on Economy and Efficiency. These scholar-activists, like their Progressive predecessors, were concerned with the fate of democracy and with promoting it through reconciling a strong executive with democratic accountability. At the same time, Gulick himself, who had long disavowed the notion that administration could be separated from politics, feared a weak government more than he feared a loss of impartiality. Owing to the fact that Committee principals Brownlow, Merriam, and Gulick were deeply involved in urban government reform, it is not surprising that the Brownlow model of a strong executive imitated the concept of the city manager.

Release of the Brownlow Report was accompanied by the publication of the report's background papers, *Papers on the Science of Administration*, edited by Gulick and Lyndall Urwick (1937) (which first brought Henri Fayol's ideas to an American audience). Both the report and the background papers served as lightning rods for critics of a centralized, depoliticized scientific managerialism. Scientific management in a narrow sense had never been as dominant an idea in democratic America as is often supposed (Dunsire 1973), not even with Gulick. Moreover, human relations scholarship, the debate between Herman Finer (1940) and Carl Friedrich (1940) – Finer argued for detailed control of bureaucracy by legislation, Friedrich for managerial professionalism and self-control – and works such as Pendleton Herring's *Public Administration and the Public Interest* (1936) and Chester Barnard's *The Functions of the Executive* (1968 [1938]) were bringing to the fore the human and political dimensions of management.[18]

Though the Brownlow Report faded to political obscurity, especially after Roosevelt's ill-conceived proposal to enlarge the Supreme Court antagonized a wary Congress, the most basic of the reorganization proposals were nonetheless achieved in 1939 when Congress passed a bill authorizing creation of the Executive Office of the President, which recognized the executive role of the president and the concept of administrative management: "the most profound contribution in our generation to the progress of administrative science" (Emmerich 1950, 80).

FROM NEW DEAL TO GREAT SOCIETY

Throughout its first half-century, developments in American public administration were motivated by the urge to complete the modernization of the administrative state and of all levels and functions of government, together with the associated shifts of political power toward governing elites (Bertelli and Lynn 2006). The goal was to strengthen administrative capacity and to broaden the bases of its legitimacy through responsible management. The Brownlow Report was a powerful expression of these tendencies toward executive government. In the immediate aftermath of World War II, however, Congress struck back at a presidency perceived to have grown so powerful that it threatened to reduce Congress to irrelevance (Rosenbloom 2000).

Through an ongoing series of enactments beginning with the Administrative Procedure Act (APA) and the Legislative Reorganization Act (LRA), both of 1946, Congress sought to tether public management as tightly as possible to legislative intent and values by establishing the bureaucracy as a working extension of the legislature (Rosenbloom 2000). These efforts were countered by two "Hoover Commissions," appointed successively by Presidents Truman and Eisenhower and chaired by former president Herbert Hoover, which "asserted the need for a hierarchy of authority and responsibility in administrative organization" (Millett 1949, 745).

With the Cold War in full swing, America's reformist spirit was revived by presidential initiatives in the form of John F. Kennedy's New Frontier, Lyndon Johnson's Great Society, and Richard Nixon's New Federalism. Confronted with an accelerated pace of transformation reminiscent of the Progressive era and the New Deal, American government began to be inundated by what Paul Light (1997) has called "tides of reform," some initiated by the executive branch, some by Congress, some by judges, all reflecting the competitive dynamics of "separated institutions sharing power," in Richard Neustadt's (1970) memorable phrase.

Personnel reforms, reorganizations, efforts at productivity enhancement and budgetary discipline and greater fiduciary accountability, cost control, and paperwork reduction alternated with specific reform "techniques": the Planning–Programming–Budgeting System (PPBS), Management-by-Objectives (MBO), Zero-Base Budgeting (ZBB), all aimed at ensuring the efficiency and effectiveness of governments that had become increasingly complex, expensive, opaque and unaccountable. The results in terms of public service delivery have hardly been impressive. Rather, "[t]he bulk of the improvements in government efficiency that have taken place in recent years," wrote George Downs and Patrick Larkey in 1986, "have resulted not so much from overt, grandiose reform schemes as from a host of modest, tactical reforms" (Downs and Larkey 1986, 259).

Francis Rourke offers a synoptic view of developments in governance during this period. According to him (1987, 218),

the growth of national bureaucracy in the United States since the 1930s has been a far less important phenomenon than the simultaneous emergence of new ways by which the traditional institutions of American national government – the presidency, Congress, and the courts – have been able to meet and contain the challenge of a bureaucracy that many people prior to World War II anticipated would actually become a fourth branch of government in the postwar period.

These adjustments included a collegial or collective presidency of the president and the White House staff, to preserve executive hegemony over bureaucracy, and the increased utilization of experts from the private sector to advise policy makers and managers;[19] expansion in the size and proficiency of legislative staffs, an enhancement of the legislature's capacity to do its job; judges becoming "major actors in the policy process, largely as a result of statutes that provide broader opportunities for private parties to challenge the decisions of executive agencies in the courts" (Rourke 1987, 226); and the proliferation of "iron triangles" and "issue networks" linking bureaucrats, interest groups, legislative staff members, and others with a stake in governmental outcomes.

There were more specific developments, too, that, as will be discussed further in Chapter 6, anticipated what was to become known as New Public Management.

- The US federal government began systematically to privatize public services, using such instruments as contracts, user charges, vouchers, and alternative delivery systems, beginning in the mid-1950s, a practice pursued with even greater enthusiasm by state and local governments (Ott, Hyde, and Shafritz 1991, 110).

- A concurrent development was the deinstitutionalization of state and county hospital and other institutionalized populations owing to the fortunate coincidence of the growing concern for the civil rights of dependent people and the development of drugs and treatment approaches permitting community-based care for those with chronic conditions.

- The accelerating popularity of hybrid organizations beginning in the 1960s – early examples included ComSat, the Manpower Development Research Corporation, and the Corporation for Public Broadcasting – reflected several factors: federal budget controls, which forced agencies to seek new sources of revenue; evasion of general management laws such as statutory ceilings on personnel and compensation; and the popularity of generic, business-focused values and, in particular, the belief that entity-specific laws and regulations facilitate management flexibility, "even at the cost of accountability to representative institutions" (Moe 2001, 291).

- In the aftermath of the Watergate scandals of the Nixon administration, the Civil Service Reform Act of 1978, in a historic departure from "protection" as a principle of public personnel administration, abolished the Civil Service Commission and reorganized its function. The act also created a Senior Executive Service of experienced career managers who might be assigned wherever needed by an administration. That the act failed to accomplish its goals largely reflects competitive politics of controlling the bureaucracy, in effect vindicating the protection principle.

If, as we shall see in Chapter 6, New Public Management did not produce the *frisson* in America that it did in much of the rest of the world, it was because most if not all of its features had already become widely used "tools of government" in American public management.

AMERICAN LEGACIES

American intellectual leadership has brought more organized and detailed attention and a high degree of academic prestige to a continuously evolving field (Lepawsky 1949) both in the US and elsewhere. The emergence of a profession of public administration and management in the United States and of a productive academic enterprise both within and independent of the discipline of political science has inspired and been imitated in Europe (Dunsire 1973; Kickert 1997). The American approach has given legitimacy to ideas and methods that the reigning European legalism regarded as irrelevant (Rugge 2004). "The orientation of Dutch, German, British and Scandinavian [public administration] scholars on the Northern American study of Public Administration is striking," argues Walter Kickert (1997, 28). Thus, as will be discussed at greater length in Chapter 8, while American public management policies and practices retain their distinctive character, American scholarship, with its social scientific foundations, has made significant contributions to the emergence of public management as an international field.

American public management structures and practices are another matter, however. They are, as often claimed, exceptional.

In Europe, argues Mark Rutgers (2001, 222), "the state provides a common denominator; in the United States, it does not."[20] In Europe, the state is synonymous with public administration; in the US, it is not. "Pluralism, representation, and a debating tradition," says Rutgers (224), "characterize stateless societies" such as that of the United States. An older appreciation of the American administrative state which complements this insight was provided by Schuyler Wallace (1941, 12, 13):

> At the outset . . . early pioneers in the study of administration assumed the existence of a democratic society, popular government through a representative assembly and elected officials and the perdurance of the conception that the purpose of administration is to serve the requirements of such a society with the utmost efficiency and economy. . . . No aspects of administration were ever treated as something existing in a vacuum. . . . Every system of public administration forms a part of a social organization, and its structure and procedure bear and must bear intimate relations to the spirit, form, and purposes of the government to which it belongs.

Inevitably there is delegation of sovereign power to unelected public officials. Congress, for example, delegates authority to (imposes a duty on) subordinate officers,

99

thereby providing them with independence from the president in specific situations defined by statute. But such delegation hardly confers independence and self-control on such officers. "[A]ccountability to Congress," argues Rohr (2002, 101), "severs the hierarchical chain of command in the executive branch and exposes the subordinate to the full force of Congress's impressive powers to investigate the public administration and to subject it to the rigors of legislative oversight." Thus executive officers are not simply the president's men and women but officers of the law. As a consequence, argues Rohr (2002, 83), "participation, transparency, and accountability [and protection of individual rights] – are legislative characteristics that set a tone quite different from efficiency, effectiveness, and economy, the traditional hallmarks of administrative orthodoxy."

In a very real sense, then, American executive agencies are extensions of the legislative branch (Rosenbloom 2000). In contrast, in Europe, says Edward Page (1992, 89),

> the legislature is largely dominated by the executive. Legislatures in France, Germany and Britain do not initiate legislation to any significant degree, they are peripherally involved in the budgetary process and party cohesion and institutional limitations serve to restrict the scope of powerful scrutiny of executive actions by the legislatures.

Owing to the separation of powers, American public managers not only are beholden to legislative authority, but must cope with continuing competition among all three branches of government for control over the extent and uses of managerial authority. In Rutgers's (2001) view, public administration does not legitimately exercise any *independent* influence within this scheme.

What are perceived to be European solutions to the centrifugal forces of democracy – a mandarinate obedient to parliament or bureaucracy-and-*Rechtsstaat* – have been rejected as un-American. Even the Progressive American idea of executive management based on scientific principles has been discredited as a governing philosophy, even if scientific management remains a tool of governance. The United States, moreover, "lacks the integrative mechanisms found in European nations such as a central and powerful treasury or finance ministry as well as, in Great Britain, a strong service-wide civil service ethos" (Page 1992, 63–4). Instead, the American solution is Madisonian: the interplay of interests who seek influence through all three branches, the whole ultimately governed by administrative law.

A consequence, as Joel Aberbach, Robert Putnam, and Bert Rockman have noted (1981, 243), is that "the American separation of powers means that face-to-face encounters . . . are actually more frequent in Washington than in European capitals. . . . Institutions and history have pushed American bureaucrats toward more traditionally political roles as advocates, policy entrepreneurs and even partisans, and have led congressmen to adopt a more technical role. Communication is thus a key managerial aspect of American exceptionalism" (although there are others, including the tolerance of enormous variation across states and municipalities and the fluidity of the legal framework (Peters 1997)). Norton Long (1949, 258) said, "The mandate that [American political] parties do not supply must be attained through public relations and the mobilization of group support."

In the face of what often appears to be a vacuum of governing values, many public management scholars are prone to invoke idealizations of public service values, from equity to individual rights to democratic participation to constitutional trusteeship. A classic example is Long (1952, 811), who argued that "important and vital interests in the United States are unrepresented, under-represented, or mal-represented in Congress. These interests receive more effective and more responsible representation through administrative channels than through the legislature." The representative bureaucracy, in this view, becomes an alternative and independent forum for Madisonian governance.

In practice, however, the governing values must comport with the constitutional separation of powers, and that scheme is founded on delegation. Those officials who attempt to place themselves beyond the pale of legislative mandates and intent are likely to find themselves either under increasingly detailed statutory supervision or cast as defendants in institutional reform lawsuits whose objective is to curb their autonomy and capacity to abuse their discretion. In America, the separation of powers rules.

NOTES

1 As a "presidentialist" state, America can be distinguished from "parliamentary" states, but such a categorization is over-broad for most of the comparisons in this book.
2 The Constitution was sketchy at best concerning the status of administration, although the authors of *The Federalist* certainly were aware of the issue. See Rohr (1986, 1987, 2002).
3 However, the Treaty of Paris (1783) ending the revolutionary war with Great Britain languished in the Continental Congress for some time because members failed to attend its sessions.
4 At the time, Edmund Burke (in *Thoughts on the Cause of the Present Discontents*) was, says Gaus, "describing for the first time a consistent theory of party government in which the responsibility for the direction of administration is vested in the leaders of the majority party of the legislature" (Gaus 1936, 30).
5 In E. N. Gladden's account (1972b), the Tenure in Office Act of 1820 limited to four years the terms of office of officials handling moneys. "Although of limited operation, the Act endorsed a principle that was to gain increasing support thenceforward" (1972b, 309), culminating in the spoils system of the Jackson era, which replaced a basically aristocratic system with a fully democratic one.
6 The term "red tape" derives from "the ribbon once used to tie up legal documents in England" (Kaufman 1977, 1). "Because the common law gives great weight to precedent, every judicial decision must have been preceded by a thorough search of the records for guidance and authority. Such a system presumes that records of every transaction are punctiliously filed and cross-filed. We may surmise, therefore, that legions of clerks and lawyers spent a good deal of their time tying and untying

the ribbon-bound folders. Meanwhile, citizens and administrative officers trying to get action must have fretted and fumed while they waited for the meticulous minions to complete their patient unwrapping and rewrapping. And they must have exploded in outrage when after all that, action was blocked on grounds of some obscure ancient decision or, still, worse, because no unequivocal precedent could be found. Hence the emergence of red tape as a despised symbol. The ribbon has long since disappeared, but the hated conditions and practices it represents continue, keeping the symbol alive" (Kaufman 1977, 1).

7 The nineteenth-century spoils system, Carpenter notes (2001, 41), "bore curious similarities to the medieval European notion of property-in-office," having degenerated into "political clientelism, nepotism and corruption" (Kickert 1997, 19).

8 Karl further notes that "[u]ntil well into the [twentieth] century, a standard format for studies of municipal revenues and taxation, welfare and social security, opened with a survey of foreign plans" (Karl 1976, 493).

9 Von Stein had argued that "[t]he further the culture of our era progresses, the clearer becomes the significance of the statement that we have essentially overcome the epoch of constitution-building and that the critical area for further development lies in administration" (von Stein 1876, 1, quoted by Miewald 1984, 21).

10 Goodnow is important for several reasons: his grasp of administrative law and of the separation of powers; his articulation of the importance of administration; his practical interest in municipal reform; and his familiarity with European thought and practice. Before Goodnow, the field of government was considered to comprise a recounting of constitutional powers and limitations. He first directed attention to the operations and techniques of the governmental mechanism, his administrative law course substantially the same as a typical public administration course in the 1930s (Haines and Dimock 1935).

11 Goodnow points out that the emergence of a significant system of federal taxation brought the issue to the fore. Judicial remedies were made unavailable in the case of taxes voluntarily paid, and the exemption of administrative determinations from judicial control has been incrementally expanded.

12 Under the influence of Kant, according to Willoughby, "the Prussian people are taught, and have very generally come to believe, that, viewed metaphysically, the affairs of this world are so ordered that it is irrational for them to demand the right to determine for themselves the form of government to whose control they shall submit, or to claim a participation in its operation. . . . [T]he typical German is content to have his life minutely regulated if he can feel himself secured from the interference or annoyance of the unregulated actions of others" (Willoughby 1918, 274, 275).

13 "By discretion is meant the exercise of choice involving not the scientific application to the facts of objective standards but a subjective evaluation of the advisability of alternatives" (Hart 1925, 28).

14 Irene Rubin makes the point that while the accounting and budgeting reforms associated with the Bureau of Municipal Research were touted as applications of business methods, nearly the reverse was the case. Business accounting and budgeting were not nearly so well advanced, but, owing to business sponsorship of the Bureau and its spin-offs, much lip-service was paid to business models and methods, and those, such as William Allen, who were critical of business practices might be marginalized or fired (Rubin 1993).

15 "The outstanding lessons of the war in respect to the organization and functions of the government bear chiefly upon the problem of readjusting the division of powers

between the national government and the states and upon the problem of reorganizing the system of checks and balances within the national government itself" (Fenwick 1920, 584).

16 Some argue that the apogee was actually reached with the first post-World War II Hoover Commission. According to Harold Seidman (1998, 4), "[t]he [Hoover] commission's report on 'General Management of the Executive Branch' represents the most categorical formulation of the orthodox or classic organization doctrine derived largely from business administration and identified with the scientific management movement during the early decades of this century and the writings of Gulick, Urwick, Fayol, and Mooney."

17 Louis Brownlow chaired the committee, whose other two members were Charles Merriam and Luther Gulick.

18 Urwick, coeditor of the special studies for PCAM, saw clearly the tradeoff between "scientific management" and democratic self-government, "which places an overriding emphasis on the consent of the governed secured through representative institutions" (Urwick and Brech 1945, 14). Urwick believed the Brownlow Report to represent scientific management at its best, "not [in] the details of their recommendations . . . but [in] the intellectual method, the outlook which illuminated their whole enquiry" (Urwick and Brech 1945, 161). Urwick believed centralized, scientifically managed administration to be the protector, the shield of democracy.

19 "The lesson of the last half-century of American politics," said Rourke in 1987, "has thus been unmistakable – as the power of the White House staff grows, the power of departmental bureaucrats recedes" (Rourke 1987, 225).

20 Stillman (2001) argues that the concept of "state" disappeared from American public administration discourse only after World War II and the advent of behavioralism, pluralism, functional specialization, incrementalism, the reassertion of American liberal tradition, etc.

Chapter 6

New Public Management: reform, change, and adaptation

INTRODUCTION

Historical legacies in the structures, practices, and values of public administration and management from 1660 to the 1970s notwithstanding, something "new" unquestionably began coming into the picture both in the United States and in Europe. Economic crises, fiscal scarcity, demographic change, immigration, and the resultant concerns with the financial appetite of the welfare state gave impetus to public policies emphasizing government retrenchment and efficiency. Public-management-cum-private-management came to be viewed by neo-liberal reformers, if not by citizens at large, as a means, even as a panacea, for achieving more frugal, more efficient, and, as a hoped-for consequence, more effective and politically popular governments.[1]

As earlier chapters have shown, state building involving far-reaching changes in governance had been proceeding apace on both sides of the Atlantic throughout the twentieth century following the revolutionary changes of the nineteenth. France and Germany rewrote their constitutions twice, Great Britain's incipient bureaucracy evolved from Fabian beginnings into a socialist welfare state, and America's local, parties-and-courts-dominated government gave way to governance overshadowed by federal executive power and delegated authority. Throughout Europe as well as in the United States, the growth of welfare states and the democratization of political participation were accompanied by the strengthening of executive authority at the expense of parliaments, the judiciary, and the professionalization of public sector personnel.

Except for the American reforms, however, most of these twentieth-century developments are not usually regarded as "managerial," that is, as concerned with the effective organization, control, accountability, and performance of public service delivery. What was regarded as new in Europe, and as of heightened importance in the US, beginning in the 1970s was the sharply increased preoccupation, in some cases the obsession, on the part of policy makers with reduced-cost public service delivery. Intentional, programmatic public sector reform became commonplace rather than a rarity (Raadschelders and Toonen 1999).[2] Advertent or inadvertent, maintenance of the status quo in public management institutions began to be viewed as *déclassé*, the unfortunate condition of "laggard" states. Nations mindful of the implications of globalization and of the wishes of their own citizens were encouraged to embrace what came to be widely known as New Public Management. An era of managerialism had rather suddenly begun.

This chapter first discusses the origins and meanings of the term New Public Management and of managerialism more generally. Then public management adaptation and change in the United States, the United Kingdom, France, and Germany, including specific consideration of the growing influence in Europe of the European Union and Commission, are reviewed. Finally, a variety of critical perspectives on New Public Management and managerialism are summarized.

THE BIRTH OF MANAGERIALISM

While managerialism had been, as noted in Chapter 5, an element of what may be regarded as American administrative ideology for nearly a century, the idea of management gained new force on both sides of the Atlantic beginning early in the 1970s.

A literature of managerialism began to emerge in Great Britain as early as 1972 with the publication of Desmond Keeling's *Management in Government*. Interest in public management broadened and accelerated in the 1980s with the publication of works such as Jan Kooiman and Kjell Eliassen's *Managing Public Organizations: Lessons from Contemporary European Experience* and Les Metcalfe and Sue Richards's *Improving Public Management*. As Kooiman and Eliassen (1987b, 1, 16) explained at the time, "[p]oliticians have taken up a new interest in so-called management solutions. The call for *management* and *managers* has slowly penetrated public administration itself. . . . We feel a change is in the air" (emphasis in original).[3] In 1991, notes Johan Olsen (2003), the World Bank knew that it was necessary to shift from centralized, hierarchical, rule-driven administration to a management and market orientation (World Bank 1991).

Observers began to note the ideological cast to the new emphasis on management in government. "[B]oth in public debate and scholarly writing," say Kooiman and Eliassen (1987b, 8), "the vague concept of 'management' in the private sector has been borrowed more or less uncritically."[4] Metcalfe and Richards elaborate (1987, 35):

> [T]he explicit or implicit assumption of most management reformers is that management offers a more logical, rational and orderly approach to improving performance in government than existing administrative practice. The superiority of a management approach is supposed to reside in applying proven principles to create neatly structured organizational hierarchies with well-defined tasks and clearly allocated responsibilities. Orderly management is superior to muddling through because it establishes firm control, streamlines processes and defines purposes.

In his 1990 book *Managerialism and the Public Services: The Anglo-American Experience*, Christopher Pollitt explicitly referred to the new phenomenon of managerialism as an ideology, whose foundation is the private sector, where the importance of management to performance seems virtually self-evident (cf. Lane 1987).

In America, Kennedy School professor Mark Moore in 1984 summarized the emerging state of the new public management art that was emerging in the recently formed public policy schools (Moore 1984, 2, 3):

> Our conception of "public management" adds responsibility for goal setting and political management to the traditional responsibilities of public administration. . . . Our conception of public management adds some quintessential executive functions such as setting purpose, maintaining credibility with overseers, marshaling authority and resources, and positioning one's organization in a given political environment as central components of a public manager's job.

Taking stock of the work of Moore and others from the new public policy schools, James Perry and Kenneth Kraemer (1983, 1) said that "[p]ublic management as a special focus of modern public administration is new," a view echoed by Hal Rainey (1990, 157): "In the past two decades, the topic of public management has come forcefully onto the agenda of those interested in governmental administration," perhaps, he suggested, because of the growing unpopularity of government.[5]

Meanwhile, in the real world an accelerating series of global changes was placing new pressures on governments while creating new opportunities for governmental transformation. In Gerald Caiden's (1991, 1) view, "inherited administrative systems were proving to be sluggish, inflexible and insensitive to changing human needs and novel circumstances." Martin Minogue (1998, 19) argues that "[w]hat cannot be doubted is that a generic wave of reforms must have a generic stimulus: this we can find in the consistency and similarity across systems of the pressures for change." These pressures include the (political) necessity for expenditure and cost reductions; consumerist orientations and the demand for quality; and ideological factors in solving conflicting pressures both to improve and to reduce the state (with the risk that the gains may go to individual and group interests rather than to "the public").[6] As Theo Toonen (2004, 188) sees it, the reforms are "commonly understood as a reaction against a perceived economic threat" in the second half of the 1970s and the end of the 1980s and mid-1990s, a "quest for resilience, economic sustainability and innovating capacity."

Many governments took full advantage of these opportunities, and the world-wide pace of governmental change accelerated. The neo-liberal politics of many of these governments introduced a pronounced emphasis on managerialism as an ideology of change and reform. This ideology also proved congenial to international organizations such as the World Bank and the United Nations, which were engaged in promoting economy and efficiency on a world-wide scale. As national governments had once converged on bureaucracy and the rule of law, some observers now went so far as to claim that nations, facing similar transforming pressures, were converging on incentives, competition, and performance as a paradigm for managing the operational side of government, enabled by a real separation of politics from administration (Toonen 1998).

The term "New Public Management" (NPM) was coined in 1989 by Christopher Hood to retrospectively characterize the "quite similar administrative doctrines" of Australia, Canada, New Zealand, the United Kingdom, and (with a different emphasis) the United States of the 1970s and 1980s (Hood 1989, 349). NPM referred to a simulacrum of the allocation of resources by competitive markets that suited neo-conservative times, in König's terms "a popularised mixture of management theories, business motivation psychology and neo-liberal economy" (1997, 219). NPM has, in its uppercase form, come to characterize what many scholars of public management regard as a "universal administrative reform movement" (Aucoin 1990, 115). "Since the 1980s," says Donald Kettl (2000, 1), "a global reform movement in public management has been vigorously underway."

Christopher Hood's seminal characterization (1989, 349; reprised in Hood 1991) of NPM's principal themes included a shift away from an emphasis on policy toward an emphasis on measurable performance; a shift away from reliance on traditional bureaucracies toward loosely coupled, quasi-autonomous units and competitively tendered services; a shift away from an emphasis on development and investment toward cost-cutting; allowing public managers greater "freedom to manage" according to private sector corporate practice; and a shift away from classic command-and-control regulation toward self-regulation.

Definitions of NPM have proliferated as experts have sought to put their own "spin" on the subject (for example, Pollitt 1990; Hood and Jackson 1991a; Dunleavy 1994; OECD 1993, 1995; Kickert 1997; Carroll 1998; Minogue 1998; Kettl 2000; Lane 2000; Koppenjan and Klijn 2005). The analytical model of NPM depicted by Toonen (2001, 186) is particularly useful for evaluating contemporary developments:

- a business-oriented approach to government;
- "a quality and performance oriented approach to public management";
- an emphasis on improved public service delivery and functional responsiveness;
- an institutional separation of public demand functions (councils, citizens' charters), public provision (public management boards) and public service production functions (back offices, outsourcing, agencification, privatization);
- a linkage of public demand, provision, and supply units by transactional devices (performance management, internal contract management, corporatization, intergovernmental covenanting and contracting, contracting out) and quality management;
- wherever possible, the retreat of (bureaucratic) government institutions in favor of an intelligent use of markets and commercial market enterprises (deregulation, privatization, commercialization, and marketization) or virtual markets (internal competition, benchmarking, competitive tendering).

NPM was only one of the "mega-trends" forecast by Hood in 1989, however. He also foresaw sustained efforts to reduce the size of governments and continued moves away from what he termed "the public bureaucracy state" (Hood 1989, 358, n. 5) in favor of para-governments, the "subsidiarity principle" in service delivery (that is, devolving service delivery to quasi-autonomous entities close to those affected by their operations)[7] and reliance on the private sector for service delivery. While these mega-trends are primarily managerial and not easily distinguishable from his characterization of NPM, Hood was nonetheless taking note of broader patterns of adaptation and transformation than NPM-oriented managerialism. Vincent Wright (1994a, 6) characterized this wider policy ferment as concerned with "reducing the size and reshaping the role of the central state . . . allocating resources and wealth differently, and . . . providing collective goods in a different fashion."

There is in these accounts a strong suggestion, if not outright assertion, of a con-vergence in the forms and aims of governance (Lynn 2001a). The implication is that isomorphism of governing relations across states is or will be the resultant of national efforts at reform. In other words, the national sovereignty of administrative reform has been shattered by globalization in its many guises.

While there is no denying that there is much that is new in public management, it is also true that many recent developments may not be original so much as adaptations of old institutions to new circumstances. The popularity of NPM as a theme for recent changes has distorted understanding of public management adaptation, change, and reform in three important ways. First, there has been a tendency to use similarities in the rhetoric of reform across countries to exaggerate similarities in the actual trans-formation of managerial institutions, for which the record is decidedly mixed (Pollitt and Bouckaert 2004). Second, there has been a tendency to neglect transformations in administrative institutions, notably devolution and deconcentration, which, while not regarded as managerial, nonetheless have significant ramifications for the practice of public management. Finally, and as a consequence of the first two distortions, the path dependence of change – the fundamental continuity of administrative institutions – has been obscured, with a resulting loss of insight into the change process itself and the future prospects for reform.

To gain a perspective on such issues, it will be useful to survey the character and fruits of managerialism in the four countries examined closely in this book.

REINVENTING AMERICAN GOVERNMENT

Owing to the separation-of-powers-inspired competition for control over executive agencies (see Chapter 5), a competition that intensified following World War II (Rosenbloom 2000; Bertelli and Lynn 2006), American public management became the object of a seemingly continuous but disjoint sequence of reform initiatives, each with ambiguous legacies. As Paul Light (1997) sees it, these reforms, which he traces in detail from 1945 through 1994, reflected various themes: "scientific management," "war on waste," "watchful eye," and "liberation management," each with its own distinctive theory of what kinds of reforms might improve governmental performance. Initiatives reflecting these differing emphases have not so much succeeded each other as created additional, poorly articulated layers of governing structures and values.

At the same time, as noted in Chapter 5, governments at all levels in the 1960s had begun to utilize a variety of new tools of action: privatization, hybridity, deinstitutionalization, devolution, revenue sharing (or block grants), and personnel reform. Charles Schultze's 1977 *The Public Use of Private Interest* assayed the possibilities of performance contracting – an early innovation in this vein was health maintenance organizations – and the several varieties of new tools were soon labeled "third-party government" by Lester Salamon (1981). Donald Kettl (1988) explored the increasing reliance of the federal government upon a variety of intermediaries – non-profit organizations, hybrid entities, other levels of government, the proprietary sector (including banks and insurance companies): in effect, a "quasi government" – to implement national policies. Policy implementation in general and the phenomenon of third-party government in particular were among the early staples of what was emerging as a public management movement in US universities.

The movement began inauspiciously enough as an academic and curricular innovation, although one inspired by the scientific-management-oriented reforms, such as the Johnson administration's Planning–Programming–Budgeting System (PPBS), which sought to centralize and professionalize executive policy making and the supervision of its implementation.[8] When choosing to complement technocratic training in policy analysis with an emphasis on policy implementation as a subject for research and teaching, public policy scholars at places such as Harvard, Princeton, and the University of California rebuked "traditional public administration" for having too little regard for the public manager as a strategic political actor (Lynn 1996). The emphasis of these schools was on how public managers could "realize the potential of a given political and institutional setting" (Moore 1984, 3), that is, on public management as statecraft, an emphasis underplayed, although (as noted in Chapter 5) far from ignored, in traditional American literature.

Craft-oriented pedagogy and scholarship in the policy schools was designed to prepare a new breed of trained professional for service in advisory capacities at the highest levels of federal, state, and local governments, primarily, but not exclusively, in the executive branch. The new curriculums featured experiential learning such as workshops, internships, and the extensive analysis of teaching cases. The goal was identifying "best practices" and universal principles (based now, however, on "experience" rather than "science"), rules, and checklists for effective public management conceived as a craft (Bardach 1987; Majone 1989). Works that distill managerial principles from personal experiences and case analyses have subsequently become one of the most popular genres in the field, in academic publications, in prescriptive management literature, and in government reports such as those of the Government Accountability Office (GAO).[9]

Although this largely unhistorical, "institutions-are-given" approach to public management drew criticism from traditional public administration scholars, eventually it caught the wave of popularity enjoyed by the "best practices" perspective in business management literature owing to the success of the "Japanese management" movement (Pascale and Athos 1982) and of Thomas Peters and Robert Waterman's *In Search of Excellence: Lessons from America's Best-Run Companies* (1982). The latter book's no-nonsense principles – a bias for action, closeness to the customer, productivity through people, simple form, lean staff – inspired numerous public-sector-oriented imitators motivated to arrest government's declining popularity following the Nixon-era Watergate scandal, the economic crises of the 1970s, and the ineffectual presidency of Jimmy Carter.

American public management reforms are, as Light (1997) demonstrated, distinctly non-linear. With a kindred spirit, British Prime Minister Margaret Thatcher, providing an inspiring example, President Ronald Reagan embarked on his own "war on waste" with the goal of shrinking the size and increasing the economic efficiency of government. Although neo-liberal in spirit, Reagan's reform strategy was quintessentially American and bore little resemblance to what was soon to become known, as Thatcher's initiatives evolved (see below), as New Public Management. Reagan's chosen instrument, a throwback to the kinds of initiatives launched by Presidents Theodore Roosevelt and William H. Taft early in the twentieth century, was the President's Private Sector Survey on Cost Control in the Federal Government, known as the Grace Commission after its chair, businessman J. Peter Grace.

The Commission's objective was to demonstrate how the intrinsically superior methods of the private sector might save billions of dollars by eliminating waste, fraud, and abuse (Downs and Larkey 1986; Grace 1984). Its 1984 report called for measures such as objective-based management, goal clarification, better planning, and the development of performance measures, without, however, acknowledging that prior reforms of similar character had not accomplished much by way of changing a government dominated by separated institutions sharing power (Downs and Larkey 1986). This particular report generated no legacy of sustained reform activity, of enduring ideas.

Less ephemeral American contributions to the public management reform movement were the publication in 1992 of two influential books, David Osborne and Ted Gaebler's best-selling *Reinventing Government* and Michael Barzelay's *Breaking Through Bureaucracy*. With its universal "steer-don't-row" prescription and canonical principles, *Reinventing Government*, reinforced by Barzelay's proclamation of a post-bureaucratic paradigm of public management, was to provide the text for a new generation of reform-minded activists, including officials associated with the Clinton administration's National Performance Review[10] and the practitioner-dominated National Academy of Public Administration.

Beginning in 1993, Vice President Al Gore led an eight-year effort, popularly known as Reinventing Government, to create a government that was smaller, cheaper, and more effective. Its four themes were:

- **"cutting red tape,"** including streamlining the budget process, decentralizing personnel policy, reorienting the inspectors general, and empowering state and local governments;
- **"putting customers first,"** including demanding that service organizations compete and using market mechanisms to solve problems;
- **"empowering employees to get results,"** including decentralizing decision-making power, forming a labor–management partnership, and exerting leadership;
- **"cutting back to basics,"** including eliminating programs, investing in greater productivity, and reengineering programs to cut costs.

"[T]he people who work in government are not the problem," proclaimed Osborne and Gaebler, "the systems in which they work are the problem." Echoed Vice President Gore, "The Federal Government is filled with good people trapped in bad systems: budget systems, personnel systems, procurement systems, financial management systems, information systems. When we blame the people and impose more controls, we make the systems worse" (Gore 1993, 2).

It is important to note, however, that while the American "reinvention movement" was managerial in its ideological orientation (Aberbach and Rockman 2001), it placed far less emphasis on the kinds of neo-liberal, market-mimicking reforms that, as noted in Chapter 5, had long been popular in America, especially with state and local governments. Reinvention-inspired reforms employed strategies emphasizing the "liberation management" theme of managerial deregulation, quality, and managerial entrepreneurship. Moreover, as Guy Peters (1997, 255) notes,

> [p]erhaps the one defining feature of reinvention is a disregard of some of the conventions associated with traditional public administration and an associated desire to rethink government operations from the ground up. . . . These practices certainly would not be acceptable to more legalistic administrative systems such as those found in Germany and other countries operating in the Germanic administrative tradition. These reinvention concepts have not even translated easily to the Canadian federal government with its well-institutionalized public service ethos.

Peters continued (1997, 255): "The deregulatory movement differs from the widespread use of market models in Europe in part by not having any clear substitute for the rules and hierarchy that are being abolished by reform."

The one initiative that was clearly NPM-inspired failed to make more than minor inroads on the status quo. The reasons are instructive because they were political and, more significantly, constitutional. The Clinton administration sought to imitate Great Britain's Next Steps reform (discussed further below) by promoting the creation of Performance Based Organizations (PBOs). But, as Andrew Graham and Alasdair Roberts note (2004, 146), the separation of powers meant that "an influential third party –

111

Congress – threatened to complicate negotiations over the content of annual performance agreements." Regarding funding predictability, performance agreements required commitments to budgets for the period covered by the agreements, but future Congresses cannot be bound by the decisions of a sitting Congress. A third problem arose from provisions restricting the termination of Chief Operating Officers for other than performance-related reasons; Congress "may not limit the ability of the President to remove appointees, unless those appointees exercise quasi-legislative or quasi-judicial functions that require some independence from the administration" (147). The three PBOs that were created were denied significant flexibilities.

The more important, and surviving,[11] American public management reform of the 1990s was the Government Performance and Results Act (GPRA). Enacted in 1993 largely on the initiative of Congressional Republicans, GPRA is now a routine aspect of public management at the federal level and a key building block of America's expanding practice of performance management at all levels of government (Radin 2001). The act requires each federal agency, in cooperation with Congress and in coordination with the budget process, to formulate forward-looking performance plans and to conduct performance evaluations using agreed-upon performance measures. John Rohr (2002, 84) sees GPRA as an example of traditional legislative preeminence within the American separation of powers: "By law it requires nothing less than close cooperation between executive branch agencies and congressional subcommittees, first in developing goals and plans and then in evaluating performance measured against these same goals and plans." The US Government Accountability Office (GAO), an agency of the US Congress tasked with monitoring implementation of GPRA, was less than pleased after a decade of executive branch effort, viewing with concern the less than wholehearted use of performance information in government-wide or agency management (USGAO 2004a).

In the most recent of America's uncoordinated public management reforms, this time by the executive branch, the just-elected administration of President George W. Bush promulgated the President's Management Agenda (PMA), which emphasizes performance-driven, outsourced management in federal departments and agencies. Little publicized by the administration and only slowly acknowledged by the academic field, the Bush administration's approach features the quarterly scoring of all federal agencies against PMA priorities and other administration initiatives, and a Program Assessment Rating Tool (PART) to evaluate individual program accomplishments in coordination with preparation of the president's annual budget. The GAO somewhat haughtily declared that PART assessments are "not a substitute for GPRA's strategic, longer-term focus on thematic goals, and department and government crosscutting comparisons" (USGAO 2004b, summary), thus revealing the separation-of-powers tensions that pervade American public management and its reform.

From Theo Toonen and Jos Raadschelders's European vantage point, American reforms such as the ones just described represent a continuation and refinement of earlier attempts to improve government by professionalizing the policy process (1997). Reinventing government, in their view, represented a rediscovery of classical American public administration. What was new with reinventing government was its pro-government spirit as against what went before, especially in the Reagan administration. Their assessment only highlights the difficulty of appraising New Public Management in America. American Ezra Suleiman (2003) sees the same reforms as a landmark in combining sweeping scope with an anti-government agenda associated with the political right wing. "[A]t the heart of the reinvention-of-government movement lies a skepticism about the existence of a public-service institution" (Suleiman 2003, 47; cf. Frederickson 1996).

Supporting Suleiman's darker view of reinvention is the fact, noted by Lombard (2003), that in 1994 Congress, at the administration's request, amended the Government Employees Training Act of 1958 to change the legal purpose of government training from "training related to official duties" to "training to improve individual and orga-nizational performance." Also, in compliance with administration directives, the Office of Personnel Management (OPM) reorganized and cut its staff by 50 percent, abolished many mid-level positions, reduced personnel in its training policy, procurement, information technology, financial management, and human resources functions, closed many of its field offices, and privatized its nation-wide training and investigation programs (Lombard 2003).[12] The Bush administration's distinctly Thatcherite hostility to the traditional civil service was further demonstrated in its insistence that the permanent personnel of the new Department of Homeland Security be exempt from civil service rules and managed toward the goal of performance, a model they intended to extend to the entire federal government.

Joel Aberbach and Bert Rockman (2001) argue that, while some National Performance Review (NPR) recommendations were unarguably good ideas, the main thrust comprised slogans and nostrums that could not withstand critical scrutiny. For example, they note that, although many of the inefficiencies and restrictive rules decried by NPR were legislatively mandated, NPR largely ignored the need for legislative reforms, de-emphasizing the role and importance of Congress. As for successes, they cite NPR claims concerning "more contracting out, streamlining the hiring process, use of various devices to gauge agency customer opinion and respond to it, greater and more effective use of information technology, streamlining some aspects of procurement, and attention to a variety of internal agency management reforms" (2001, 31).

James Thompson has attempted to summarize the accomplishments of the National Performance Review. He notes that NPR incorporates a diverse set of interventions directed toward the achievement of multiple objectives (2000, 509). First, he sum-marized and classified the objectives of the National Performance Review as of first, second, and third order importance. Of first order importance were downsizing, reducing administrative costs, and reforming administrative systems. Of second order importance were decentralizing authority within agencies, empowering front-line workers, and promoting cultural change in agencies. Of third order importance were improving the quality of public services and improving the efficiency of agency work procedures.

Thompson conducted a broad review of the results of NPR in terms of satisfying these objectives based on survey research conducted by a US government personnel agency. A broad conclusion, he says (2000, 510),

> is that while some success has been achieved with regard to lower, first-order goals, only limited progress has been made toward critical, higher second- and third-order reinvention objectives. Thus, downsizing and cost reduction objectives have been substantially achieved . . . but there is no evidence of any significant, systemic improvement in quality of services or culture.

As noted earlier, another tide of reform has surged under President George W. Bush. Almost unnoticed, even in the US, is the President's Management Agenda (PMA) and the many measures taken to effect its implementation. Mr. Bush has shown more of the essential spirit of New Public Management than any other recent American president. Promulgated in 2001, the PMA features five business-like initiatives: strategic management of human capital, competitive sourcing, improved financial performance, expanded electronic government, and budget and performance integration. In February 2003 a new method for evaluating the performance of federal programs called the Program Assessment Rating Tool (PART) was introduced. PART is represented as an effort to get agencies to report consistently on their programmatic goals and results in order to facilitate funding decisions and the integration of budget and performance information. Evidence concerning the effects of the PMA was accumulating slowly, especially with regard to higher-order objectives. The PART process, however, appeared during Mr. Bush's second term to be having some influence on incremental budgetary allocations if not on the overall shape and size of the budget, where what was termed "big government conservatism" was enlarging the federal budgets and payrolls.

SOMETHING NEW IN EUROPE

Something "new" was abroad in Europe as well, beginning in the 1970s (Eliassen and Kooiman 1993; Aucoin 1990; Kickert 1997; Löffler 2003; Lynn 2005; Pollitt 1990). In Peter Aucoin's view (1995, 113), new public management comprised "efforts to roll back the state through some combination of privatization, contracting out, deregulation, expenditure reduction, program termination, downsizing the public service, and measures to contain pressures on the public purse."

While perhaps most obviously inspired by the economic crises of the mid-1970s, in which expenditure and revenue trajectories began to diverge sharply, the broader background of the new managerialism in Europe includes the complex challenges of sustaining the post-war welfare state, the conservative reassertion of the market as an ideal institution for social resource allocation, ongoing decentralization and decon-centration of national administration not associated with managerialism but affecting it, and the effects on national administrations of the policies of the European Union. The ambitious neo-liberal reforms of Margaret Thatcher's government, "whole-of-government" reforms in New Zealand, and Australian managerialism sought to transform traditional ministries and the civil service by introducing market-like discipline and business practices – a private sector mentality – to public service delivery.

In contrast to America, managerialism in Europe was a less familiar concept, a fortuitous fusing of ideological, practical, and scientific ideas (Kooiman and van Vliet 1993).[13] Management could be seen as "a new way of conducting the business of the state" (Pollitt and Bouckaert 2004, 12). Whereas Europeans could and did draw on American ideas concerning the application of business management techniques to government as well as on its public choice and public administration intellectual traditions (Kickert 1997; cf. the discussion in Chapter 7), European approaches to public management tended to reflect the indigenous concepts of administrative science and public administration whose evolution was described in earlier chapters (Pollitt and Bouckaert 2004).

Thus public management and managerialism in Europe have come to mean something different than in the United States. In Europe, these terms refer primarily to the delivery of public services and to the organizations responsible for service delivery: in effect to those organizational and functional aspects of government that, because they are founded on repetitive tasks, are most business-like or that could be made to be so. European scholars, especially in the UK and Northern Europe, do case studies, too, but their focus is on specific agencies or on specific management reform programs, leading toward insights into how reform processes work and what doesn't work and why. At the same time, many Europeans have become enamored of American public choice theory and the new economics of organization, and there are numerous attempts to apply them in their empirical work, ironically probably more so than in mainstream American public management research.

From an intellectual perspective, Aucoin (1990) sees two distinct sets of ideas underlying the new emphasis on public management in Europe: "managerialism," which establishes the primacy of managerial principles over bureaucracy, and public choice theory, which establishes the primacy of representative government over bureaucracy. These two sets of ideas, Aucoin argues, are having "a profound impact" on governance structures despite their being in sharp tension: managerialism requires a separation of administration from politics whereas public choice theory repudiates such a separation. Aucoin's insight warrants elaboration.

To Christopher Pollitt (1990), managerialism is an ideology, a set of beliefs and values centered on the role management can play in promoting social progress. A clear statement of this ideology is that of Peter Drucker (1974, x): "[I]t is managers and management that make institutions perform. Performing responsible management is the alternative to tyranny and our only protection against it." Managerialism appeals to neo-liberal policy makers for its critique of bureaucracy, for its celebration of the achievements of the corporate sector, and for the fact that "it has been packaged in ways

115

which have addressed issues from the perspective of managers rather than from the perspective of the theorist" (Aucoin 1990, 118). In Aucoin's view (1990, 127),

> [managerialism] sees politics as present essentially in the determination of the basic values or missions, and thus the policies, of an organization. It assumes that the realization of these values through a process of implementation can be achieved without the need for direct intervention by those who have set the basic values; at most, a monitoring role is required to ensure that there have not been departures from basic values.

The other perspective inspired by public choice theory and the economics of contracts is more political than managerial (Lane 1993; Greve and Jesperson 1999). Though conceived for American Congressional government, public choice theory is widely applied in Europe, especially to Westminister models of cabinet government where the minister is cast as the principal, civil servants as agents. This theoretical perspective is appealing for its account of the "crisis" of contemporary government, too much bureaucratic power, and because it supports the basic principle of government by elected representatives and a chain of delegation extending through ministers and their agents. The public choice approach, according to Aucoin (1990, 127), "sees politics as pervading management, that is politics is present in both the formulation and the implementation of policies." Not surprisingly, then, "[g]overnment bureaucrats are thus prone either to be seen by their clients as unresponsive to them or to be seen by political authorities as captured by their clients" (129).

Christopher Hood and Michael Jackson provide a contrasting analysis to that of Aucoin. In many ways, they argue (1991b, 179), "NPM can be seen as a development of the international scientific management movement, with its concern to eliminate waste and measure work outputs as a precondition for effective control." While traceable to Frederick Taylor and, farther back, to Bentham's ideas about public administration, its origins are even earlier, in cameralism (discussed in Chapter 3). In essence, cameralism assumed that the foundation of the state lay in economic development, which in turn required the active management of government, whose administrators should, therefore, be trained and loyal to a strongly led state. Cameralism and NPM are similar in their use of the term "public management" (*staatswirtschaft*, *haushaltungskunst*); stress on administrative technology; separation of policy making from its execution; emphasis on thrift; avoidance of direct state management of complex processes; centralization; and acceptance of the existing social and economic order. NPM could, in Hood and Jackson's view, be called a "new cameralism" (Hood and Jackson 1991b, 182).

There were still other motive forces behind managerialism in Europe. Similarly to their American counterparts, some European students of bureaucracy and management sought to repudiate a seemingly entrenched paradigm: the legalistic thinking that had continued to dominate training and practice since the nineteenth century (Kickert 1997). In France especially, owing to the influence of Michel Crozier, Erhard Friedberg and other sociologists, the concept of *management public* became central, and the *Institut de Management Public* was created in the 1960s (Crozier and Friedberg 1980). An awakening interest in public administration in Germany, and such latent interests as existed in Great Britain, were not to bear fruit until later.

Within this broad perspective of developments in European managerialism, however, is contained a set of quite different stories associated with individual country experiences.

Great Britain

Prior to the economic crises of the early 1970s, public management in Great Britain had as its foundation the least politicized civil service of any country discussed in this book – an unsegmented, government-wide service that enjoyed relatively high social and political status. Moreover, reflecting the distinctively philosophical and humanist "British philosophy of administration" (see Chapter 1), there was little in the way of a managerial tradition in the public sector in the administrative science sense.

How, then, could a British government exhibit greater enthusiasm for business-style managerialism than, for example, the United States, becoming, as Walter Kickert has put it, "the prototypical example of managerial, client-oriented, competitive public service since Margaret Thatcher became prime minister in 1979" (Kickert 1997, 20)? From the analytic perspective of this book (further developed in Chapter 7), such a development, while far from inevitable, is hardly surprising. More than the US, France, and Germany, Great Britain's form of constitutional governance enables an elected government determined to do so to implement managerial reforms so extensive as to alter constitutional arrangements themselves. Prime Minister Thatcher and her successors have been determined to do just that.

Mrs. Thatcher's reform program was inspired by disdain for the civil service, an ideological orientation toward the market, and a determination to cut public spending (Rhodes 1997). Despite her determination to reduce the role of the central government – evident in the extensive privatization of national enterprises (energy, steel, transport, shipbuilding, ports, airports, water, gas, electricity, and telecommunications) beginning in 1979 – intervention, centralization, and managerialism were prominent, even decisive, characteristics of the Thatcher years.[14]

Mrs. Thatcher's reforms were carried out incrementally via a number of initiatives of varying consequence, such as the Scrutinies by the newly established Efficiency Unit, Management Information Systems for Ministers, the Financial Management Initiative, Program Analysis and Review, and the Next Steps initiative, which is discussed more fully below (Barberis 1995). Concurrent initiatives for locally delivered services occurred in 1988 with the creation of an internal market in the National Health Service and the introduction of compulsory competitive tendering (Löffler 2003). In a deviation from her "war on waste," the government of Mrs. Thatcher's successor, John Major, introduced the Citizens' Charter in 1991 to encourage a customer-and-quality orientation in public service delivery. The Competing for Quality White Paper of 1991 promoted contracting out, followed by exercises on comparative costs known as market testing. Other reforms were occurring in the civil service, including decentralizations of personnel and finance to all civil service units, whether Next Steps agencies or not, and massive reorganizations of departments and ministries (Talbot 2004).

The creation of the Next Steps agencies beginning in 1988 is undoubtedly the UK's most celebrated NPM program and the most visible manifestation of managerialism (Rohr 2002). The agency idea, the central feature of Next Steps, had been broached in the 1968 Fulton Report (see Chapter 4), and the 1988 "Next Steps Initiative," whose foundation was the so-called Ibbs Report titled "Management Reform: The Next Steps" (Efficiency Unit 1988; see also Efficiency Unit 1991), drew as well on studies conducted by management consultants.[15] It is revealing of British governing traditions that Next Steps was, according to Colin Talbot (2004, 105; cf. Hogwood, Judge, and McVicar 2004), "conducted without any formal basis (legislation, secondary legislation, or even a simple policy statement) on which to judge it. Ms. Thatcher made a short statement to Parliament which endorsed the conclusions of the [Next Steps report] and announced a decision to go ahead."

Mimicking corporate management was the clear objective of the Next Steps Initiative.[16] Individual agencies headed by chief executive officers (CEOs) were created to handle distinct governmental activities on behalf of ministries, each within a regulatory framework designed to solve principal–agent problems, including features such as performance requirements and targets (James 2001). Although they are civil servants, the pay of CEOs was in principle performance-related, and removal for poor performance was to be possible. Annual reports and business plans based on performance targets and the "framework document" were to be prepared. The civil service itself was broken up into permanent and temporary elements and assigned activities that are prospectively subject to market testing and transfer to the private sector.

The goal of the Thatcher government was to change the ethos of the civil service and to make it more managerialist in style (Fry 1997). Civil servants, on the whole, tended to see (Metcalfe and Richards 1987, 216)

> management as a dull, routine, uncreative task, not really worthy of their talents. Their impoverished concept of management sprang out of a perception that management was what the lower, executive grades of the civil service did. [Their attitudes] also sprang from a stereotyped and uninformed view of management in the private sector.

The Civil Service Department was abolished in 1981, and the Treasury formalized its control over the management of resources with a new Management and Personnel Office. In 1987, the Treasury assumed formal authority over the civil service. In implementation, however, there were numerous deviations from the Thatcher ideal. Talbot (2004, 106) notes, for example, that in four out of five of the agencies employing around two-thirds of those working in agencies (the Employment Service, the Prison Service, Customs and Excise, the Inland Revenue), "there was little change either to the task focus of the organization, or to its structure."

It is ironic, then, that public management, at least in Colin Talbot's analysis, became more, rather than less, subject to principal–agent problems. Instead of simple accountability, agencies in effect had two principals: the permanent secretary of their government department as well as the chief executive. The framework document omitted resources and performance, which were settled through the normal public expenditure survey processes and through separate negotiations or impositions. Thus the framework became, according to Talbot (2004, 108), "a complex and cumbersome set of overlapping steering and accountability systems involving multiple 'principals' (parent departments, Ministers, Cabinet Office, the Treasury)."[17]

Performance against key indicators was, moreover, a mixed picture. Many targets were set below the level of current performance, reflected internal processes rather than outputs and outcomes, and included too few measures of real efficiency. James (2001, 248) notes unwanted side-effects: "the separation of agencies with separate pay systems and working practices has made cooperation across organizational boundaries to achieve jointly provided programs more difficult" – for example, in the Social Security Benefits Agency, where joint provision of welfare payments became more difficult. However, Talbot (2004, 111) concludes, "[t]here probably has been an overall improvement," especially at the service delivery end.

The spirit of far-reaching reform continued under Prime Minister Tony Blair's New Labour government. In 1994, Blair promised to his party's conference "the biggest program of change to democracy ever proposed" (Hazell and Sinclair 2000, 379). Unlike those of his predecessors, his program included far-reaching constitutional change.[18] Notable were Blair's proposals, only partially enacted, for reforming the House of Lords toward making it more democratic; the voting rights and membership of the hereditary peers, for example, were abolished. Of significance is the Blair government's introduction of the "Best Value" initiative, which became a statutory requirement in April 2000, to replace the compulsory competitive tendering program (Löffler 2003). Local councils are mandated to review all services and plan on service improvements. Local authorities, moreover, are being encouraged to take leadership roles in creating joined-up government: strategic partnerships and community strategies.[19]

Mr. Blair was seemingly determined to make UK governance more "presidential" in the US sense. His cabinet, for example, was arguably moving, as Bagehot would put it, from the "effective" to the "dignified" part of government. According to Robert Hazell and David Sinclair (2000, 379),

[a] highly centralized system of government is being replaced by a form of quasifederalism. This and other changes will lead to more checks and balances on the UK executive; parliamentary sovereignty is likely to be further eroded; there will be tighter rule of law, with a shift of power to the courts; and the British majoritarian, two-party system will be replaced by more pluralist forms of democracy.

119

The record of actual change in managerial operations and performance has been mixed (Hazell and Sinclair 2000). The agencies created by the Regional Development Agencies Act of 1998, for example, are appointed by ministers; they are not answerable to a local electorate. Countering this decentralization is centralization of power in the Cabinet Office and the prime minister's own office. Proposals to increase proportionality of representation in the House of Commons have not yet been enacted (as of January 2006). In the House of Lords, the hereditary peers, as noted, lost their power to vote and are being phased out, but further reforms were on hold. Regarding the civil service, there has reportedly been little change, although new executive agencies have been created; "best value" continues to be stressed; the number of temporary civil servants and political advisers has grown substantially.[20]

Despite the UK's reputedly strong local government traditions, these governments have largely been the passive objects of reforms rather than collaborators in their design. Although changes require an act of parliament (because of the *ultra vires* doctrine), parliament can give and take power at will. According to Helmut Wollmann (2002, 9, fn. 14),

> While England was historically the "mother country" and much admired exemplary case of politically as well as functionally strong local government well into the early part of the 20th century, it has been politically and functionally dwarfed by the Thatcherist interventions and reforms in a development which seems to have hardly been mitigated and reversed under "New Labour."

The Local Government Acts (Housing, Education, Finance) in the 1980s reinforced the center's right to control and limit local government by forcing local authorities to sell housing stock and land, deregulate local transport, and generally rely on contractors to deliver services. The 1988 Local Government Act compelled local authorities to introduce competition for garbage collection, maintenance, and management of sports facilities (Silver and Manning 2000b). The Urban Development Corporations were created in 1980 as corporate structures with jurisdiction over land acquisition, environmental improvement, infrastructure, fire fighting, public health, and other activities previously organized by the local authorities. Toonen and Raadschelders note that John Stuart Mill's idea of "local government as the school of democracy" has lately been realized more on the European Continent than in the UK itself (1997, 5–9).

In Great Britain, then, the managerial level has been the starting point for public management reform, with significant consequences for the constitutional and policy levels of governance. In several respects, managerialism in Great Britain has become a vehicle for structural reform, in contrast to the US, where, owing to a constitutional scheme of formally separated powers, managerialism is more concerned with operational issues within a given structural context. The kinds of changes brought about by Mrs. Thatcher and Mr. Blair, many on the basis of a mere determination to bring about change, are unthinkable in the United States. They are, as well, unthinkable on the Continent.

120

Continental Europe

Following the pre-World War II emergence of executive government discussed in Chapter 3, administrative reform was a theme of Continental governance beginning with European reconstruction following World War II. The aftermath of the war saw in particular the rapid expansion of welfare states, which created the preconditions for the new managerialism of the 1980s and beyond.

On the Continent, and especially in France and Germany, the ideology of managerialism – the Anglo-Saxon model codified by the OECD – encountered constitutionally legitimized administrative systems which, as noted in Chapter 3, had endured crises and socio-economic changes over centuries. In times of national collapse, public bureaucracies had borne the burden of maintaining a semblance of stability in public services. "It was the public administration [in West Germany] that enabled the new democratic policy on East German soil to function beyond the peaceful revolution," notes Klaus König (1997, 216). Thus Continental reactions to managerialism were bound to be far more compromised than was the case in the United Kingdom. Toonen and Raadschelders (1997, 5–10) argue that

> [t]he emphasis in Europe has been on loosening up administrative systems, making them more flexible, responsive to (changing) external conditions and perhaps somewhat more entrepreneurial, but all in an overall context of an integrated administrative 'Rechtsstaat' . . . tradition. The (managerial) reforms may affect the operation of these systems and perhaps perceptions of tasks and functions of the state in society, but hardly the constitutional nature of the various state systems.

The strength of the *Rechtsstaat* tradition is, according to König (1997, 226), that legalistic reasoning, even political reasoning, may be superior to economic reasoning; "[a]ssessments of effects and successes, analyses of costs and benefits fall short of what legal argumentation is able to perform." He continues: "[W]hen we are talking of executive management here, this does not mean anything other than that the continental European administration must give more scope to effectiveness and efficiency on the socio-technological side without completely breaking with the values of the classical executive" (227). Given the nature of public goods, "the primacy of politics and democracy as well as the constitutional system of order appear secured" (228).

Germany

The Federal Republic of Germany presents a picture of managerialism that is nearly, although not completely, the opposite of what is found in Great Britain. According to Löffler (n/d),

> [g]iven the more equal balance between the legislative, judicial and executive branches in the German system as compared to Westminster-system countries, the pursuit of

121

managerial reforms should not have been expected to — and did not in practice — override the prevailing fundamental legal and political processes in the German system.

In general, argues Eckhard Schröter (2004, 72), at the federal level, every effort has been made "to keep any organisational change as compatible as possible with the existing machinery of government." Since 1989, moreover, the federal government has been preoccupied with creating a democratic public service in the former German Democratic Republic and moving the capital from Bonn to Berlin.

As is the case with the US, there have been numerous German reform initiatives in recent decades. A "first wave" (Wollmann 2002) included the Federal Project Group for Governmental and Administrative Reform (1969–1975), the Independent Federal Commission for Legal and Administrative Simplification (1983), the Federal Commission for Administrative Efficiency, and a Deregulation Commission (1988). Helmut Wollmann characterizes the goal of this wave as a politically controversial amalgamation of local units of government to create larger, more efficient units, to which *Land* functions were delegated (deconcentrated), as well as intra-administrative reforms within local governments.

A "second wave" of reforms included the Lean State Advisory Committee (1995), the Action Program for the Further Improvement of the Effectiveness and Efficiency of the Federal Administration (1997), the "activating state" theme of the twenty-first-century Schröder government and, most significantly, the NPM-influenced New Steering Model (inspired by the Dutch Tilburg reforms) in local government. The second wave of reforms was motivated in large part by budgetary pressures, including those brought about by the 1992 Maastricht criteria, and gained momentum from EU deregulation and market-liberalization policies (Wollmann 2002).

As noted, however, these reforms have done little or nothing to change the machinery of government. For example, the Lean State Advisory Committee ultimately proposed only cautious departures from the status quo, remaining "caught in the grid of the traditional accounting rules and civil service laws" (Schröter 2004, 62). To the extent that there were structural changes, the impetus was provided by moving the seat of parliament and the government from Bonn to Berlin, as well as by rising budget deficits. The bargaining over the relocation resulted, according to Schröter, in "the worst of both worlds," a "combination model" that left functions in both locations but did not seriously call into question existing bureaucratic structures. These structures are generally criticized as incorporating non-ministerial functions that could be hived off to executive agencies or the private sector. "Viewed in terms of their reform objectives," concludes Seibel (2001, 86),

over the last fifty years it is the administrative response to dealing with the aftermath of war and the establishment of federal ministerial administration which are the notable successes among reforms. The same can be maintained, albeit with less conviction, of the 1969 financial reforms, the territorial reforms of the late 1960s and early 1970s, and of the construction and reorganisation of public administration in eastern Germany since 1990. The failures, on the other hand, include the attempts to reform the organisation of ministries in the late 1960s and early 1970s and the bid to reform public-service law, which in fact turned out to be an unmitigated disaster.

That significant efforts at public management reform arose at the local level of government reflected the dissatisfaction of German city managers with the administrative system (Reichard 2003). As was the case with many federal reform initiatives, local government reform was not inspired by politicians, citizens, or the central government, where managerialism and neo-liberalism had never really caught on. "[I]t is precisely the lack of attention for neo-managerialism and 'new public management' and sweeping reforms," argue Toonen and Raadschelders (1997, 1–5), "which is a striking feature of the German case." Economic and business management concepts have, however, inspired operational reforms in Germany at the local level throughout the post-war period, including post-war reconstruction, the PPBS concepts of the 1960s, cost–benefit analyses and policy analysis and evaluation concepts in the 1970s, and quasi-market and managerial concepts in the 1980s and early 1990s (Toonen and Raadschelders 1997).[21]

In 1991, a *Neues Steuerungsmodell*, New Steering Model (NSM), was published by the Joint Local Government Agency for the Simplification of Administrative Procedures and, according to Christoph Reichard, "disseminated like brushfire" (2003, 349). The primary external influence was the Dutch city of Tilburg, which had adopted a corporate-management model involving a product orientation, responsibility centers, performance indicators, separation of politics and administration, and internal contract management. With very little influence by political/administrative science or business management academics (Reichard 2003), the NSM involved decentralization and autonomy of resource management and responsibility, cost-efficiency mechanisms, strengthening the influence and control of local elected councils through reshaping the budgetary process, while restricting local government to an enabling role through marketization, outsourcing, and privatization. All of these measures encountered serious problems (Wollmann 2002).

The reforms were controversial. "Critics of NSM," says Werner Jann (1997, 90), "stress its pre-occupation with concepts and visions, its affinity to commercial consultants, its naive reform-euphoria, its neo-liberal belief in the market and its neglect of the cultural premises of public administration." After ten years of reforms, moreover, "there are not many visible results; too much is still moving and is 'on the way'" (Reichard 2003, 356), although there is some evidence of improved customer satisfaction in survey results. Nor has there been any interest in government or academia in systematically evaluating the NSM reforms.[22]

In general, external pressures, administrative innovations, and internal dynamics are largely accommodated within given managerial structures, which means that only policies and standard operating procedures change, and then only gradually (Toonen and

Raadschelders 1997). The substance of public sector activity may change considerably within a given framework, however. The model of "cooperative federalism" has so far illustrated that stability can be a dynamic concept, not to be confused with immobility or absence of change (Toonen and Raadschelders 1997). Germany is "the archetypical example of a system that pairs dynamics, flexibility and innovation to a gradualist, and adaptive mode of public sector reform" (Toonen and Raadschelders 1997, 1–6).

Other observers emphasize the extent of change, however. Klaus Goetz argues, for example, that "the two main pillars on which bureaucratic legitimacy has long rested [rationality and orientation to the public good] are crumbling" (1999, 168). He continues: "[O]utside the realm of the Federal ministerial administration, the signs of advancing privatisation, corporatisation and economisation are unmistakable" (168), albeit with an unfortunate consequence: "Opportunities for organisational choice and the diversity of administrative organisation at the Länder level are . . . diminished" as legal and practical frameworks for action narrow (170).

In a similar vein, Thomas Ellwein (2001, 44) argues that "[c]ompared with the 19th century, the 'unity' of administration has become more fragile, administrative management has become more difficult, the resulting need for internal coordination greater, and the scope of discretion in decision-making broader." Such changes may well affect attitudes about what is mandated by law. "What results," says Ellwein (2001, 44), "is 'administration by negotiation', something which has always existed but has been veiled in a cloak of secrecy. However, this is now no longer history, but the current situation." Eckhard Schröter adds (2004, 70):

> This constellation of a highly decentralised and fragmented, but at the same time tightly interwoven politico-administrative system may also help to explain the preponderance (and persistence) of political bargaining as well as legal rule-setting as instruments of political steering and coordination as opposed to managerialist contract management.

But this political bargaining is not at all like that in separation-of-powers America. Schröter notes that the executive (at all levels) completely dominates the legislative branches in the field of administrative reform. For example, the parliament has no legal instruments to combine financial appropriations with binding performance goals. America's Government Performance and Results Act is inconceivable in Germany.

France

French public management has long been regarded as "dominated by a belief in the need for a strong, centralized authority, capable of containing the centrifugal forces that constantly threaten the integrity of the state" (Hayward 1982, 116), reflecting the French "conception of authority as an absolute that cannot be shared, discussed or compromised" (Crozier 1967, quoted by Hayward 1982, 114). Recent scholarship sharply challenges that stereotype. According to Jean-Claude Thoenig (2003), France is *not* an ideal-type centralized unitary state and, in fact, not a very well-coordinated government. Mayors and regional presidents are more powerful in their domains than president and prime minister are in theirs. The state's main tools are policies and approaches constituted and co-constructed with local private and public partners. "Many decision processes are close to paralysis, but it also happens that the system makes fast and radical choices in total secrecy" (Thoenig 2003).

The story of recent public management reform in France is dominated by the debureaucratization and decentralization reforms of the Mitterrand government in the early 1980s. Prior to the Law of March 2, 1982, the *préfets* wielded power over administration in the communes and departments. The 1982 Law "was a deliberate break with the French centralizing tradition" because it enshrined in legislation "the 'rights and liberties' of regional authorities" (Douence 2003, 83).

Decentralization created regional organizations to exercise many formerly prefectorial powers. "The transfer of jurisdiction to these territorial bodies was accompanied by the transfer of services and credit and compensated for by the conferral of taxes and allowances" (Silver and Manning 2000a). Of this process, Thoenig (2004, 14) observed that whereas "[c]hanges occur in quite soft ways [in France,] [t]he 1981–1984 policies of the socialist government under President Mitterrand are an exception. They were handled in a very brutal and comprehensive manner." Neither parliament nor local authorities had any voice in their adoption and implementation, and there was little opposition. As to consequences, Philippe Bezes (2004, 60) argues that the new policies

> accentuated the historical and territorial path of the French model and favoured the emergence of institutionalization of a highly fragmented territorial governance model with great interdependence between State reform policies and local authorities' policies. . . . This results in opting for incrementalism as a strategy and the setting-up of lowest-common denominator policies that select the least ambitious option.

Subsequent French reforms have included the *Xème Plan* (1989), intended to recast the *État de procédure* into an *État de responsabilité*, and the *Xième Plan*, intended to change France from a traditional to a strategic state. In a 1989 *circulaire Rocard*, called by Philippe Bezes France's version of NPM, a program of "Public Services Renewal" introduced reforms such as *cercles de qualité*, *projets de service*, and *centres de responsabilité* to improve client orientation and service efficiency and quality. Bezes says (2004, 48), "The reform revalued human resources management, training, and the social dialogue within the administration, each of which was to become a regular programme for several years." Moreover, continuous policy evaluation has been established in France since 1990 and has moved beyond performance indicators into the assessment of programs and government policy effectiveness.

It is notable that reforms initially aimed at changes in the operational level of governance (for example, the position of the *préfets* or the management of urban centers

125

and regions) in time seem to have had consequences at the constitutional level (Toonen and Raadschelders 1997). Experimentation has been recognized since 2003 by the French parliament as a constitutional right of local authorities (Thoenig 2004). To some extent the state recognized what was already occurring and provided an impetus for even wider initiatives.

In Luc Rouban's analysis (1997, 143), state modernization and reform in France is an attempt "to articulate personnel management and the development of public management." The objectives are to ameliorate state-centered, top-down decision making, to confront the civil service with greater competition from the private sector, to disrupt traditional patterns by varying points of entry to public service, and to de-emphasize generalist-dominated hierarchies in favor of specialists and flattened organizations. Thus top-down decision making is giving way to "partnerships with locally-elected leaders, business firms and authorities of Brussels" (Rouban 1997, 143), and there are new horizontal procedures and network management and new forms of collective action seeking direct contact with public services rather than mediation by politicians. "[T]he left and the right now both agree," Robert Elgie (2003, 161) argues, "that the state needs to be brought closer to the citizen and that citizens should be viewed as customers of public services and treated accordingly." In particular, "[f]or the left, the qualities of civil servants are stressed and an emphasis is placed on negotiated reform. On the right, there is still a certain hostility towards public servants and at times this hostility manifests itself in a certain anti-technocratic populism" (158).

Not surprisingly, there has been resistance by the traditional administrative elites in, for example, budget and civil service ministries. "Managers in field offices are generally more favourable to the modernisation policy than managers working in central admin-istrations or members of the administrative *grands corps*" (Rouban 1997, 152). Higher civil servants favored reform to the extent that "it was a means to reaffirm the moral and noble dimension of their role" (Bezes 2004, 56). In the end, however, "no separation really exists in France between national and local political arenas and issues in the domain of sub-national public affairs. . . . France has no specific full time national political elite" (Thoenig 2004, 30) because the national class comprises regional and local admin-istrators. But the accumulation of mandates can lead to confusion between local and national agendas. "Multiple mandate holders as a class behave as a conservative veto group" (Thoenig 2004, 32). They fight as the guardians of local autonomy.

Early twenty-first-century reforms further decentralized the civil service, devolving certain responsibilities and the personnel associated with them to local authorities. However, "[w]hile authority has quite massively been transferred from the State to sub-national institutions in the early 1980s and in 2003, no relevant decentralization has been made from the local politicians to the population" (Thoenig 2004, 33). As a result, "The French state is a weak actor, at least in ordinary times. It is less centralized and unitary than Great Britain. . . . Formal institutional mechanisms work rather less than more" and are supplemented by "subtle informal processes" (Thoenig 2004, 34). The multiplicity of administrative actors, Hayward and Wright (2002) argue, creates the perception among them of a zero-sum game, generating resistance to change and high coordination costs.

The European Union

No account of public management reform in Europe can ignore the European Union (EU). With their long history of ambivalence toward international organizations, Americans generally fail to appreciate the EU's extraordinary influence on member states' national managerial institutions. With respect to Great Britain, according to John Rohr (2002, 50), "Parliament is no longer sovereign, and the rule of law is transformed in such a way that an act of Parliament is voided because it fails to conform to an administrative regulation of an international organization." Europeanization has strengthened supranational at the expense of national powers, leading to a gradual EU-wide convergence of national institutional arrangements and subjecting national constitutional traditions to "major adaptive pressures" (Goetz 1999, 163). It has meant, in particular, the continuous sectoral extension of supra-national powers; more extensive EU rights of command, prohibition, and control; extension of EU promotional policies; growing EU coordination of national policies; and the emergence of the EU as an actor in the international system (Goetz 1999). Indeed, it was these characteristics of EU influence that contributed to the crises of legitimacy that erupted in 2005 in France and the Netherlands.

The EU constitution comprises the Treaty of Rome (1957) and the Maastricht Treaty (1992). Members of the European Union agreed in June 1989 to form a European Monetary Union. According to the ensuing Maastricht Treaty, member states would be required, albeit with considerable latitude, to maintain an acceptable level of public debt and of deficit spending, limited in principle to 3 percent of gross domestic product. Member states are responsible for a professional, impartial, and efficient public administration, governed by the rule of law. Civil servants are not to be viewed merely as "state workers" governed by general labor laws. The entire body of legislation of the European Community is known as the *acquis communautaire*, comprising substantive, sectoral administrative law provisions. Member countries are obligated to "transpose EC legislation into the domestic legal order and then implement and enforce it" (EPPA 1999, 5). Failure of a member state to do so is a cause of legal action.

These provisions nonetheless leave member countries with a great deal of managerial autonomy.[23] Various countries have used external economic and European pressures to deal with traditional deficiencies within their jurisdictions. Integration changes national politics. Central governments now share the institutional arena with sub-national governments, public and private interest groups, multinational firms, and international and regional institutions. The privatization of telecommunications, banking, and transport monopolies, for example, is now justified by the emerging European market. It is no longer primarily a national and ideological question.

The role of NPM in the EU has nonetheless been modest, argues Johan Olsen (2003). He notes the Common Assessment Framework, which "allows the sharing of experiences, comparison, and bench-marking and learning, yet gives many degrees of freedom when it comes to how improvement is to be achieved" (2003, 518). Thus, he concludes, there has been "no general trend from Old Public Administration to New Public Management [to] be observed in the Union" (523).

No structure exists to set standards for horizontal systems of governance or for national public administrations. Over time, however, a general consensus has emerged concerning key components of good governance: rule of law principles of reliability and predictability (legal certainty, administration through law, *Rechtsstaat*, *État de droit*), accountability, openness and transparency, and efficiency and effectiveness; technical and managerial competence; organizational capacity; and citizens' participation. They have been defined and refined through the jurisprudence of national courts and, subsequently, the jurisprudence of the European Court of Justice (ECJ) (EPPA 1999). Under the European Communities Act of 1972, the opinions of the European Court of Justice on matters of EU law are binding on national courts (Rohr 2002). While modeled on the civil law tradition, the ECJ has proved compatible with the common law traditions of the UK, although it has taken a more interventionist approach, questioning advocates more aggressively and adopting a narrative rather than Socratic style of writing opinions (Rohr 2002).

These shared principles, especially visible in the case of administrative law principles, constitute the conditions of a "European Administrative Space" (EAS): common (convergent) standards for action within public administration which are defined by law and enforced in practice through procedures and accountability mechanisms, expressed in administrative procedures acts, administrative process acts, freedom of information acts, and civil service laws and values. "The EAS represents an evolving process of increasing convergence between national administrative legal orders and administrative practices of Member States" (EPPA 1999, 6). The convergence is influenced by economic pressures from individuals and firms, regular and continuous contacts between public officials of member states, and, especially, the jurisprudence of the European Court of Justice. Within the EU, standards of administrative performance are becoming increasingly supra-national. For example, "the EC directive on public procurement has proven to be an important source of homogenization of legal principles throughout the EU" (EPPA 1999, 14), and there is significant judicial cooperation and mutual assistance in law enforcement and in specific fields of law.

Concerning the question of an "emerging EAS," there are skeptics. The idea has roots in Continental public law tradition and in traditional public administration, notes Johan Olsen (2003). "The [Old Public Administration] assumes that the core of political life is law-making, interpretation, implementation and enforcement," he says (2003, 510). "Law and hierarchy govern the public administration." He notes, however, that the draft constitution of the Union states that the Union shall respect the national identities of its member states, including the organization of public administration at national, regional, and local levels. Administrative impositions have been nationally unpopular, whereas discretion is popular. "The growth in specialized autonomous European agencies has

. . . been combined with a reluctance to give them discretion and national representatives have been placed on their governing boards" (514).

A DISASTER WAITING TO HAPPEN?

While popular with policy makers, the managerialism of recent decades has drawn sharp criticism from scholars on both sides of the Atlantic for the blurring of the distinction between the public and the private spheres, with associated dilemmas of accountability, the surrender of sovereignty, and the dilution of the power of the state in favor of powerful private actors and interests.[24]

That British governments have been leaders in NPM reforms has provoked strong reactions from British scholars. Richard Rhodes, for example, describes the trends in the United Kingdom toward a smaller public sector with a reduced role in service delivery, a loss of functions to the EU, and the reductions in civil service discretion – developments which he terms the "the bold new era of the hollow state" – as risking institutional fragmentation, a loss of accountability, and a decline in the center's ability to "steer the system" (Rhodes 1994). Rhodes quotes Christopher Hood and Michael Jackson (1991a) as opining that "NPM does appear to contain several of the organizational ingredients which have been associated with socially-created disasters. At the worst, NPM could be a disaster waiting to happen" (Rhodes 1994, 149). Rhodes himself appears willing to contemplate the possibility of "catastrophe" (1994, 148).[25]

Similar concerns are expressed, if less hyperbolically, by Martin Minogue (1998) and by Carsten Greve and Peter Jesperson (1999). Minogue fears that deregulation, contracting, and market testing in the United Kingdom will sacrifice important values such as equity, community, democracy, citizenship, and constitutional protection. "The traditional public service system," he says (1998, 30), "with its mix of political leadership and bureaucratic professionalism, is a careful balancing of interests, both internal and external." Deregulation, for example, requires mechanisms for ensuring efficiency, for setting standards of service, and for exercising financial audit, and thus "represent[s] a shift away from the traditional oversight values of probity and professionalism towards a primary concern with efficiency and value for money" (Minogue 1998, 31). As Greve and Jesperson (1999, 146) see it, NPM threatens "traditional values like equity, due process and general public interest." The shift of public services to more autonomous forms excludes or minimizes democratic forms of accountability, and efficiency may come at the expense of service to difficult clients, patients, and citizens.

Of NPM, Greve and Jespersen are especially critical. "There is clear conflict," they argue (1999, 144), "between elements aiming at strengthening the market and elements aiming at the transformation of governmental organisations in the direction of more flexible, innovative and flat hierarchies," which require "soft" human relations strategies. "[W]hen it comes to quality improvements," they continue, "innovation, responsiveness and flexibility results are disputed and ambiguous and there is virtually no solid

129

documentation concerning the outcomes of the administrative reforms in the NPM strategy" (145). One reason is that organizations decouple their operations from top-down administrative reforms: superficial implementation but unchanged daily routines. NPM removes "the normative foundation which is intimately connected with fundamental principles of equal rights, fair process and redistribution of wealth governed by elected politicians" (148).

Ezra Suleiman (2003) associates New Public Management – privatization, the shrinking of the state – with a loss of legitimacy. By renouncing bureaucracy, their most important instrument of legitimacy ("by undermining the governing instrument" (2003, 7)), politicians, motivated by a false notion of efficiency, are undermining their own legitimacy and that of the democratic state. Suleiman is especially critical of developments in the US. While even in Europe there is growing recognition of the need for efficient, courteous service, he says, this is a far cry from developing a "cult of the customer," as in the US, where, owing to the reinvention movement, the concept of a public interest has lost force. "No country in Europe, not even the United Kingdom (which comes closest to the U.S.), approaches the disdain of the public sphere that has been attained in the United States" (Suleiman 2003, 57).

Other American scholars have been similarly critical. Robert Gilmour and Laura Jensen (1998), for example, note that the current emphasis in the US on criteria such as cost-effectiveness, customer satisfaction, and economic efficiency mutes interest in more traditional accountability measures such as non-performance, misfeasance, and outright fraud. Ronald Moe, noting that the question of "constitutional values" or "entrepreneurial values" is not one of either–or but "a matter of precedence in the event of conflict" (2001, 305), says that "[f]or constitutionalists, the quasi-government tends to represent a retreat from democratic values and accountable management." Joel Aberbach and Bert Rockman (2001) cite James Carroll's (1995, 309) criticism that the emphasis on customer satisfaction ignores all the purposes of government proclaimed in the preamble to the American Constitution.

Not just the new policies but the new ways of thinking about governance have been sharply criticized as well. Individualism as a premise for governance, taken for granted in the United States, falls on rockier soil in Europe. Les Metcalfe and Sue Richards, for example, argue that public choice "largely fails to contribute usefully to our under-standing of real world public management problems" (1993, 115). Klaus König (1997) claims a superiority of legalistic reasoning over the economic reasoning of New Public Management. The proper unit of analysis for Metcalfe and Richards and for König is the system as a whole, not the individual or the transaction. Metcalfe and Richards prefer a network perspective,[26] and König argues for "the primacy of politics and democracy as well as the constitutional system of order" (1997, 228).

Others, however, are more sanguine about recent developments. Ian Holliday (2000, 175) flatly rejects Rhodes's "hollow state" hypothesis, insisting that coordination "is very much within the grasp of core actors . . . although control is a more distant prospect. . . . [T]he British core is more substantial than ever before." In Continental Europe, argues Suleiman (2003, 49), "the concept of the 'public interest' still retains considerable force, in part because it is in many instances the raison d'être of government and in part because the application of universal norms is tied to the stability of society and to the legitimacy of government." In France, for example, the relationship of the citizen to the republican state is paramount, the antithesis of the multicultural society that adopts a competition–entrepreneurship–customer orientation to public service.

MANAGERIALISM IN PERSPECTIVE

It is perhaps advisable to take the more hyperbolic judgments about managerialism and New Public Management with a grain of salt. Hood himself (1989, 356) noted the precariousness of the field of public administration, owing in part to "the multiplicity of paradigms and academic takeover bids which constantly sweep the field." A paucity of careful and critical documentation of facts and of systematic analysis and evaluation enables the more speculative ruminations of ideological advocates and critics to claim an aura of confirmed truth that they do not deserve. Thoughtful assessments are nonetheless useful to maintaining perspective on elusive questions of management reforms and their consequences.

Vincent Wright (1994a, 1994b), for example, is subtly insightful concerning the European embrace of privatization. He notes numerous paradoxes: socialist governments indulging in privatization, right-of-center governments being skeptical of the same practice, states embracing pro-EU rhetoric of the free market while protecting their own industries, and privatizers denouncing the inefficiency of state enterprises but then privatizing only those activities that are already efficient. To attribute ideological coherence to such political behavior is clearly inappropriate.

Wright's summary judgment (1994b, 102) makes a point that is too often obscured by proclamations of new paradigms: the influence of national context:

[C]onvergent pressures which are reshaping the states of Western Europe, combined with other convergent pressures, have inevitable direct or indirect effects on their public administrations, squeezing governments into reforms which are broadly and increasingly similar. However, significant differences remain in the nature, intensity, timing and pace of the reforms. These differences may be explained in terms of the opportunities afforded by the politico-institutional and cultural environment in which they are being pursued.

Wright notes that in terms of the style of national reforms, "there are marked differences, for instance, between the evolutionary and internally motivated program of the Germans, the reformist and negotiated program of the French . . . and the imposed radicalism of the British" (Wright 1994b, 117). Pollitt and Bouckaert (2004, 147) add the insight that Anglo-Saxon regimes are more inclined toward managerial reforms because the instruments of the state are held in lower esteem than in Continental Europe.

The reality of historically conditioned national variation is even more evident to Jos Raadschelders and Theo Toonen (1999, 60), who argue that European public management reforms illustrate "how more or less uniform challenges may result in rather different responses and solutions" and thus in considerable national variation. The post-World War II expansion of European welfare states, they argue, has been redirected, not terminated. (Wright (1994b) similarly notes that many countries seek to modernize their states, not denigrate and dismantle them.) Raadschelders and Toonen continue (1999, 61):

> Public sector reforms generally leave the existing state and administrative institutional structure intact. They do not, and probably cannot, fundamentally alter the constitutional principles upon which the welfare state could be built. In a globalizing world governmental response to social change will resort to familiar avenues until the citizenry decides it is time for fundamental changes. And only then the functions of the state rather than its tools will be subject to evaluation.

In the meantime, they argue, states proceed by trial and error, gradually, incrementally, which constitutes the "best practice" and produces the most sustained results. This glass-is-half-full view stands, however, in contrast to Wright's (1994b, 128–9) glass-is-half-empty view that too much reform

> is obsessed with efficiency, narrowly defined, and is based on a simplistic view of bureaucracy, a naïve view of the market, an idealized view of the private sector, an insensitivity to the hidden costs of reform, an over-optimism about outcomes, and, perhaps more fundamentally, a misleading view of the state.

What these assessments make clear is the importance of a broad historical perspective, the systematic comparison of the new with the old, which is the subject of the concluding Chapter 8.

NOTES

1 Peters (1996) provides an overview of changes in governance beginning in the 1970s. See also Benz (1995), Raadschelders and Toonen (1999), and Wright (1994b).
2 "What distinguishes the privatizations of the last two decades of the 20th century from the long previous history of mostly incremental establishment and disestablishment of public enterprises," argue Wettenhall and Thynne (2002, 5), "is the sheer size of the recent movement and the ideological fervor with which it has been pushed."
3 In 1993, Metcalfe and Richards noted that "[p]ublic management is an idea whose time has come. Force of economic circumstances and political doctrine are combining

to push European governments into seeking ways of improving the performance of public organizations" (Metcalfe and Richards 1993, 106).

4 Lewis Gunn (1987), who declares that the term "public management" is of American origin, notes that the British Audit Commission's 1983 manual *Economy, Efficiency and Effectiveness* seems deeply influenced by the best-selling book by Peters and Waterman (1982), which created pressures to imitate business management.

5 This concession by some of the most respected scholars in the American traditional public administration community was puzzling. The concept of management and the term public management had long been in use even in traditional literature. Prominent traditional scholars have held that the terms "administration" and "management" are for all intents and purposes synonymous. Nonetheless there has ensued considerable discussion over the differences between administration and management, some of which were noted in Chapter 1, and over the controversial implications for public administration and democratic theory of public management's rapidly growing popularity as a theme of teaching, research, practice, and administrative reform.

6 Toonen and Raadschelders argue, however (1997, 2–1) that "[e]ver since the beginning of this century the productivity, effectiveness, efficiency and budgetary control of public expenditure have been called in as reasons for administrative reform in Western systems."

7 In an EU context, subsidiarity means that member states remain responsible for areas which they are capable of managing more effectively themselves, while the European Community is given those powers which the member states cannot discharge satisfactorily.

8 American public management reforms such as PPBS and Management by Objectives (MBO) were to have some influence in Europe, where they were viewed as imitating the private sector, but left the system basically unchanged except for increased numbers of analytical specialists in staff positions (Derlien 1987).

9 Prior to 2004, "GAO" stood for "General Accounting Office." Examples of this literary genre include Bardach (1998), Behn (1991), Cohen and Eimicke (1995), Haass (1999), Heymann (1987), Moore (1995), and Reich (1990).

10 The National Performance Review (NPR) was later retitled the National Partnership for Reinventing Government.

11 In April 2000, the Clinton administration announced that two-thirds of the 1993 NPR proposals had been completed (Lombard 2003). But the reinvention movement in America died with the following poignant announcement on the National Partnership for Reinventing Government website (http://govinfo.library.unt.edu/npr.): "The National Partnership for Reinventing Government has come to an end, but government reform continues. We thank the Government Printing Office's Federal Depository Library Program and its partner, the Government Documents Department, University of North Texas Libraries, for archiving this website exactly as it appeared on January 19, 2001. NPR's mailing address, phone numbers, and staff e-mail addresses are no longer active." Students of termination take note.

12 Interestingly, Congress, in typically American fashion, stepped into the vacuum and began to manage training resource allocations and operations by statute. Unfortunately, as Lombard (2003) notes, private sector trainers turned out to lack the special skills needed in federal appropriations, personnel, ethics, and procurement law.

13 It is worth noting, however, that English civil servant Desmond Keeling's insightful *Management in Government* (1972) appeared when the renewed emphasis on

public management in America was still in its infancy. Toonen (1998, 236, 237) notes, moreover, that "a tradition of 'governance' does not preclude an abundant use of managerial practices at the operational level of government" and that many Continental countries "have strong managerial traditions of their own, particularly at decentralized, local levels of government. Public administration as a discipline often started out at these levels," as was the case in the US.

14 Vincent Wright (1994a) notes that nationalized industries represented 9 percent of the GDP, whereas in 1993 they represented only 3 percent.

15 The Ibbs Report (Efficiency Unit 1988, 9) said that "[t]he main strategic control must lie with the Minister and Permanent Secretary. But once the policy objectives and budgets within the framework are set, the management of the agency should have as much independence as possible in deciding how these objectives are met. . . . [T]he presumption must be that, provided management is operating within the strategic direction set by ministers, it must be left as free as possible to manage within that framework."

16 Talbot (2004) says that the three essential ideas associated with agencification are structural disaggregation and/or creation of task-specific organizations, performance contracting and deregulation, each of which is often pursued separately. The idea, he says, is most closely identified with the unbundling of large, comprehensive ministries.

17 Brian Hogwood, David Judge, and Murray McVicar (2004) note that overall, as shown by the experience of the Labour government, the Next Steps agency form does not appear to hinder policy change, owing to its largely informal status; it is adaptable to new purposes.

18 The central elements of the constitutional change program were devolution (to Scotland, Wales and Northern Ireland); the modernization of political institutions: both Houses of Parliament, the civil service, and local government (including creation of a Greater London Assembly and Mayor); greater democratization of the political system; and safeguarding and improving individual and minority rights (http://www. historylearningsite.co.uk/constitutional_reforms.htm.).

19 Joined-up government was, in Oliver James's view (2004, 76), "a vague set of aspirations for performance and organizational prescriptions, suggesting that outcomes citizens and their representatives value should be delivered in a way that is not dictated by organizational boundaries." Structural integration, information exchange, joint planning, staff transfer, and improved coordinating structures can be used to accomplish this goal.

20 Robert Hazell and David Sinclair conclude (2000, 399) of the broad scheme of constitutional reform in the UK: "Devolution will introduce a form of quasifederalism. Its federal characteristics include (a) a formal division of legislative power, of the kind found in federal constitutions; (b) entrenchment, but by the political means of a referendum; (c) the creation of a new constitutional court, the Judicial Committee of the Privy Council, which is the body chosen to adjudicate in devolution disputes; and (d) formal machinery to handle intergovernmental relations, namely the new Joint Ministerial Committee on Devolution."

21 Christoph Reichard (2003) notes that the old cameralist book-keeping method, still in use in all German public sector organizations, is only now beginning to be replaced by modern resource-based accrual accounting and budgeting systems.

22 Werner Jann (2003) notes that in Germany the division between academia and practitioners is rather blurred. There has been a constant flow of advisory commissions,

reports, and reform initiatives (enumerated above), and the policy networks are closely knit. "Academics and practitioners are members of the same commissions and associations, write and read the same journals and reports, and have, at least in the past, enjoyed a rather homogeneous socialization through a highly dogmatic legal education" (Jann 2003, 97).

23 According to Johan Olsen (2003, 518), "EU arrangements have been compatible with the maintenance of different national institutional structures and practices. Established national patterns have been resistant but also flexible enough to cope with changes at the European level."

24 In its unprecedented contracting out of national security functions during the war in Iraq, for example, the US government, in the view of critics, let its monopoly on the legitimate use of force slip out of its grasp, beyond the reach of democratic controls.

25 Vincent Wright is more circumspect: "Many of the reforms, which are flawed in several ways, may have unanticipated and unwelcome consequences" (1994b, 102).

26 "[W]e propose a general definition of management as taking responsibility for the performance of a system. . . . [P]ublic management entails getting things done through other organizations. Steering the activities of systems composed of several interdependent organizations is one of the distinctive challenges of public management" (Metcalfe and Richards 1987, 37).

Chapter 7

New Public Management: delegation and accountability

INTRODUCTION

Actual changes in public management structures, institutions, and practices in the era of managerialism that began in the 1970s have increasingly been recognized as qualified, contingent, and variegated, differing markedly across nations with different administrative histories (Pollitt and Bouckaert 2004). Change has been sufficiently widespread, however, to have ignited renewed interest in "an old and tricky subject" (Barberis 1998, 451): the accountability of public management to sovereign authority, whether the authority of the ruler or of the people and their representatives. Owing to the management and institutional reforms of recent years, argue Peter Aucoin and Ralph Neintzman (2000, 46),

> all governments must now govern in a context where there are greater demands for accountability for performance on the part of a better educated and less deferential citizenry, more assertive and well organized interest groups and social movements, and more aggressive and intrusive mass media operating in a highly competitive information-seeking and processing environment.

The intensity of concern for accountability varies across countries. Historically, concern for political accountability has been less intense in democratic regimes with strong integrative institutions such as parliamentary sovereignty, *Rechtsstaat*, and corps of officials imbued with public service values or *noblesse oblige*. When such traditional institutions are perceived to be under threat, however, as is the case in Great Britain, concern for accountability has intensified, much more so than in France and Germany, where the influence of New Public Management has been diffuse. In the United States, the accountability of executive officials to democratic authority was a motivating factor in the design of the Constitution's federal organization and its checks and balances, depriving governance of strong integrative institutions. As a consequence, owing to Americans' distrust of bureaucratic power, managerial accountability has been an ongoing issue, even more so as American administrations have adopted neo-liberal public management policies.[1]

136

In their efforts to highlight the significance of the changes and adaptations associated with managerialism, many scholars have dramatized the accountability issue by viewing it as a confrontation between the clashing values of the Old Public Administration and the New Public Management (Dunleavy 1994; Peters and Wright 1996; Gilmour and Jensen 1998; Greve and Jesperson 1999; Olsen 2003). As noted in Chapter 6, New Public Management is portrayed as being in fundamental conflict with traditional public service values, threatening the control by representative institutions of an increasingly deconcentrated and "hollow state" and posing new intellectual and practical problems relating to the accountability and responsibility of public officials.

The practical problems of accountability, which are increasing in complexity as the distance between policy making and service delivery grows, may seem intractable. As Donald Kettl puts it (2002, ix):

> Elected officials find themselves delegating authority in traditional ways but discovering that the old mechanisms for ensuring accountability often work poorly, if at all. Instead they work increasingly through loose networks of service providers, but often, as government practitioners, they struggle to maintain government's legitimacy.

The intellectual problems, on the other hand, have stimulated a growing body of insightful scholarship based on public choice theory, the new institutional economics, and positive political economy. Students of politics and public management on both sides of the Atlantic have begun to think about democratic governance in new ways.

As a result of this new scholarship, issues of delegation and accountability have become more complex and more intellectually challenging. What forms should accountability take across regimes having different characteristics? How, in theory and practice, might traditional representational and hierarchical "chain of delegation" accountability, still the undoubted preference of legislators and courts in all countries, be reconciled with a managerialism variously emphasizing polyarchy and interdependence, or competition, performance, and customers, or even deliberative, direct democracy? More succinctly, how might the legitimacy of governance in the eyes of citizens be sustained in the future if the distance between constitutional authority and the actual delivery of services has grown dramatically?

This chapter attempts to place these questions in perspective. It first reviews the root cause of the accountability problem: the delegation of sovereign authority to officials empowered to act in the name of the people and their representatives and the resulting necessity to maintain control over those officials' actions. Then New Public Management is examined in the light of the doctrines and practices of Old Public Administration in order to gain an appreciation of why the accountability problem has grown in importance and difficulty in the managerial era. The following section reviews the theoretical issues posed by the problem of assuring democratic accountability in a neo-liberal state, sketching a "new political economy" of accountability involving both hierarchical control and polycentric coordination. The chapter concludes with a discussion of the extent to which the adaptations and changes comprising the new public management constitute a serious challenge to democratic accountability and what the practical responses to this challenge might be.

PERSPECTIVES ON ACCOUNTABILITY

In one sense, delegation is just another name for the division of labor that accompanies the emergence of complex activity: specialized responsibilities are assigned – delegated – to those with the expertise to perform them in a competent manner. The management problem is one of monitoring and coordinating those to whom such responsibilities have been assigned, each of whom is, in effect, held accountable for adding value that cumulates to the accomplishment of an overarching purpose.

In markets, "management" is accomplished largely through mechanisms of exchange, such as legally enforceable contracts, in which a price, wage, or fee secures the interests of the parties to the exchange. The demands for accountability by those responsible for producing value are satisfied when they have demonstrably produced or delivered the agreed-upon values. Problems arise when exchange values cannot readily be established, as is the case with public goods, and when there is substantial performance ambiguity, as is the case when value cannot be verified at reasonable cost. Thus accountability is an issue when governments or administrations are assigned responsibility for producing collective rather than private values and especially when there is performance ambiguity.

Issues associated with delegation and accountability are as old as administration itself. "The growing complexities of civil administration," noted E. N. Gladden of eleventh-century administration (1972a, 234), "would become burdensome to the leader interested in the exercise of power and he would be compelled for his own comfort not only to call in his officials for advice but to delegate responsibilities to them." Reliability and competence would also be of concern. Thus some rulers would appoint deputies for household and civil affairs with "certain managerial capacities," and some of these deputies could wield real power to the extent that "the line between the ruler, as power wielder, and the administrator as manager, cannot easily be drawn" (234). But the goal of delegation was clear: "[T]he leader who also had administrative talent at his disposal was better equipped to make his rulership effective, as well as acceptable, to the subjects whose continuing support he needed if his period of rule was to be satisfactorily prolonged" (Gladden 1972a, 235).

The advent of popular sovereignty beginning with the revolutions in the United States and France brought the issue of accountability into sharp relief. Formerly, accountability had been obscured by imperial power, royal absolutism, and crown prerogative: the relationship between sovereign authority and those charged with implementing the sovereign's will.[2] Even then, such relationships were at least potentially problematic.

Household officials could take advantage of a ruler's prolonged absences or personal weaknesses. Primitive communications contributed to the problem; according to an old Chinese expression, "the mountains are high, and the Emperor is far away." When the people are sovereign and the government, administration, or regime they empower to execute their will is a complex and impersonal amalgam of officials, organizations, and territories, the problems of accountability involve structures, practices, and institutionalized values and are difficult and costly to solve.

Previous chapters recorded the evolution of structures and institutions to assure public sector accountability. Aucoin and Neintzman observe (2000, 45) of the current situation:

> Although accountability regimes vary in important respects among political systems, taken collectively they encompass processes whereby citizens hold their governors to account for their behavior and performance directly through elections; the representatives of citizens in legislative assemblies hold political executives and public servants accountable through mechanisms of public scrutiny and audit; political executives hold their subordinate officials accountable through hierarchical structures of authority and responsibility; and, among other things, courts and various administrative tribunals and commissions hold legislatures, executives or administrative officers accountable to the law.

More specifically, the possible mechanisms of accountability include:

- **those relying primarily on executive authority**:
    - **power backed by force**, used to some extent even in democracies;
    - **accepted systems of moral values, commitments, or precepts of responsibility**, such as public service values or codes of ethics, sustained and protected by merit and tenure systems;
    - **professionalism and expertise**, certified by recognized accrediting authorities and empowered by a separation of politics from public management;
    - **representative bureaucracies**, whose personnel are broadly similar to citizens in general;
    - **performance targets, balanced scorecards, evaluations, and assessments**;
    - **incentives**, that is, systems of rewards for performance that may emulate the efficiency-inducing effects of markets.

- **those relying primarily on legislative authority**:
    - **detailed legislative (statutory) prescription**, which, in effect, minimizes and severely limits the discretion of officials;

139

- **"police patrol" and "fire alarm" and other monitoring provisions** of legislation, to include reporting requirements;
- **freedom of information, administrative procedure, sunset, and financial disclosure acts;**
- **legislated performance goals and indicators;**
- **inspectors general and ombudsmen** authorized to operate independent of executive authority.

- **those relying primarily on legal authority:**

  - **detailed and comprehensive codes of legally enforceable rules,** as in civilian (Roman) law countries;
  - **the liability, in common law countries, of public officials before courts of common law,** an approach which rejects the distinction between public and private sectors;
  - **judicial review,** in which courts or judicial officers are empowered to review legislation and to uphold rights expressed in constitutions and guidelines;
  - **separation of governmental powers** combined with systems of checks and balances.

- **those relying primarily on popular authority:**

  - **constitutionally established elections, referendums, and recalls,** in which officeholders and those beholden to them are periodically subject to the sanction of being turned out of office;[3]
  - **participatory democracy,** in which citizens share the authority to deliberate about and reach managerial decisions affecting their well-being.

In general, accountability in practice relies on all of these approaches, but the selection and balance vary across countries with different administrative and legal traditions. "Accountability," says Peter Barberis (1998, 464), "is essentially about institutions, mechanisms and procedures set to work in a world of hard, practical realities."

In the Anglo-American tradition, primary reliance for curbing official abuses of power was placed on the legal authority of courts of common law, which retained jurisdiction over all disputes, public and private (Bertelli 2005).[4] Thus A. V. Dicey (1885, 215–16) famously rejected the distinction between public and private legal accountability that, for example, characterized French administrative law, writing:

[T]he notion which lies at the bottom of the "administrative law" known to foreign countries, that affairs or disputes in which the government or its servants are concerned are beyond the sphere of the civil courts and must be dealt with by special and more or less official bodies (*tribunaux administratifs*), is utterly unknown to the law of England, and indeed is fundamentally inconsistent with our traditions and customs.

140

The formal doctrine of accountability in British government, argues Barberis (1998, 451), "remains in the shadow of A. V. Dicey. . . . [M]inisters are accountable to the public via Parliament, for their own decisions and for the work of their departments; civil servants are accountable internally – and only internally – to their political chiefs."[5] In national government, doctrines of parliamentary sovereignty and unified powers reduce the potential for administrative drift and incentives for external political control over the bureaucracy.

In the guise of what is known as the non-delegation doctrine, the British model was operative in the United States well into the twentieth century (Bertelli 2005), especially during the patronage era in which administration was dominated by political parties and common law courts (Skowronek 1982).[6] "Law paralysing administration," said John Dickinson (1928, 280) quoting Roscoe Pound, "was an everyday spectacle. . . . We seemed to have achieved in very truth a *Rechtsstaat*. . . . It was fundamental in our policy to confine administration to the inevitable minimum."[7] Such court oversight on behalf of private rights arose especially after the Civil War, when officials were held liable for damages.[8]

As the administrative state grew in scope and complexity, however, the three branches, reflecting the constitutional structure of checks and balances, began competing for the control over delegated authority. The fact that the Constitution itself failed to define a role for administrators has created the existential problem of American public management. "It is clear," argues Norton Long (1949, 258),

> that the American system of politics does not generate enough power at any focal point of leadership to provide the conditions for an even partially successful divorce of politics from administration. Subordinates cannot depend on the formal chain of command to deliver enough political power to permit them to do their jobs.

Thus, in Long's view (1949, 258), a "structure of interests friendly or hostile, vague and general or compact and well-defined, encloses each significant center of administrative discretion. This structure is an important determinant of the scope of possible action." By the 1970s, "the main thrust of administrative law," David Epstein and Sharyn O'Halloran (1999, 21) write, "was to make agencies look like pluralistic enterprises, open to the public and reviewable by higher courts." As a consequence, "the focus of the administrative law literature was the role of interest groups and courts as checks on bureaucratic power" (21).

Between British parliamentary dominance and French concerns for administrative effectiveness, argues Anthony Bertelli (2005), lies German administrative authority, which is subjected to a strong form of *ultra vires* based on constitutional rights guarantees and the *Rechtsstaatsprinzip* (principle of the rule of law in Article 20 of the German Basic Law): "[A]ny state action interfering with the rights of individuals must be authorized by parliamentary statute" (Groß 2000, 587, quoted by Bertelli 2005). Moreover, under Article 80, any statutory grant of administrative rule-making authority must be stated explicitly and with precision. As Thomas Groß (2000, 587) characterizes it, "[a]ny independent regulatory power of the administration has been abolished. Only internal affairs of the administration and beneficial actions, like subsidies or the creation of public services, are excepted from that principle."[9]

In general, note Theo Toonen and Jos Raadschelders (1997), in Anglo-American (common law) systems, detailed, instrumental control by statutes is the rule. In Westminster systems (with the important exception of the Next Steps program), an act of parliament is generally necessary to legitimate state activity and induce change. American legislation is notoriously, albeit inconsistently, detailed. "In systems of statutory regulation by means of framework-law[, however,] the basic idea is that laws and regulations may shape outcomes, but not determine them" (Toonen and Raadschelders 1997, 1–10). In many Continental systems, they say, with their tradition of executive preeminence over the parliament, there is potential for non-legislated reform of even constitutional proportions; the legislature may not even pay attention.

The general problem of accountability has, as discussed in Chapter 6, been brought into sharp focus by the changes and adaptations of managerialism. Pressures for governance reform have taken three forms, according to Aucoin and Neintzman (2000): devolution or debureaucratization; shared governance and collaborative management; and demands for both results and demonstrated performance. Accountability and performance may, although they need not, pull in opposite directions. "Devolution and debureaucratization increase discretion; shared governance and collaborative management disperse responsibility; and managing to outputs and outcomes gives preference to results over compliance with input controls and prescribed processes" (Aucoin and Neintzman 2000, 47).

OLD PUBLIC ADMINISTRATION VS. NEW PUBLIC MANAGEMENT

Governance in any country may be defined as the way sovereign power and responsibility are distributed, both formally and informally, among that country's institutions. How much of the people's sovereign power has been delegated, to which institutions, and under what enabling and constraining conditions? How are the continuing reliability and legitimacy of this distribution of power assured? When tensions or conflicts of governance arise, what kinds of solutions are held to be legitimate? Finally, within each nation's institutional context, what is the responsibility of public management? Old Public Administration and New Public Management propose different answers to these questions.

Old Public Administration, in Johan Olsen's view (2003, 510), "assumes that the core of political life is law-making, interpretation, implementation and enforcement." Public managers are governed by rules and hierarchy and by the public service values of reliability, consistency, predictability, and accountability to legislatures and courts in executing and maintaining the rule of law (constitutional, administrative, jurisprudential) or the principles of *Rechtsstaat*, all on behalf of the common good or the public interest. Authority is not the opposite of democracy, argued Carl Friedrich (1976), but complementary to it. "[R]ational bureaucracy," he believed, "needs strongly inspirational democratic leadership. . . . Bureaucracy which serves such leaders will . . . strive for responsibility as well as efficiency" (1976, 51).

In contrast, New Public Management implies that "the public sector is not distinctive from the private sector" (Olsen 2003, 510). Public managers are assumed to be entrepreneurial "rational actors" who, in their pursuit of their interests, create public value much as actors in private markets do. The original assumption of NPM was that introducing relatively uniform, market-like incentives – competition and rewards proportional to performance – would produce more accountability than the rule-bound bureaucracies of the Old Public Administration. The values of administrative integrity, democratic joint decision making, transparency, and external accountability, which animated reformist concerns of the 1960s, were less central to the efficiency-oriented reformist concerns of the 1980s and 1990s (Toonen and Raadschelders 1997, 7–10).

The accountability issue raised by NPM is not so much delegation *per se* as the extensive sub-delegation of authority to lengthening chains of subordinate agents in both the public and the private sectors. These elongated "chains of delegation" increase the distance between the sovereign authority of the people and their representatives, on the one hand, and those service-delivery agents acting in the people's name and financed by their resources, on the other. By increasing power at the lower reaches of administration, NPM arguably strengthens centrifugal forces of democratic governance, weakening the hold of traditional command-and-control and other integrative institutions, all of this with indeterminate consequences.

A related issue, as discussed in Chapter 6, concerns the increasing popularity of quasi-governments (essentially, formally unaccountable public entities) and their implications for accountability (Moe 2001; Bertelli 2005). Ronald Moe (2001) writes of literally hundreds of increasingly popular "hybrid organizations," the existence of which raises important questions: To whom are these hybrids accountable? How is the public interest being protected against the interest of private parties? "New Public Management" – ironically in a Diceyan spirit – spurned the notion that the public and private sectors are legally distinct. The idea was to give managers the flexibility to improve performance measured in terms of outputs or results, that is, to let managers manage in a "nobody-in-charge-society" (H. Cleveland 2000). Departmental integration and cohesion, canons of Old Public Administration, are replaced by organizational dispersion, and managerial autonomy is separated from political accountability.[10]

Though proponents of New Public Management have viewed it as an inevitable consequence of the forces of globalization – of trade, communications, technology, and the movement of factors of production – proponents of Old Public Administration have mounted a strong defense. According to Carsten Greve and Peter Jesperson (1999, 146), for example, NPM threatens "traditional values like equity, due process and general

143

public interest." The highly developed formal *systems* of accountability that are central to New Public Management, Barberis (1998) notes, may negate the *spirit* or *morality* of accountability. Guy Peters and Vincent Wright elaborate on the virtues of traditional accountability (1996, 639):

> The fundamental social loss arising from the change away from the old public administration, with all of its apparent rigidity and seemingly outmoded assumptions, is that at least that old model contained a consistent set of ideas that had proven their utility over time. . . . They were able to create . . . a public service with an ethos of service, and with a clear idea of the limits of its role. Further, this . . . approach to the public sector provided the means for linking bureaucracy and democracy in a clearer way than do the contemporary characterizations of the field. . . . If nothing else, the traditional model did provide a clearer normative standard, and one that was oriented to the public interest, than is available from much of the new public management.

The shift of responsibility for public service delivery to more distant and autonomous agents excludes or minimizes constitutionally authorized forms of accountability, and efficiency gains, if such there are, may come at the expense of equity and other values upheld by representative institutions.

Toonen and Raadschelders (1997) have questioned whether governments will be willing to pay the price for real performance management, by which they mean the abandonment by representative institutions of traditional hierarchical controls over public service delivery. Perhaps especially in performance-oriented government, moreover, managers need direction, goals, and performance standards, which remain the responsibility of constitutional policy makers. Thus, as Kettl suggests, new accountability mechanisms will be needed as well. An appropriate balance between performance and compliance auditing must be struck.[11] Aucoin and Neintzman (2000, 48) argue that "diminished attention to probity, fairness and impartiality, as illustrative of critical public service values, ought not to be traded-off for improved performance." Letting managers manage has never been a viable alternative, in their view. "Systems of devolved authority and responsibility only work well when accompanied by other kinds of constraints, such as comprehensive systems of administrative law, backed by judicial or administrative review, strong legislative oversight, or the disciplines of the market or professional codes" (2000, 48).

In summarizing the lessons of both New Public Management and the German experiment with the New Steering Model, Christoph Reichard (2003) lays out an analytic agenda for the issue of accountability:

- a politics–administration dichotomy may create principal–agent conflicts;
- "one-dimensional, self-interest guided, efficiency-driven values . . . may cause oversimplification of complex policy issues and may end in one-sided solutions" (358);

144

- decentralization may lead to fragmentation;
- a performance-based orientation, together with agencification and corporatization, may cause accountability problems.

It is this agenda that is being addressed using the theoretical tools of institutional economics and political economy.

THE POLITICAL ECONOMY OF ACCOUNTABILITY

From early in the development of American public administration, problems of delegation and accountability were intuitively perceived as what we now call "principal–agent" problems: that is, problems associated with ensuring that an agent's actions comply with the principal's expectations – including actual use of the terms (Hart 1925; Friedrich 1946; Morstein Marx 1949). Frederick Taylor himself seemed to recognize that specialized hierarchies posed principal–agent problems when he noted that workers kept employers ignorant of how fast work can in fact be done (Crainer 2000). A British scholar of the American administrative state, Harold Laski (1919, 1923), had similar intuitions:

> [T]he sovereign people is too large for continuous action. Its powers become delegated to the complex of institutions we call government.
>
> (1919, 25)

> Administrative discretion is of the essence of the modern State.
>
> (1923, 92)

> To call forth initiative in the public servant is perhaps the first task to which a member of the Cabinet must address himself; but that initiative must work always within the ambit of a conscious control. . . . For only by making discretion effectively responsible can we hope to give the modern state the instruments of which it stands in sore need.
>
> (1923, 100)

Public management reforms during the era of managerialism, which, as Joel Aberbach and Tom Christensen (2003, 491, 492) see it, are "more extensive than ever before in history," are, in their view, "quite self-consciously theory driven . . . [and] rest on a well-articulated body of academic writings." Their reference is primarily to what they refer to as "new institutional economic theory," which assumes the rational pursuit of self-interest by individual actors and makes extensive and formal use of the principal–agent logic.[12] This analytic literature encroached on habits of thought which Lewis Gunn (1987, 33) has characterized as reflecting a concern with "changing settings, structures and staffing in the public sector" through "a mixture of description, comparisons with other

European countries and prescriptions for reform in the machinery and formal procedures of government."

Not everyone sees theory as preeminent in the new managerialism. "[T]he new public management is not a theory in any meaningful sense of the term," insist Peters and Wright (1996, 638–9). "It does not provide a coherent and integrated set of propositions about running the public sector, but rather appears more to generate 'principles' that are compatible with the political thinking of the day." Theo Toonen (1998) and Peter Bogason and Toonen (1998) argue in contrast that diverse intellectual developments in international public administration accelerated following devastating critiques of traditional public administration by Herbert Simon, Robert Dahl, and Dwight Waldo and others during the late 1940s (Bertelli and Lynn 2006). According to Toonen (1998, 235), "[d]ifferent theories, explicitly or by default, are based on different assumptions about the relations among the various levels of 'government in action'. Some postulate a hierarchical order while others think in terms of networks and interdependency relations or of more atomistic and symbolic interactions." These two types of theories are taken up in turn.

The new political economy

While what may be termed the "new political economy" is only one of the managerial era's intellectual developments worth noting, it goes to the heart of issues of delegation and accountability. Patrick Dunleavy (1992, 259) lauds "the development and refinement of public choice into behaviourally realistic and theoretically diverse explanations of broad classes of political phenomena," among them, issues of accountability.

Peter Aucoin (1990, 126–7) has made the interesting argument that "[t]he public choice paradigm emphasizes the role to be played by political authorities as elected representatives in governance. It does not admit to a policy/administration dichotomy that would carve out spheres of responsibility for politicians on the one hand and bureaucrats on the other." The public choice approach sees politics as pervading management, that is, politics as being present in both the formulation and the implementation of policies. Public-choice-based approaches have sought to diminish the capacities of special interest groups to dominate the policy process of the administrative state.

In contrast, according to Aucoin (1990, 127), the managerialist paradigm

> reasserts the policy/administration dichotomy with a vengeance. [Managerialism] sees politics as present essentially in the determination of the basic values or missions, and thus the policies, of an organization. It assumes that the realization of these values through a process of implementation can be achieved without the need for direct intervention by those who have set the basic values; at most, a monitoring role is required to ensure that there have not been departures from basic values.

The managerialist paradigm, says Aucoin, gives a high priority to the responsiveness of bureaucrats to their policy constituencies (again citing Peters and Waterman).

"Government bureaucrats are thus prone either to be seen by their clients as unresponsive to them or to be seen by political authorities as captured by their clients" (129).

That such an analytic approach might seem "new," that the various concepts associated with political economics have in recent decades become a dominant framework for analyzing issues of public management, is attributable not only to recent developments in formal theory but also, as Chapter 6 showed, to increased public sector reliance on quasi- and non-governmental entities (contracting, privatization, subsidiarity, hybridity) and to increased central government reliance on sub-national governments (devolution, deconcentration, decentralization) to fulfill sovereign purposes, the very circumstances the theory was intended to illuminate. Thus there has been a convergence of interest in the principal–agent problem across countries, although differently viewed as a problem of political control in the US and as a problem of managerial control in Europe.

Because this theoretical approach assumes rationality on the part of political actors, its application to actual problems of governance is controversial. To what extent can individual or organizational behavior be plausibly assumed to be motivated by "self-interest" and, therefore, to be rational in a utilitarian sense? Creating a predictive science of politics based on rational choice assumptions is defeated, argues Colin Hay (2004), by the indeterminacy of human behavior, although rational choice models can be useful as heuristic devices.

Another source of objections is that typical rational choice formulations ignore crucial details. "Although in most parliamentary systems incentive compatibility between members of parliament and cabinet is high," argues Thomas Saalfeld (2000, 373), "it is rarely complete. One important dimension of legislative oversight, the interaction between government backbenchers and cabinet members, is often neglected, especially in many rational-choice accounts of modelling parliamentary parties as unitary actors." West European governments fall because of lack of backbench support, he argues. "Future studies will have to incorporate the agency relationships, conflicts of interest and information problems *within* parliamentary parties more systematically into the general principal–agent framework of executive–legislative relations" (373).

So long as at least some political actors pursue their own interests through engaging the institutions of government, then it can be insightful to use public choice theory as a source of heuristics to frame and analyze accountability issues.

The chain of delegation

In the new political economy, the policy process is conceptualized as "a chain of delegation, in which those authorized to make political decisions conditionally designate others to make such decision in their name and place" (Strøm 2000, 266).[13] The chain can be said to have four discrete steps: from voters to elected representatives, from legislators to the head of government, from the head of government to the heads of executive departments, and from the heads of these departments to civil servants. Agents are accountable to their principals (1) if they are obliged to act on the latter's behalf, and (2) if the latter are empowered to reward or punish them for their performance in this capacity. In a democracy, the citizens' role is to control officials, but when we "consider the incumbents of political office as agents of the citizens, we have to acknowledge that they are *constrained* and frequently *common* agents, whose responsibilities may thus be manifold" (268).

"The very raison d'être of delegation is a constraint," argue John Brehm and Scott Gates (1999, 191). Supervisors require assistance if they are to carry out all the tasks assigned to them, so they delegate to subordinates who, because their activities cannot easily be monitored, make the supervisor vulnerable to moral hazard, and, because their "type" cannot be clearly identified, render the supervisor vulnerable to adverse selection. "Subordinate preferences, the repertoire of responses available to subordinates, and the means by which subordinates learn to implement rules, procedures, or policy all significantly constrain the supervisor" (192). Focusing on amenable subordinates may be the most rewarding strategy for supervisors.

A synthesis of neoclassical and institutional economics based on the concept of transaction costs (prominently including the work of Douglass North) was employed by Thráinn Eggertsson (1990) to explain the purpose of the state, in a cameralist spirit, as creating a regime of property rights and transaction costs that enables it to maximize its technical economic potential. "[T]he willingness of individual owners to supply specific appropriable assets, essential for economic growth and full utilization of advanced technologies," Eggertsson argues (1990, 320), "depends directly on the social rules structure, including the availability of relatively consistent and impartial dispute processing by a third party, which in most cases can be supplied only by the state." States may fail to provide the most appropriate institutional structures, however, thus jeopardizing or fatally limiting their wealth-creating potential.

Jan-Erik Lane's *Constitutions and Political Theory* (1996) is an application of public choice theory and neo-institutional ideas to questions concerning the existence, origins, and consequences of constitutions. He notes that institutionalizing constitutions enhances national stability by recognizing unalterable rights, by creating veto players (individual or collective decision makers whose agreement is required to change the status quo; see below), and by creating highly qualified majorities to amend them. He further notes, however, that these kinds of features of constitutions may tend to privilege the status quo at the expense of more participatory and responsive forms of democracy.

States and their constitutions comprise the institutional framework for public choice, the articulation and pursuit of what may be broadly termed "the public will" or "the public interest" through politics. In the chain of delegation, theoretical attention is on "the people" or "voters" as principals and their elected representatives as agents, and on elected representatives or, alternatively, on organized interest groups as principals and bureaucrats as agents, and so on down the chain.

Employing principal–agent logic, John Ferejohn (1999) identifies three serious limits to accountability within democratic institutions. First, electoral heterogeneity makes it possible for officials to play voters off against each other. Second, officials can group unpopular with popular actions, thereby achieving significant parts of their own agendas. Third, the complexity of modern government means that officials enjoy enormous informational advantages over voters, who might vote differently if this information disadvantage did not exist.

Using a similar theoretical orientation, Michael Laver and Kenneth Shepsle (1999) focus on parliamentary rather than presidentialist democracies. Accountability in such democracies depends on the credibility of the mechanism whereby a majority of legislators can express "no confidence" in the government and, in turn, on alternative ways of replacing a cabinet or one of its ministers. In parliamentary democracies, they argue, political officials are not directly accountable to citizens but, rather, to representatives of citizens. Accountability may be said to exist when parliament, although having the means to do so, has no inclination to replace a government with a feasible alternative. Accountability exists, therefore, when the system is in equilibrium. Laver and Shepsle conclude that parliamentary governments have as a result rather broad discretion in the making of policy.

In a similar vein, Strøm (2000) views parliamentary democracy as a particular regime of delegation and accountability that can be understood with the help of agency theory. "Parliamentary government is a system of government in which the prime minister and his or her cabinet are accountable to any majority of the members of parliament and can be voted out of office by the latter through an ordinary and constructive vote of no confidence" (265). It is the threat of being voted out of office, *ex post* accountability, that produces party cohesiveness in parliamentary systems. Parliamentary democracy is a particularly simple form of delegation, argues Strøm, in contrast to presidential systems, where there are multiple, competing agents. Civil servants have a single principal, their minister.[14] It is in the relationship between the legislative majority and the executive that the two regime forms most clearly diverge.

Agency problems associated with delegation arise if the interests of principals and agents differ. According to Brehm and Gates (1999), these problems are of two basic types: omission ("shirking") and commission ("sabotage"). Agency "losses" are contained through contract design, screening and selection mechanisms, monitoring and reporting requirements, and institutional checks. If adverse selection is feared, then *ex ante* screening and selection are appropriate. "Parliamentary democracy implies a particular choice of instruments to control agent behavior, which systematically differ from those of presidential systems" (Strøm 2000, 272). Parliamentary democracy relies more on indirect delegation, less on competing agents and on institutional checks, more on *ex ante* control mechanisms, especially prior screening, than on either "police patrols"[15] or "fire alarms."[16] The key is that "[t]he institutions of parliamentarism empower political parties to an extent that is not generally found under presidentialism" (274); parties are the screening mechanisms.

Thus, in Strøm's view, parliamentary democracy implies potential advantages in administrative efficiency, in providing incentives for principals to monitor and for agents not to shirk. But the likelihood of overall agency loss is heightened because of the absence of competition; principals cannot bypass their agents. The lack of constraint and competition diminishes the ability of principals to learn from their agents' behavior from the signals they receive. Thus they are exposed more to moral hazard,[17] less to adverse selection.[18] Parliamentary regimes have less transparent politics.

Strøm cites George Tsebelis's (2000) argument that regimes differ in the number of veto players. In the UK there is always one veto player, in the US always three, in Germany two or three, and so on. For example, because presidential systems have more such players, their capacity for policy change is diminished. Tsebelis's proposition is that stability is associated with many veto players, big ideological distances between them, or high qualified majority thresholds in any collective veto player. Policy stability means "inability to adapt to exogenous shocks" (Tsebelis 2000, 464).

This finding leads to the interesting argument that the greater the stability in this sense, the more likely that the judiciary will step in and play an important role and the greater the independence of bureaucracies. According to Tsebelis, if the court makes constitutional interpretations, it is a veto player itself. If it makes statutory inter-pretations, then it is not, but its independence increases with the number of other veto players, and it can "legislate" without fear of being overruled. Tsebelis (2000, 466) discusses the example of the European Union:

> From the sixties until the mid-eighties the legislative decisions required unanimity of the countries' members. As a result, the political system was unable to take significant decisions, and European integration was pushed through by the European Court of Justice, which handed down its most important decisions. From the mid-eighties on, qualified majority replaced unanimity in the EU, and the role of the European Court of Justice declined.

As for bureaucratic independence, single veto players do not need to micro-manage bureaucracies through formal, legal procedures; ministerial decisions are sufficient. Moreover, such procedures could not bind the next government. Multiple veto players, as in separation-of-powers regimes, will, in contrast, attempt detailed restrictions on bureaucracies when they are in disagreement. Arthur Lupia and Mathew McCubbins (2000) show how democratic institutions adapt to the problems created by delegation. Legislatures, for example, use *ex post* mechanisms such as revocation of authority, sanctioning of agency officials, reductions in agency budgets, and reversals of agency decisions to influence bureaucratic behavior. Policies can be assigned to multiple agents, agency procedures can be manipulated to make certain that winners in the legislative arena will also be winners in the implementation battle, and police patrol and fire alarm oversight mechanisms can be legislated.

An alternative to the emphasis on elected representatives as principals to bureaucratic agents looks "behind" legislative choices to the interests that motivate them. "In ordinary times," noted Norton Long (1949, 260), "the manifold pressures of our pluralistic society

150

work themselves out in accordance with the balance of forces prevailing in Congress and the agencies. Only to a limited degree is the process subject to responsible direction or review by President or party leadership." "Actually," he continued, "the competition between governmental power centers . . . is the effective instrument of coordination" (261). A more recent expression of these ideas takes the form of common agency models of delegation in which interest groups, rather than elected officials, are the dynamic force behind the configuration of public policies and their implementation (Bertelli and Lynn 2005).

Problems of agency deepen as the chain of delegation reaches into government organizations themselves. Patrick Dunleavy (1992) systematically applies public choice reasoning to behavior inside organizations. He contests the assumptions that decision makers are fully informed and that their preferences are exogenously determined and unchanging.[19] In Dunleavy's model, "bureaucrats' preferences are not exogenously fixed, but endogenously determined within the budget-setting and bureau-shaping processes which underlie agencies' activity" (1992, 254). Bureau shaping refers to activities directed at influencing the nature of the work and the work environment. Senior officials do not act like a unitary actor because they choose differently between individual or collective modes for improving their welfare. Bureau-shaping strategies present fewer collective action problems than, say, budget-maximizing strategies. Thus bureau-shaping strategies are superior ways of pursuing personal goals.[20]

In a more sociological view of what Dunleavy called "bureau shaping," Brehm and Gates argue that organizational cultures form when subordinates look to each other for appropriate behaviors. Cultures are common stocks of information. "Subordinate performance depends," they argue, on the basis of their empirical research (1999, 195), "first on functional preferences, second on solidary preferences, and lastly on the efforts of the supervisor." They continue: "The chain of command looks to be a weak mode for principals – ultimately, democratic publics – to influence the performance of bureaucratic agents" (196). Reflecting Michael Lipsky's earlier (1980) insights concerning street-level bureaucrats, Brehm and Gates find that clients have a substantial influence on the performance of bureaucrats, especially of social workers. Moreover, they found no evidence for "shirking"; bureaucrats want to work. They argue that "the principal–agent models which have made their way into the political science literature have over-emphasized the importance of moral hazard and ignored issues of adverse selection" (1999, 199). "[T]he strongest and most positive role that our research identifies for the potential of supervisory control over bureaucracy is in the process of recruitment" (202). The arguments of organization theorists bear scrutiny more than those of economists. Bureaucracy works in the US because, they say, of "principled agents."

The Brehm and Gates empirical argument for a more sociological approach to organizational and interorganizational behavior suggests why non-economic or socialized choice approaches to problems of delegation and accountability have become popular, especially in the study of networks and partnerships.

Horizontal democracy

When Vincent Ostrom wrote about the "intellectual crisis in public administration" in 1973, his message, according to Theo Toonen (1998, 232), was that

> [a] monolithic, uniform and monocentric concept of governance characterized by a streamlined, integrated organization and unity of command had to be replaced by a differentiated, plural and polycentric notion. Fragmentation, checks and balances, self-organizing and self-governing networks, competition for services and a differentiation of demand, provision and supply agents in the organization constituted the alternative – for Europeans at the time futuristic and highly unlikely.

As Toonen interprets Ostrom, "self-government and co-production by citizens in non-market, non-governmental forms of collective action required more attention" (232–3).

Democratic administration, Toonen argues (1998, 233), "has become a fairly close description of contemporary European public sector reform movements." In fact, Toonen believes that Ostrom's type of reform has materialized more in the European than in the American context: "In the US, 'reinventing government' only seems to have scratched the surface, whereas in the European context, various state systems are going through fundamental changes, all amounting to a more differentiated, pluralistic and 'decentralized' operation of government and public administration" (Toonen 1998, 233). Interestingly enough, Lupia and McCubbins (2000) argue in support that linear chains of delegation are more subject to agency loss than chains of delegation involving network relationships. Thus, says Toonen, "network analysis generally brings a new focus to the analysis of traditional questions and issues from a bargaining and exchange perspective. . . . The network concept takes public administration out of the narrow tunnel of formally designed structures and mandated organizations" (Toonen 1998, 250). Networks comprise "the varying interactions that link each pair . . . of social actors in the system" (Knoke 1994, 235), variations which explain the behavior both of individual actors and of entire social systems.

Interorganizational analysis emerged as an important subfield of American sociology beginning in the 1970s (Perrucci and Potter 1989), as scholars sought to understand how and with what consequences already powerful organizations pooled their resources in order to influence actors outside the network and how network participation influenced individual participants. Subjects of investigation included international relations, elite influence, community power, social movements, and political influence and participation. Under the influence of managerialism, network analyses in Europe and America began to encompass a wide variety of topics with governance and managerial orientations, as noted in Chapter 1. Networks evolved from more or less spontaneously occurring phenomena into intentionally chosen and designed agents of public management. According to Provan and Milward (2001, 414), "[r]ecently, the focus has broadened from a concern with individual relationships among organizations to an examination of the multiple interactions that comprise full networks, including discussion of how public policy is implemented through networks of cooperating service providers."

Thus the network has become a vigorous competitor with hierarchy as a paradigm for managerial reform, albeit not one without its skeptics. "Public policy is made and implemented in networks of interdependent actors," say enthusiasts Walter Kickert, Erik-Hans Klijn, and Joop Koppenjan (1997, 2), thus presenting a major challenge to public management. These authors go so far as to claim that "[p]ublic management should therefore be seen as network management" (3). Arthur Benz (1993, 171) argues, however, that

> the informal, emerging patterns of interaction which create intraorganiza-
> tional networks cannot be completely separated from formal structures of decision
> making and governance. . . . Actors who are not able to coordinate informally
> can . . . switch to formal mechanisms in order to reach a solution. The availability of
> this opportunity is often a necessary prerequisite for the working of informal
> mechanisms.

Yet a third view is that of Laurence Lynn, Carolyn Heinrich, and Carolyn Hill (2001, 54), who argue that "formal and informal coordination mechanisms may be incompatible, each inhibiting the effective operation of the other."

To Theo Toonen (1998, 250), a network is "a dynamic constellation of interdependency relationships which governs itself, *sometimes using governments as its agents*" (italics added). He continues (1998, 250):

> Few dare to question, for example, the relevance of official government policy for
> the way in which social, political or administrative networks actually operate. In many
> cases, the constitution, governance and management of networks is treated as if we
> are dealing with a new category of policy instruments.

Bogason and Toonen (1998, 208) are concerned that "[o]rganizations, law, constitutions, power, courts, governments, formal mandates and legal competencies don't seem to matter any more. History and institutions seem almost to have been lost." In fact, they argue, networks are not new; they are only newly discovered and named.

The network concept is not a sufficient basis, in Toonen's view, "for refounding the study of public administration as a more or less integrated field of study. . . . Network analysis is a useful analytical tool but on the whole it provides only divided ground for rediscovering public administration in the study of public administration" (1998, 251).

TENSIONS

Whether one is inclined to view problems of delegation and accountability through the perspective of a rationally ordered chain of delegation or of overlapping communities of socialized cooperation and coordination – or a combination of the two – the practical implication is the same. Managerialism has both lengthened chains of delegation and created more complicated and less transparent networks of interdependence. In so doing, it has made the problem of democratic accountability much more complex, creating increasingly vexing challenges to the effective functioning of representative institutions.

Peter Barberis (1998, 463) puts his finger on the key issue of delegation and accountability in the British context, but the point is a more general one:

> [T]he force of proposals for constitutional change is to restructure roles and rela-
> tionships as between the various organs of state and, in so doing, to bring the executive
> under control through a more open, decentralized, disaggregated and essentially
> pluralistic system of accountable government. In any such system Diceyan notions of
> parliamentary sovereignty [or American notions of legislative-centered administra-
> tion] could not survive and the traditional doctrine of ministerial accountability would
> be rendered moribund.

But what might replace traditional doctrine, in law and practice? The question concerns whether the steadily lengthening and broadening chains of delegation and coordination that are, across regime types, the combined resultant of territorial deconcentration and managerial disaggregation undermine traditional concepts of control and accountability to such an extent that wholly new structures, practices, and institutions of democratic governance, including radically revised doctrines of representation and administrative law, will perforce emerge? This question is taken up in the concluding chapter.

NOTES

1 The Clinton administration's National Performance Review, although centrist in spirit, ignited sharp debate over threatened losses of accountability to representative institutions. In contrast, as Chapter 6 noted, the management agenda of Clinton's successor, George W. Bush, as compared to the agendas of either Clinton or Ronald Reagan, is downright Thatcherite in its attitudes toward civil service protections and its belief in the market.
2 "It is the pattern of public accountability of previously 'invisible' organizational functions which strengthens at one time the formal organization, those specialists who monopolize the accounting process itself, and the leader(s) of the organization" (Merkle 1980, 143).
3 In a 2005 interview with *The Washington Post*, President Bush said, "We had an accountability moment, and that's called the 2004 elections. The American people listened to different assessments made about what was taking place in Iraq, and they

looked at the two candidates, and chose me." According to the story, Bush indicated that there was no reason, for example, to hold any administrative officials accountable for mistakes or misjudgments in pre-war planning or managing the violent aftermath. In other words, it is through the electoral process that American public officials are finally and summarily held accountable to the people, not through media pressure or investigating commissions or Congressional hearings. Let the people decide.

4 Harold Laski in 1923 advocated tort liability on the part of the civil service to protect against "bureaucratic zeal," arguing that the safeguard of supervision by parliament itself is not at all adequate. He went on (1923, 99–100): "We are seeking to bring administrative discretion into public view. . . . Certainly the constant criticism of the administrator is essential to the success of the democratic adventure. . . . Every degree of his removal from the scrutiny of the public is a serious infraction of its liberties."

5 But "to apply Diceyan or neo-Diceyan notions of accountability in anything like their pure form would mean the abandonment of much that is widely valued by way of recent developments in openness, accessibility and greater transparency" (Barberis 1998, 461).

6 Leonard White (1935b, 418) summarized pre-bureaucratic America: "So long as American administrative systems remained decentralized, disintegrated, and self-governmental and discharged only a minimum of responsibilities, the necessity of highly developed machinery for its control was unknown. Administration was weak and threatened no civil liberties; it was unorganized and possessed no power of resistance; it was elective and quickly responsive to the color and tone of local feeling."

7 The quotation is from Roscoe Pound (1914). Pound was hostile to what he called "executive justice" as well. "[E]xecutive justice is an evil, even if sometimes a necessary evil. It has always been, and in the long run it always will be, crude and as variable as the personalities of officials" (1914, 8).

8 According to Dickinson (1930, 305), "[t]o make intelligence effective in government requires primarily that the members of government shall be guaranteed a certain independence, a certain freedom to rise above especial interests and make positive contributions of their own toward the adjustment of such interests." Precisely anticipating what we now call collective action problems, Dickinson continued: "Voluntary adjustments are ordinarily possible only between a relatively small number of interests, and between interests which have already come to know one another's measure" (308). With a large number of interests, when new interests emerge, old interests are almost certain to refuse them room.

9 German courts are organized into five divisions – ordinary, administrative, fiscal, labor, and social – to create a pluralistic expertise in scrutinizing Germany's famously detailed code. The administrative courts, which perform the bulk of judicial review of administrative action, are confined to questions of law – not the quality of administrative decisions – and Germans enjoy a right of review in all cases alleging rights interference by the administration (Groß 2000, 589–90, cited by Bertelli 2005).

10 Moe notes that the question of "[c]onstitutional values" or "entrepreneurial values" is not one of either–or but "a matter of precedence in the event of conflict" (2001, 305).

11 Torres and Pina (2002, 44) note that European Supreme Audit Institutions (SAIs) "do not carry out audits or opinion surveys to analyze the degree to which the needs of the users are satisfied by the public services delivered." While some aspects of contracts are monitored – staff and financial policies, investments, environmental production – little attention is given to the credibility of the buyer, protecting citizens

155

against abuses by the company and unjustified cost and price rises. Thus there are "serious deficiencies in accountability" (44).

12 Aberbach and Christensen (2003) contrast this "emergent" approach with two "traditional" approaches: a collectivist approach which emphasizes the conscious design of the state based on collective or homogeneous goals, strong central government, and rule of law in the *Rechtsstaat* sense; and pluralism, which views the state and civil service as founded on the competition for influence, in a Madisonian sense, by the multiple group interests that arise in a heterogeneous society.

Aberbach and Christenson argue that the collectivist model is best suited to a homogeneous society with strong egalitarian norms, the pluralist model to a heterogeneous society with complex social organization and competing interests, an individual economic model to a highly fluid environment in which capital, labor, and technology "flow easily across national boundaries, upsetting traditional notions of citizenship, public regulation systems, and even national independence, and generating a strong demand for efficiency in order to compete for capital and employment opportunities" (2003, 505). They conclude that "the individual-economic model will add to the complexity of the public apparatus and that elements of it will ultimately find a place in a new and melded organizational form and culture" (506).

13 The chain of delegation is termed "a logic of governance" by Lynn, Heinrich, and Hill (2001).

14 Talbot (2004) notes, however, that instead of simple accountability, under the Next Steps program, agencies have two accounting officers: the permanent secretary of their government department as well as the chief executive. The Framework Document omitted resources and performance, which were settled through the normal Public Expenditure Survey processes and through separate negotiations or impositions. Thus the framework is "a complex and cumbersome set of overlapping steering and accountability systems involving multiple 'principals' (parent departments, Ministers, Cabinet Office, the Treasury)" (2004, 5).

15 The term "police patrols" refers to proactive efforts by those in authority, say through active inspections, to search for non-compliance with policy or regulations.

16 The term "fire alarms" refers to mechanisms that permit private actors to trigger review of governmental performance.

17 The term "moral hazard" refers to the risk that policy may change the behavior of its intended beneficiaries in a way that undermines the policy's intent.

18 The term "adverse selection" refers to the possibility that an information asymmetry between actors may enable the party with superior information to exploit the other party.

19 Dunleavy notes that Anthony Downs's *An Economic Theory of Democracy* (1957) "is about an information rich world where assembling, screening and evaluating the mass of data transmitted is a costly undertaking" (1992, 251–2).

20 In Barberis's (1998, 455) interpretation of Dunleavy, officials, especially those in strategic positions, "assume a sense of ownership. They need not have a personal interest but they may enjoy professional enhancement in steering through some of the changes by which the NPM has come to be recognized – for example, the creation of executive agencies."

Chapter 8

Of wine and bottles, old and new

INTRODUCTION

Beginning in the 1970s and quickening in the 1980s, the ideology of managerialism began to infuse European public administration. In America, where management and managers had been respected for generations, an invigorated emphasis on public management was pervading public affairs education and practice. There ensued an era of public management reforms so international in scope that the term New Public Management (NPM), coined for that subset of neo-liberal policies initiated by Westminster governments, came to describe public management reforms of every kind, everywhere, including civil service, budget, and territorial reforms that had long histories under other names.[1] Almost any deliberate effort at organizational change and development began to be counted as NPM.

An international tribe of scholars and consultants arrived on the scene to take the measure of these widespread, some said convergent, reforms and even to participate in designing and promoting them. New, globalized paradigms featuring incentives, competition, results, and, for intellectual foundations, a "new institutional economics" or, somewhat later, partnerships, networks, decentralization, and participation were declared to be replacing outdated national habits of administrative thought and action. These obsolescing habits were most commonly characterized as "traditional public administration," with its emphasis on hierarchy, bureaucracy, and separation of administration from politics.[2] The field's policies and its vocabulary have since been enriched by new terms of art, such as hybridity, subsidiarity, joined-up government, hollow state, quangos, agencification, and consociation. Powerful theories that assume rationality on the part of political actors have been invoked to analyze traditional problems of delegation and accountability. If this talk of change and transformation is to be believed, there is, indeed, a "new" public management.

For all the excitement, empirical evidence of actual change in the management of governmental operations, much less of improvements in governmental performance and of changes in official habits of thought, which were goals of the various reform programs and activities, has been accumulating only slowly. The evidence is, moreover, inconclusive concerning the hypothesis of international transformation and convergence.

157

National developments that in the 1990s had been confidently proclaimed to be harbingers of a universal new approach to democratic governance have begun to be seen as nationally variegated adaptations to various forces for change rather than as transformations of constitutional institutions: as new wine in old bottles. Indeed, argues Theo Toonen (1998, 236), the application of business-like approaches at the operational level of government "may bring back an interest in 'traditional [public administration] questions' of supervision, integrity, primacy of politics, control, accountability and due process." Out with the old – in with the old.

It would be easy to conclude that yet another managerial fashion is running its course. The New Public Management of the 1990s might be little more than the Japanese Management of the 1970s, celebrated for a season before fading to obscurity, or the many other fashions of the past century (Downs and Larkey 1986; Light 1997). Such a conclusion would be premature, however. Toonen (2004) employs the concept of "induced reforms" to argue that changes in one part of a political-administrative system, for example, at either the operational or the institutional level, may prompt or induce reforms over time in other (higher or lower) parts of the system. "The notion of 'induced reforms'," he concludes, "makes clear that one should not use too limited a timeframe for comparing reform processes" (2004, 193).[3] He continues: "[M]anagerial reforms, if effective, in the end require political decision-making" (194). It follows that the efficacy of managerial reforms may gradually be either magnified or eroded by the presence or absence of the requisite political action.

As Elke Löffler (2003) and others have pointedly noted, the requisite political decision making to sustain NPM has not been occurring. Though there have been structural and operational reforms, little significant change has occurred in the organization and practices of legitimizing institutions: in parliaments and legislative councils, in judicial systems and administrative law, in political conventions and traditional notions of oversight and accountability. In the face of inertia in the political and judicial branches of government, the question is whether managerialism can do any more than supplement the repertoire of managerial structures and practices that is the cumulative legacy of centuries of efforts to create modern administrative states. In the long run, as suggested in Chapter 7, legislatures and courts may not be willing to tolerate the loss of traditional accountability implied by performance management.[4] That the *status quo ante* may no longer be a preferred option, as Guy Peters (1996) suggests, overlooks evidence of path dependency in national institutions and the political dynamics that account for it.

Any attempt to step back from more than three decades of intense concern with public management and its reform in order to appraise the extent and significance of change needs a context, although many such appraisals have been made without one. The argument of this book is that the proper context for such an appraisal is the long history of governing by organized states. That history might be interpreted in at least two different ways, however, depending upon which historical "facts" one chooses to emphasize. As subsequent discussion will suggest, history might be interpreted as confirming the essential durability, adaptability, and constraining influence of Old

Public Administration. Alternatively, it might be viewed as demonstrating that fundamental changes – the most popular term for characterizing such changes is "paradigm shifts"[5] – do occur, and they not only alter historical trajectories in significant ways, but may even tend towards at least partial convergence across nations.

Recent scholarship has addressed the tensions between the proponents of incremental models of decision making, who tend to predict, or argue in a manner consistent with, path dependency, and the proponents of comprehensive rationality models of decision making, who are more inclined to predict, or at least not rule out, paradigm shifts. Bryan Jones and his associates have developed a model adapted from evolutionary biology that synthesizes the incremental decision model with the arguments that there is occasional non-incremental change (True, Jones, and Baumgartner 1999; B. Jones 2001; Jones, Sulkin, and Larsen 2003). They argue that decision makers, particularly in organizational environments, are "boundedly" rational,[6] which leads to patterns of under- and over-reaction to exogenous developments. The result is what they term "punctuated equilibrium."

For long stretches of time (inequilibrium), according to this logic, decision makers may stray very little from their previous commitments, and changes may be small and incremental/decremental. Occasionally, however, "punctuation" occurs, and decision makers must change strategies radically. The new strategy or strategies become the basis of a new equilibrium. Determining whether or not such a punctuation or paradigm shift has occurred requires a good deal of evidence concerning not only the widespread adoption of new strategies but also changes in "habits of thought" throughout the political-administrative system. Those who claim that such shifts have occurred seldom produce the kind of evidence that would justify their claims, but these failings do not negate the possibility.

This chapter first explores the issue of continuity or path dependence and of "punctuation" or (possibly convergent) paradigmatic change in Old Public Administration in the US, the UK, France, and Germany. Based on historical accounts, two different sub-narratives of change – continuity and punctuation – are plausible. Next the so-called new wine that has been brought to market in the era of managerialism is reconsidered in the light of these two narratives: does managerialism most resemble path-dependent adaptation or do its relative novelty and seemingly widespread adoption suggest punctuation on a global scale? Finally, the future of managerialism both as an ideology of policy and practice and as an international field of teaching and scholarship is considered. Though the triumph of a globalized, stateless capitalism cannot be conclusively dismissed as the primary cause of recent governmental change, the greater likelihood is that the continuing triumph of democracy, institutionalized in reliable and legitimate instruments of state action, better accounts for both historical and recent experience with public management reform. What is new is that from here on out, discussion of such matters will be carried on by a self-aware international community of scholars and practitioners.

159

OLD BOTTLES

As discussed in Chapter 3, public management has roots deep in antiquity and in pre-industrial Europe: in the evolution of organized societies and their governments. Traditional, classical, or "old" public administration as we know it today had its first modern progenitors in post-Westphalian European states, where bureaucracy, the basic instrument of traditional governance and the structural setting for public management practices and values, evolved into its present institutional forms and uses.

Old Public Administration

Beginning in the seventeenth century, the institutions of contemporary public management began to emerge, first in relatively rudimentary form and, subsequently, following popular revolutions on both sides of the Atlantic. "The rise of formal bureaucratic administration," says Judith Merkle (1980, 279), dates "from Europe's 'age of absolutism,' when great kings consolidated power by substituting the work of hierarchies of servants of humble origin, directly dependent upon the monarch's power, for the services formerly rendered by contentious barons." The next significant development was the separation of this administrative structure from the person of the monarch, for which the initiative was provided by the French Revolution and its aftermath. The industrial revolution further rationalized and structured both corporate and, partly in imitation, public administration.

As Ezra Suleiman (2003, 7) elaborates on this story,

[p]olitical leaders of the emerging democratic states from the early nineteenth century to the late twentieth century recognized that whatever the goals of the state – controlling a vast empire, creating an educational system, guaranteeing democratic procedures, conducting war, establishing the welfare state, collecting taxes – each necessitated a highly organized, basically nonpolitical instrument at its disposal.

The structural form of that non-political instrument was bureaucracy, which, as it became institutionalized, became infused with values such as responsibility to democratic political authority, loyalty, integrity, reliability, and legal conduct, manifest in the practices of an increasingly professionalized civil service.

While Merkle (1980, 280) argues that gradual professionalization of the civil service placed "the new labels of democratic theory upon the ancient struggle between the king and his servants," Fred Riggs (1997a) takes a different view. He argues that bureaucracy is symbiotic with industrialization rather than with democracy. The basic principle of democracy as an aspect of modernity, in Riggs's account, involves the replacement of top-down monarchic authority with bottom-up representation: dominated subjects were replaced by free citizens able to participate in governance and choose their governors. But "[i]t has never been easy in even the most democratic countries for the organs of representative government to sustain effective control over their bureaucracies" (1997a, 350), and it became more difficult as those bureaucracies were being rationalized in order that they might approach industrial reliability and efficiency.

As part of this rationalization, in Merkle's account (1980, 280), future president Woodrow Wilson initiated what Merkle held to be a new idea, a new ideology: "power wielded without regard to persons [either monarch or the people] but rather to attain social ends whose usefulness and means of attainment could eventually be determined by science itself." She continues: "It was a theory of politics that proclaimed the victory of the experts and defined 'politics,' or the contest for power, as obsolete" (281). An implication of this idea is that all the pathologies of bureaucracy that were also coming to be widely recognized would influence the premises of political choice. "All of these modes of influence [by bureaucracies] tend to break down the ability of the political system to control bureaucracy, while at the same time they introduce the values and the vested interests of the state's own administrative 'servant' into the political process itself" (Merkle 1980, 282; cf. Karl 1976). Attempts at democratic control, as Riggs notes, only undermine the effectiveness of administrative action, ensuring a fundamental tension between them.[7]

The issues that arise from these tensions are by no means of the same policy significance across industrialized democracies, however. Klaus König notes (1997, 217) that

> [w]hile bureaucracy in the classical administrative systems [such as Germany and France] may be said to be older than democracy, the development of public bureaucracies in civic culture administration countries such as Great Britain and the United States was governed from the outset by the political régime, the historic continuity of which has been maintained up to the present day.

Thus the legislative dominance of public bureaucracies in the latter countries contrasts with what is found in the countries of Continental Europe, which "have had to learn by experience that, in certain historical situations, people may expect certain things from the administration which cannot be provided by the political sector such as, for instance, certain basic supplies in times of political confusion" (217). There are risks to this faith in executive institutions, notes König: "In Weimar Republic Germany, for instance, the administrative bureaucracy was not among the defenders of democracy" (218).

At the dawn of the era of managerialism, then, four distinctive national administrative traditions – four different configurations of public management institutions – had emerged in the US, the UK, France, and Germany. These emergent differences reflected the fact that the pace and character of change had varied across these four countries as each contended with external and internal forces peculiar to its own historical circumstances. Thus we have a meta-narrative of differentiation that presages distinctive futures for these and other countries' public management institutions.

161

Path or punctuation?

The meta-narrative of emergent differentiation is consistent with the two quite different sub-narratives of how and why national institutions evolve.

The first of these sub-narratives emphasizes path dependence, the evolutionary emergence of national administrative traditions and durable institutions whose function is to provide stable and reliable performance of the functions of the state. These durable institutions include national versions of constitutional and administrative law; representation and participation; administration, regulation, enforcement, and accountability; and merit and qualifications. This is essentially a narrative of fundamental continuity in the institutions of public management.

The second sub-narrative emphasizes the often dramatic, occasionally revolutionary, changes that have occurred in each country as its managerial institutions have evolved. Within frameworks that represent the institutionalization of policy choices made during succeeding eras of adaptation and change, there nonetheless occur, albeit infrequently, discontinuities that transform the structures, practices, and cultures of public organizations. Constitutional principles may endure, but their reflection in public management institutions, values, and practices can take different forms.

A narrative of continuity

Narratives of continuity that link each country's institutional evolution to seminal events in its history – to a Glorious Revolution, a Peace of Westphalia, a War of Independence – are convincing, but almost trivially so. It is inarguable that distinctive national identities have emerged, and these identities characterize all aspects of national institutional life. Nations may learn from each other, voluntarily or forcibly, but that which is distinctive about them is not thereby extinguished. What is remarkable in the narratives of continuity is the specific durabilities of administrative institutions and the ways in which these durable institutions have framed the processes of evolution and change.

In the American case, for example, the separation of powers has shaped the emergence of the American administrative state and its managerial institutions right down to the level of local service delivery. While the preeminence of the different branches of government has waxed and waned over two centuries, the essentially political character of public management, with its orientation toward pragmatism and balance, has not. Through civil war, world war, world-wide depression, cold war, and the threat posed by global terrorism, the three branches have continued to hold each other in check and to insist, often antagonistically, upon mutual accountability. Public management is always and necessarily responsible to polycentric political interests that are often expressed in inconsistent, even conflicting ways.

In Great Britain, in contrast, parliamentary sovereignty and its supporting conventions have enabled both a strikingly long-lived civil service increasingly characterized by independence and probity and, at the same time, remarkable flexibility and agility in national policy making. Governments can change direction with alacrity, their influence constrained perhaps primarily by the obduracy not of civil servants *per se* but of the ministries, with their institutionalized values – what Americans call the "permanent government" – of which they are a part. Paradoxically, then, what is notably enduring about British governing institutions is their potential for far-reaching change.

On the Continent, what is notable is how the bureaucracies of the eighteenth century survived first a century of revolutionary change and the shift of sovereignty from the person of the king to the state and its people, then the upheavals of European and world wars, to ensure the continuity of the very idea of the state and its ethos of public service. With the advent of *Rechtsstaat* early in the nineteenth century, bureaucratic institutions governed by the rule of law have seemed, to Americans at least (and not with particular admiration), virtually impregnable. Their differences notwithstanding, what is notable about French and German governing institutions, then, is less their capacity to change than their stability and resilience in the face of extraordinary external and internal pressures and the outright rewriting of constitutions.

A narrative of change

Changes there are, however. The four countries examined in this study have hardly been static in the modern era.

A narrative of change is perhaps easiest to observe and most instructive in the American case, not only because of its shorter managerial history but also because of the penchant of American scholars, documented in Chapter 5, for proclaiming "the new" as their administrative state evolves. The form of governance established by the US Constitution was, of course, new, representing a determination by the Founders to avoid the kinds of arbitrary administration that had in significant part fomented the American revolution (Wilson 1975). So, too, was the Jacksonian practice of rotation in office, with its accompanying, albeit rudimentary, protections against corruption, which replaced the elite-dominated administration of the federalist era.

In contrast to these unmistakable breaks with America's colonial and federalist past are the incremental, adaptive processes that, beginning in the Jacksonian era, eventually produced an American administrative state which, at least by the time of Franklin Roosevelt's Depression-era New Deal, represented a clear departure from the nineteenth-century spoils system controlled by political parties and courts of common law. John Gaus proclaimed "the new administration" in the early 1920s, Leonard White referred to "the new management" in the early 1930s, and John Pfiffner coined "the new public administration" a few years later (Bertelli and Lynn 2006).[8] It is these claims of an emergent new reality (the fundamental character of which, incidentally, is still in dispute; see Lynn 2001b) that most resemble the claim that a "post-bureaucratic paradigm" is, perhaps in drip-drip fashion, inexorably transforming public management on a national and a global scale (Barzelay 1992; Osborne and Gaebler 1992).

163

A more discrete change within the broader state-building process, arguably qualifying as a paradigm shift, as Chapter 6 suggested, was the relatively rapid emergence of a "scientific management" movement in both public and private sectors (and on both sides of the Atlantic), based on the research of Frederick W. Taylor and on the practices of forward-looking industrialists. Complemented by Progressive reform notions such as separating politics and administration, ensuring the neutral competence of administrators, and identifying administrative principles of universal applicability, scientific management remained popular among administrative reformers through the New Deal and, in a variety of other guises, retains its influence as a paradigm of governance (being reflected, for example, in the measurement and analysis needed to sustain the performance management systems of George W. Bush's administration).

In contrast to the United States, Great Britain, with an uncodified constitution that has been evolving for over a millennium, is a harder case. British governance is, as Chapter 4 indicated, a tapestry of acts of parliament, principles of common law, conventions of politics and statecraft, and scholarly treatises that might be said to be emergent in its totality. A "new" paradigm for the British civil service – a new answer to the question as to who is qualified to provide staff support for the government – was adumbrated by the 1853 Northcote–Trevelyan Report on civil service reform and ensuing acts of implementation, but reforms with similar motivation were still being advocated as sorely needed in the Fulton Report over a century later. Nonetheless, the classic British model of a civil service of broadly educated gentlemen infused with *noblesse oblige* had become iconic by the end of the nineteenth century without ever having actually been "new." Incrementalist adaptation rather than notable paradigm shifts characterizes Old Public Administration in Great Britain.

France and Germany present a richer array of candidates for what *was* new in historical perspective. Surely the most striking of these candidates are, first, the emergence of the nation state beginning in the seventeenth century and, at the end of the eighteenth century, the emergence of popular sovereignty as a basis for state power, first in France and over the next half-century or so elsewhere in Continental Europe.

As with America and Great Britain, however, many of what can now be seen as paradigmatic transformations were largely emergent, rather than discrete historical episodes, including the two just noted. "Prussian bureaucracy," another iconic example of a public management paradigm, was centuries in the making as feudal administration was replaced with the modern administrative state, although, as Chapter 3 showed, successive rulers decreed significant reforms – competitive examinations, methods of state finance and administration, systems of training – that cumulated to the modern bureaucratic state and to its sense of transcendence and unity. The emergence of the modern French bureaucratic state, in contrast, was undoubtedly expedited – punctuated – by Napoleon's *Code* and principles of administration (discussed in Chapter 3).

More likely candidates for the kinds of paradigmatic change said to be represented by New Public Management are, first, the emergence of cameralism – the sciences of the state – a precursor to twentieth-century scientific management and, arguably, to New Public Management, and, second, the emergence of *Rechtsstaat* as the basis for the legitimacy of public management, especially in Germany.

As noted in Chapter 3, cameralism, which enjoyed a relatively long run on the Continent, reflected the scientific, rationalizing, and economizing spirit of the age. In order to ensure the wealth of the state and the happiness of its people, cameralists applied principles of economic rationality to issues of state policy and administration. Cameralism featured identifiable habits of thought: meritocracy, administrative science, universal principles, and formalism. In that respect it was, in every sense, a paradigm promoted as such virtually from its inception.

Beginning early in the nineteenth century, cameralism began to be eclipsed by the formalities of *Rechtsstaat*, which reconciled the continuing need for bureaucratic competence with the increasingly urgent need to concede popular control of, and confidence in, that capacity. The French revolution and the governance of Napoleon were seminal to the emergence of *Rechtsstaat* on the Continent. In Germany, under Napoleonic influence public administration came to be viewed as an application of law, and legal training became *sine qua non* for public service. Officials' putative incapability of committing injustice earned a large measure of deference and respect from citizens, honor which had been withheld a century earlier.

These narratives of punctuated equilibrium might be said to constitute a larger narrative of convergence: on rational-legal bureaucracy in a Weberian sense as the primary instrument of state action. It is not a stretch to argue that, their differences notwithstanding, the US, Great Britain, France, and Germany at the end of the nineteenth century were committed to bureaucratic public administration governed by the rule of law and deriving its legitimacy from representative institutions.

The question is whether the new wine of late twentieth-century managerialism, in its various national manifestations, is being adapted to the institutions of Old Public Administration without difficulty or whether, instead, new institutions are being revealed as necessary if these particular forces of change are to yield their benefits. Which narrative, then, path dependence or punctuation (possibly accompanied by convergence), characterizes the era of managerialism?

NEW WINE

An accelerating series of changes in the world beginning in the 1970s placed unfamiliar pressures on governments, with the effect of creating new opportunities for governmental transformation. As discussed in Chapter 6, many governments attempted to take advantage of these opportunities, and the world-wide pace of governmental change accelerated. The neo-liberal politics of many of these governments introduced a pronounced emphasis on managerialism as an ideology of change and reform, an ideology that also proved congenial to international organizations engaged in promoting economy and efficiency on a world-wide scale, especially in the deeply indebted developing world. As national governments had in the nineteenth century seemingly converged on rational-legal bureaucracy as their primary instrument of governance, some observers now go so far as to claim that nations, because they face similar pressures, are converging on incentives, competition, and performance as a paradigm for managing the operational side of government and, to effect it, on a real separation of politics from administration (Toonen 1998).

Sweeping claims have been made concerning these changes (Lynn 2001a). In their best-selling *Reinventing Government*, David Osborne and Ted Gaebler (1992, 19) say of change in American government that "the reforms represent a paradigm shift." According to the Priority Issues Task Force of the US National Academy of Public Administration (NAPA), "[g]overnance, in the United States and around the world, is undergoing a fundamental transformation [that] is redefining institutional roles and straining the capacities of all those involved in the pursuit of public purpose" (NAPA 2000, 3). "[R]ecent public sector reforms in Western countries," argues Elke Löffler (2003, 486), "have changed the nature of the state, which in most Western countries has now become more diversified." In a similar vein, say Toonen and Raadschelders (1997, 6–10),

> [i]t is safe to say that the challenges to governance in this century and government's response to them are without precedent in European history. . . . While the gap between state and citizen may have increased, the gap between government and society has never in history been smaller than today.

Donald Kettl (2002) believes that governments are confronting an accelerated prolif-eration of problems that transcend organizational and jurisdictional boundaries and virtually demand a new paradigm of governance.[9]

At the same time, the diversity and differentiation of recent national developments has been widely noted. Mark Bevir, R. A. W. Rhodes, and Patrick Weller argue that (2003a, 203) "[g]overnance is constructed differently and continuously reconstructed [across countries] so there can be no one set of tools." Of their own empirical research, they say (pp. 202–3) that

> [w]hat shines through most clearly is the contrast between European parliamentary systems and Westminster systems. All the Westminster systems share a tradition of strong executive government that could force through reform in response to economic pressures. . . . Westminster systems with executives subjected to few constraints can legislate almost at will.

In European countries, public sector reform rests on the consent of those about to be reformed, and they often refuse to grant it.[10] As between the US and Great Britain, Toonen (1998, 237), argues that

166

[f]rom a public administration perspective – *government in action* – there is probably more that sets the British new public management apart from American managerialism and efforts to reinvent government than brings the two together. An entrepreneurial public choice approach is more easily converted into some new kind of corporate and business-like neo-Taylorism in the context of a centralist government structure than in a much more pluralist constitutional structure which, by the way, also characterizes several continental systems. Other than for polemic reasons, it makes little sense to combine the British and American experiences and contrast them with continental ones.[11]

The implication of differentiation, contrary to the more sweeping claims on behalf of a global institutional isomorphism, is that convergence on a new paradigm of public management is, at best, an open question. Nonetheless, convergence has its champions.

Convergence or differentiation?

In many accounts of managerialism, as already noted, there is a strong suggestion, if not outright assertion, of a convergence in the forms and aims of governance (Lynn 2001a). According to Patricia Ingraham (1997, 326), despite obvious differences in national experiences, "the commonalities are more important than the differences." Christopher Hood argues that there has been "the spread of what at least on a superficial level are remarkably common doctrines about the direction of reform and good practice in public administration" (Hood 1989, 348).

A weaker version of this argument is that, because of the globalization that "engulf[s] the world in virtually every dimension of life" (Fosler 1999, 495), all governments face the same challenges and tasks and the same paradigm of change, even if their precise responses differ. According to Martin Minogue (1998, 19), "[w]hat cannot be doubted is that a generic wave of reforms must have a generic stimulus: this we can find in the consistency and similarity across systems of the pressures for change." These pressures include the (political) necessity for expenditure and cost reductions; consumerist orientations and the demand for quality; and ideological factors in solving conflicting pressures to both improve and reduce the state (with the risk that the gains may go to individual and group interests rather than to "the public").[12] Minogue (1998, 20) identifies three categories of responses to these pressures: "public sector restructuring (privatization); civil service reform; and the introduction of competitive disciplines into the provision of public services."

The provocative suggestion of convergence, of common responses to common causes, draws at least superficial support from the widespread use of a powerful new language in the discourse on administrative reform. Formerly dominated by the language of public law and classical public administration's emphasis on structures and procedures, the new "talk," as noted in Chapter 7, is based on the discipline of economics: markets, customers, transactions, competition, equilibrium, and value, including even technical concepts

167

associated with the "new economics of organization," such as transactions costs, principal–agent models, and game theory/collective action. Unlike the traditional languages and concepts of public law and public administration, whose descriptions imply the differentiation and path dependence of national administrative forms, the conceptual language of economics suggests interdependence and paradigmatic behavior among national – and universally (at least among industrialized states) rational – actors.

Convergence is a complex and controversial issue, as Christopher Pollitt notes (2002). The implication is that isomorphism of governing relations across states is or will be the resultant of national efforts at reform. In other words, the path dependence of administrative reform has been interrupted – punctuated – by globalization in its many guises. But isomorphism presumes that nations reconcile the tensions between the demands of the globalization of national economies and the demands of citizens for greater democratic accountability and participation in very similar ways.

A preponderance of opinion among public management scholars is that convergence is an unproven hypothesis at best. Variations in state traditions are a powerful explanatory factor in the national interpretations of managerialism. Though exogenous pressures on national political-administrative systems may be broadly similar, their force is diffracted into the differentiated adaptations that have been described in detail in Chapter 6.

Some doubt it altogether. "With marked national variations and despite all rhetoric about 'postmodernist' public administration," argue Toonen and Raadschelders (1997, 8), for example,

> the overall constitutional pattern of Western European administrative systems at the end of the 1990s still very much resembles the Weberian bureaucratic model identified to have emerged about a century earlier. Many of the attempts to arrive (again) at general civil service "core departments" actually seem to amount to an effort to restore the traditional elite of general administrative specialists once labeled "bureaucracy."

These same authors (Raadschelders and Toonen (1999, 47)) argue that "[t]he different European bureaucratic patterns still do not really seem to have changed or converged." In general, they argue, "[p]ublic sector reforms generally leave the existing state and administrative institutional structure intact" (61).

Ezra Suleiman (2003, 5–6) makes a similar point. "Neither globalization nor greater cooperation through international organizations, regimes, treaties, or the European Union seem to have produced a convergence of conceptions on how best to organize the policy-making instruments of the state." Christopher Pollitt's (2002, 481) hypothesis is that "the extent of convergence declines sharply as one moves through the discursive to the decisional to the practice and finally to the results categories." He continues: "There may be a considerable convergence of discourse and/or of decisions without anything like the same degree of convergence of practice (and still less of results). . . . [F]or constructivists, the main payoff may be in the decision to do something rather than the actual doing of it" (487).[13]

168

What is happening in theory?[14]

These particular accounts of the character and direction of global public management reform are essentially descriptive. An international group of scholars has, over the years, attempted to understand the comparative development of states within various theoretical frameworks. To strengthen the foundations for drawing conclusions concerning New Public Management in historical and comparative perspective, it will be useful to review a selection of these theories and consider their implications or predictions.

Consider that democracies depend on an institution, bureaucracy, which arguably is inherently undemocratic (proponents of representative bureaucracy, for example, would disagree). The dynamics of public management traditions, as well as much scholarly and public policy discourse, reflect the tensions associated with this dependency. What is it about the needs of diverse democratic states that has given rise to an institution which is seemingly alien to its nature? A variety of logics, drawing primarily on the disciplines of economics, sociology, and political science, have been adduced to account for comparative institutional change.

Among the most well-known of these theories is Douglass North's account of institutional change, which is based on the economic concept of transactions costs. "There are two forces shaping the path of institutional change," he argues (North 1990, 95), "increasing returns and imperfect markets characterized by significant transactions costs." Actors seeking to exploit opportunities offered by a governing framework will confront a variety of information and signaling problems, costly constraints, and differences in power and resources. Because these problems, constraints, and differences tend to be historically specific, there is, by this logic, every reason to expect continued differentiation among nations. "Marginal adjustment [to change]," concludes North, "*does not lead to convergence*" (1990, 101, emphasis added). One would immediately expect, for example, that the paths of change in common law and positive law countries, or in unitary and separation-of-powers countries, would differ significantly; all other things being equal, actors are confronted with different transactions costs associated with differences in constraints, power, and resources. As discussed elsewhere in this book, the US, the UK, France, and Germany also differ in quite significant ways from each other.

Sociologist Gianfranco Poggi (1978) employs an altogether different conceptual vocabulary. Also featuring path dependence, Poggi derives his logic from politics, which originates in the efforts by a collectivity to create and sustain itself through "rule," that is, through the use of the coercive powers of the state to achieve collective goals. Thus there emerge different polities, each characterized by a different system of rule and by a logic of change that is governed by that system of rule. If North sees a constitution or a juridical order as an institution that affects transactions costs, Poggi sees such institutions as affecting the creation and allocation of values that sustain or legitimize the state. A more synoptic view is that of Michel Crozier and Erhard Friedberg, who argue that, for systemic change to occur, "a whole system of action must be transformed. . . . [Actors] must put new human relations and new forms of social control into practice.

169

. . . For such changes to occur . . . sufficient capacities must at least potentially be available, e.g., cognitive capacities, relational capacities, models of government" (1980, 216). Such capacities differ across nations.

R. L. Jepperson and J. W. Meyer, also sociologists, adduce a framework of explanation similar to that of Poggi. They view the evolution of the formal organization of society as governed by the modern polity, by which they mean (1991, 206)

> the system of rules conferring societal authority in pursuit of collective ends, establishing agents of collective regulation and intervention. . . . We have in mind processes such as monetarization and democratization – the construction of markets and rights – and the institutionalization of goals such as collective progress and justice.

Their framework is accommodating of global influences. "Our line of argument proposes that a wider polity (often worldwide) of universalistic collective definitions plays a governing role, combined with an expanding set of subunit national societies competing and copying each other within this frame" (1991, 209). These authors, then, suggest the possibility of a mimetic isomorphism that allows for degrees of convergence.

Of interest at this point is an integrative concept originating in sociological theory, that of an "organizational field," that is, a "recognized area of institutional life . . . involving the totality of relevant actors" (DiMaggio and Powell 1991, 64–5). Paul DiMaggio and Walter Powell argue that "[b]ureaucratization and other forms of organizational change occur as the result of processes that make organizations more similar without necessarily making them more efficient." Three forces that induce isomorphism, that is, convergent structural/functional arrangements, are: *coercive*, i.e. political influence (operating as an exogenous influence on organizations) that ensures legitimacy; *mimetic*, i.e. standardization of responses to uncertainty; and *normative*, i.e. standardization reflecting professional beliefs and values (DiMaggio and Powell 1991, 67). In other words, choices of administrative arrangements may be a resultant of socialized rather than rational choice within organizational fields, of imitation, coercion, or ideology rather than of calculation and analysis. We should not be surprised to find convergence on a functional or specific policy basis if not on a whole-of-government scale.

Elaborating on this line of reasoning is Powell's (1990) elucidation of the conditions that give rise to network forms of organization. Under certain circumstances, he argues, exchange relationships may be governed by reciprocity and collaboration rather than by (complete, incomplete, or implicit) contracts or structures of formal authority. In general, says Powell (1990, 326–7),

> networks appear to involve a distinctive combination of factors – skilled labor, some degree of employment security, salaries rather than piece rates, some externally-provided mechanisms for job training, relative equity among the participants, a legal system with relaxed antitrust standards, and national policies that promote research

and development . . . – which seldom exist in sufficient measure without a political and legal infrastructure to support them.

Cross-national variation in the frequency of network forms may be explained, Powell suggests, by variations in state policies that support and sustain collaborations. Differentiating among administrative forms, that is, being selective, may help in identifying the underlying dynamics of change.

In yet another political perspective, the contemporary administrative state is widely held to be a product of modernization. This was Weber's view, and there is wide scholarly concurrence. In *Surveillance, Power and Modernity: Bureaucracy and Discipline from 1700 to the Present Day*, Christopher Dandeker (1990) associates the growth of what he terms "bureaucratic surveillance" in modern societies – by this he means processes of information gathering, storage, processing, retrieval and their application to administrative decision making (1990, 202) – with the emergence of the modern nation state. "Both the nation state and business enterprise," he argues (1990, 196–7),

> depend upon the "visible hand" of bureaucratic surveillance for their survival. Bureaucratization of the modern state involves four distinct processes: formal-legal rationalization of social relations; non-proprietary administration of the means of administration, and especially, of discipline and enforcement; the increasing knowledgeability of organizations; and specialization as a source of advantage in competing for scarce resources.

He continues: "The outcome of these four linked processes of change has been that modern societies are now in large part under fairly dense networks of surveillance" (197). Among the sources of bureaucratic growth, Dandeker argues, are strategies of control by central authorities but also popular demands for citizenship rights (202). His logic suggests that a historical punctuation would require substitute institutions for conducting coordination and surveillance tasks.

Though modernization is paradigmatic, it by no means leads to a homogeneous configuration of the administrations of all modern states. Mediated by national differences, modernization produces differentiated bureaucracies. Bernard Silberman (1993) identifies two contributors to the dynamics and resulting structures of state building: the level of uncertainty concerning political succession, and the nature of political leadership structure, and, in particular, whether leadership is a question of social or party identification. These dynamics produce four differentiated cases: (1) high uncertainty combined with a social basis for leadership produces high levels of bureaucratic autonomy; (2) high uncertainty coupled with party-oriented political leadership produces single-party-dominated, organizationally oriented bureaucracies; (3) low uncertainty and social-network-organized leadership produces a party-dominated professional bureaucracy; (4) low uncertainty and a party system produces an American-style professional bureaucracy accountable to party-dominated politics (Silberman 1993, 82–3).

171

As a historical matter, then, political strategies reflect choices of ways to resolve tensions and problems existing between the state and civil society, to forge solutions to problems of conflicting values. Silberman concludes (1993, 425):

> [T]he rationalization of the administrative role – the creation of the norms of bureaucratic role in modern society – was the consequence of political struggles. These were struggles to redefine the structures of power and the criteria for access to them by groups of putative leaders who sought to reduce the uncertainty over their status and power and, as a consequence, their material well-being.

Farrel Heady puts the same point succinctly: "[W]hat has become more and more obvious is the extreme importance of variation among political regimes as a major explanatory factor for variation among public bureaucracies" (Heady 1996, 472).

A similar proposition is evident in the work of Robert Putnam (1993). His logic suggests that state building and the performance of administrative structures are a reflection of underlying, historically determined civic cultures; a strong civic culture produces effective administrative performance, a weak one does not. But, argues Sidney Tarrow (1996), the causal arrow may just as well go the other way: from politics as the mobilization of bias to civic culture and association based on trust as a premise for the conduct of civic affairs. If civic capacity is the by-product of politics, as Tarrow argues, then one must understand the historical bases of these politics in order to understand the character and performance of modern states, and, as Putnam's work illustrates, regions within states. The dynamics of state building are complex and differentiated. Struggles for political power are mediated by national institutions.

Cultural effects may differentiate strategic alignments and management strategies across countries. Organizational structures and processes, role perceptions, and role behaviors can be modeled as governed both by external resource dependencies and by legitimating values in the environment (Lachman, Nedd, and Hinings 1994). The importance of culture is in conferring legitimacy on organizational structures and in "the social controls and social sanctions that values exert on behavior" at organizational and individual levels (Lachman, Nedd, and Hinings 1994, 52). "'Imported' practices may fail, or be ineffectively implemented, if they are inconsistent with the core values of local settings" (53). The extent of cultural influence may depend, however, on the extent to which resource dependencies are governed by material relationships and by the degree of consensus or dissensus within the culture or environment. Predictions concerning the paths of reform must, in other words, recognize the mediating influence of culture, an influence that would predict differentiation if not divergence.

The foregoing theories are for the most part consistent with the idea that institutional change is path dependent, that comparative change is differentiated. Thus one should be cautious in concluding that we are witnessing a fundamental, convergent transformation in modern administrative states, as opposed to incremental and adaptive modifications with recognizable features.[15]

172

Even though the unitary bureaucratic paradigm is adapting to new circumstances, in other words, we are likely to observe divergent paths of state reconstitution. Guy Peters (1996), for example, constructs four models of post-bureaucratic state development based on different causes of the dissatisfaction that motivates reform: centralized power, leading toward market government; hierarchy, leading toward participative government; inertia, leading toward flexible government; and over-regulation, leading toward deregulated government. Identify the principal motivation for governmental change, he argues, and you will be able to speculate on the path that change will take.

In an approach similar to that of Peters, Patrick Dunleavy and Christopher Hood (1994), in explicitly rejecting the inevitability of a new paradigm of some sort, describe alternative, multiple futures for public management based on constitutional issues arrayed on two dimensions: the degree to which there are general, system-wide rules of procedure, and the degree to which the public sector is separated from the private sector. The future, they suggest, may hold gridlock and "headless chicken" administration, "virtual proximity systems," conventional bureaucracy, or any of a wide variety of administrative states that represent political solutions to problems of national politics measured along their two dimensions.

To argue for convergence, or, in fact, for any other dominant pattern of outcomes, one must argue that a fundamental transformation in the historic role of the nation state and of democratic institutions, that is, in the generative forces of public administration, is under way, transformation of a character that "predicts" the new paradigm or pattern. If the bureaucratic paradigm is rational/legal in the Weberian sense in order to reconcile democracy with the administrative state, then a post-bureaucratic paradigm featuring, for example, quasi-markets or participatory democracy must be founded on new sources of legitimacy and new bases for the performance of collective tasks: perhaps different forms of rationality, different jurisprudential principles, a different allocation of property rights, a different ideal concerning the role of the state in protecting individual rights and creating collective goods; new habits of thought and action not among elites but throughout the polity.

MANAGERIALISM IN HISTORICAL PERSPECTIVE

It is possible that democratic governments are in the process of a historic transformation, of reallocating power from a diversity of historical entities – the Greek polis and the Roman Senate, feudal overlords and their armies, parliaments and legislatures and their political parties, bureaucracies and their experts, dictators and their police – to the market, to the institution of capitalism with its wealth holders, investors, and customers (Lynn 2001a). Perhaps the role of the state and its bureaucracies is being constricted to that once envisioned by Friedrich von Hayek (1945): maintaining a framework of rules governing private actors in their pursuit of their own interests, the chief responsibility of the state under global capitalism. At the very least, if bureaucracy is to remain an instrument of the modern state and the modern economy, then why, advocates of managerialism argue, shouldn't it function in a manner similar to that of successful private enterprises, responding to incentives and demonstrating performance?

From one perspective, a sea change in public administration of this sort might have as its cause the triumph of more aggressive forms of capitalism, of border-erasing technologies, and of competition-based, performance-oriented social allocation, that is, of the global marketplace, over socialism, state-directed social allocation, and social democratic welfare statism.

Global capitalism, the argument continues, requires the dismantling or substantial weakening of command-and-control bureaucracy and statist enterprise and of state-sponsored distortions in prices and interference in capital and labor mobility. If nationalism once required a strong bureaucratic state, global capitalism requires the unrestricted movement of factors of production within and across borders. One would expect to see as a concomitant, as we indeed appear to be seeing to some extent, a considerable weakening of political support for redistributive policies that interfere with capital accumulation. Bureaucracy should dissolve into a series of successor institutions whose shape we may not yet fully grasp but which distribute property rights and control of scarcity rents toward private entities.

A contrary causal account, one that receives far too little consideration in public management scholarship, is plausible, arguably even more so. It is democracy, not global capitalism, which is transforming states around the world. Democracy requires the rule of law, the legally sanctioned regulation of markets, the preservation of equity, and competent bureaucracies subject to control by statute and by judicial institutions. Carl J. Friedrich (1940) once argued that democracy would have no chance to survive without bureaucracy because it would not be able to carry out the programmatic promises of its elected leaders. Weber viewed a system of bureaucratic rule in the modern state as inescapable; he could discover no known example of a bureaucracy being destroyed except in the course of a general cultural decline (Bendix 1977, 458). Bureaucratic power, says Guy Peters, "may simply be a prerequisite of effective government in contemporary society" (1992, 309).

The case for ascendant democracy is strong. Jürgen Habermas notes that "even in established democracies, the existing institutions of freedom are no longer above challenge, although here the populations seem to press for more democracy rather than less" (Habermas 1996, xlii). An OECD Ministerial Symposium on the Future of Public Services (J. T. Allen 1996) produced yet another argument, pointing to pluralism, that

[o]rganized interest groups, long a major factor in American politics, are multiplying in many countries, as longstanding benefit structures are threatened by the demand for public administrative and fiscal reform. In cases where such groups as the elderly or those with vested interests in public pensions become sufficiently mobilized, the opportunities for long-term reform may be severely constrained. This is especially

true when a political leader or his challengers finds large political advantage in playing to such groups.

In general, opportunities for the public to confront the politician have vastly expanded because of new communication technologies, and these confrontations are shaping the transformation of states.

Resurgent democracy would seem to underlie the increasing use of the term "governance" by international organizations. Richard Common argues (1998, 67) that such usage "indicates a shift in emphasis from economic to political management in affecting policy outcomes." The watershed, he says, was the publication of a report in 1989 by the World Bank entitled *A Framework for Capacity Building in Policy Analysis and Economic Management in Sub-Saharan Africa*, which led the Bank to emphasize "improvements in overall public sector management and the improvement of sectorwide institutions and service delivery" (World Bank 1992, 12).

If it is the triumph of democracy that is the story of our time, then, if historical experience is any guide, we should not expect to see bureaucracy shrivel and weaken. We should expect, instead, to see the administrative state become an even stronger and indispensable adjunct to competitive nationalism but, as in the past, in highly differentiated forms. Fred Riggs (1997a) characterizes the current period as "para-modernism," that is, a necessary confronting of the negative consequences of modernization and of bureaucracy as its instrument. In other words, "the elective affinities of the future may be driven not by new technology but rather by political culture" (Ignatieff 2000, 36).

In its narrow, corporate-mimicking manifestations, managerialism is likely to be vulnerable to the forces of democracy in significant part because it has lacked democratic legitimacy. "Rarely if ever," say Roger Wettenhall and Ian Thynne (2002, 7), "have governments consulted their electorates about whether to embark on privatization programs or adopt other elements of NPM-type reforms. Managerialism has generally appealed to political and commercial elites, and has been introduced by them as *faits accomplis* presented to mostly passive publics." In the same vein, Carsten Greve and Peter Jesperson (1999, 147) argue that "the concepts of citizen, citizens rights and citizen participation are almost non-existent in NPM debates." Public dissatisfaction with such reforms has in fact led to electoral reversals in a number of countries. The most recent reforms have shifted attention to improved citizen access and participation.

Perhaps, then, Wettenhall and Thynne (2002, 9–10) are prescient when they predict that

> as we settle into the new century, the thrust of things to come will be away from NPM-type initiatives towards a system that might be described as "enlightened public governance," a system which will even more clearly than NPM recognize the great value of flexibility and diversity, while at the same time appreciating that responsiveness to market forces must be conditioned and complemented by a commitment to enhancing the role of civil society

175

They continue: "Overall, both existing and new means of control and accountability will be invoked to ensure the openness and legitimacy of state action and of the various associated initiatives involved in the management of public affairs" (10).

Internationalizing the profession

In one respect, the era of managerialism has already produced an important convergence. Prior to recent decades, according to Christopher Hood (1989, 347; cf. Bogason and Toonen 1998), "the research field was nationally segmented." Moreover, according to Toonen (1998, 231), "[b]y the end of the 1970s international [public administration] was largely still American [public administration]," although Bogason and Toonen (1998, 207) identify "a continental European tradition focusing on legal analysis, a British tradition of pragmatic analysis based mainly on history and philosophy, and an American tradition with more ambitions to 'science'."

Entering the twenty-first century, a field of public administration and management that transcends national political boundaries was beginning to draw in prominent national scholars, a milestone in the field's history. Peter Aucoin argues (1990, 119), "[T]here has been an increasing degree of cross-fertilization throughout advanced political systems, and some considerable spread of these ideas to less advanced political systems." That what might once have been a parochial British academic coinage, New Public Management, rapidly became an identifier of public management reform among scholars, policy makers, and practitioners is evidence enough of this.

International cross-fertilization is not unprecedented. John Fairlie (1935) notes the convening of the International Congresses of the Administrative Sciences (held at Brussels in 1910 and 1923, Paris in 1927, Madrid in 1930, and Vienna in 1933). In Leonard White's early twentieth-century reporting to the profession in America on developments in Europe, he noted that "the first organized movement for the study of administration came from the continent and crystallized in the first International Congress of Public Administration in 1910" (1924, 384); at the second congress, he noted, delegates urged that an institute for public administration modeled on the British institute be created in every country. These efforts were not sustained, however.

Impressed by the apparently global nature of public management reform and by the family resemblance of its motivations and strategies, academics in recent years have once again begun creating new international forums for professional discourse on the subject, including the International Research Symposium on Public Management, the International Public Management Network, the European Group of Public Administration, and the increasing internationalization of the Public Management Research Association in the United States.[16] Klaus König (1997, 226) observes that

> management has become the . . . lingua franca in an increasingly internation-alised administrative world. It signals that public administration implies planning and coordination, staff recruitment and development, personnel management and

control, organisation, and so on, and that allowances must be made in all these respects for the scarcity of resources.

Motivations to create and participate in these forums (which, though international, have drawn less interest from the French- and Spanish-speaking worlds, Asia, and the less developed countries, which have had their own forums) have varied. Some promoted New Public Management as an ideology and sought an audience for positive assessments, however premature. Others were impressed with the apparent convergence of management institutions, practices, and values, even, as noted, seeing a global consensus that the private sector could outperform traditional institutions. Still others sought to promote a wider understanding of national institutions in responding to the managerial challenges of globalization, seeing divergence and the possibility of new theoretical insights into processes of managerial reform (Pollitt 2002). Academics sought a dialogue among scholars with the more modest ambition of encouraging both theory building and lesson drawing among jurisdictions confronting similar challenges (Lynn 2001a).

That there is a coherent intellectual agenda for the field of public administration and management is becoming more widely recognized, although perspectives on the contours of that agenda differ (Lynn 2005). Jos Raadschelders and Mark Rutgers, for example, argue that without studying three dichotomies – public/private, policy/administration, and state/society – "public administration cannot be understood at all" (1999, 30). "[A]ll governments," argue Peter Aucoin and Ralph Neintzman (2000, 46),

> must now govern in a context where there are greater demands for accountability for performance on the part of a better educated and less deferential citizenry, more assertive and well organized interest groups and social movements, and more aggressive and intrusive mass media operating in a highly competitive information-seeking and processing environment.

Among particulars, in other words, there are universals, although no agreement on what these universals are.

If there is a transcendent issue in this international discourse, it is the relationship between bureaucracy and democracy, between administrators and the people, between managerial responsibility and popular sovereignty and the rule of law, between governmental capacity and popular control of that capacity. New Public Management has only compounded this problem by greatly lengthening the chains and forms of delegation.

In the modern (or para- or post-modern) state, bureaucracy has continued to be, as it has been historically, both solution and problem, an apparatus that provides structure, stability, and capacity to modern states but, at the same time, poses challenges to institutions of democratic control and participation. Our age is characterized, according to Henry Jacoby (1973, 2), by "the forceful transformation of rational administration into the irrational exercise of power, the lack of clearly defined limits to coercion [or corruption], and the increasing incompetence of a state which arrogates independence to itself." The self-aggrandizing tendencies of bureaucratic elites have, according to Farrel Heady, heightened the issue of political control of public administration around the world. It is this suspicion of bureaucratic power that began to intensify in the 1980s, producing the changes documented by public administration scholars and inspiring discoveries of new paradigms. This intensification is occurring, however, in the context of heightened concern for national identities, the legitimacy of authority, and long-term political viability of governments, and it is this linkage that is of significance.

The fact that public management reform remains primarily a national (and constitutional) matter (König 1997; Rohr 2002) despite the globalization of resources and technology should not obscure the fact that these issues can be intelligibly studied and debated by academic and practicing professionals of widely different national experiences. National differences may be inimical to reaching that elusive consensus on the universal principles of public administration and management, but such differences are the lifeblood of scientific inquiry and thus well serve the goal of building the theories and empirical understanding that can sustain a professional field on a global scale (Forbes and Lynn 2005; Forbes, Hill, and Lynn forthcoming). While their orientations to disciplines, theories, methods, and national agendas will differ (Stillman 2001), these professionals have in common a grasp of larger issues that transcend the descriptive particulars of national regimes or tenets of disciplinary training.

New bottles?

"All administrative reform," says Werner Jann (1997, 94), "like basically all administrative theory, deals with the same set of problems: *legality* . . . *legitimacy* . . . *efficiency* and *effectiveness*." Managerialism's most plausible justification is facilitating improvements in governmental efficiency and effectiveness. As noted earlier, however, the evidence that the various instruments and techniques of managerialism have done so is mixed at best (Pollitt 2000; Pollitt and Bouckaert 2004). Depending on the effectiveness of their design and supervision, these managerial tools and techniques can be fully lawful. Insofar as the business management model is believed by citizens to be an appropriate source of ideas for public management, then their legitimacy as a matter of popular ideology may not arise.

Even under the best of circumstances, however, managerialism has a significant vulnerability: its often extraordinarily long chains of delegation, involving layers and levels of governments, contractors, subcontractors, and even volunteers. Their vulnerability lies in the sheer difficulty of ensuring the reciprocity, the fair exchange of values, essential to the integrity of any type of contractual relationship. When reciprocity fails, as when contractors behave in opportunistic ways to secure unfair advantages, the integrity of the public management regime responsible for these arrangements is called into question. These lengthening chains of delegation, then, are, as suggested in Chapter 7, a direct challenge to traditional concepts of accountability and an invitation to parliaments, elected executives, and courts of statutory and administrative review to keep them in check.

The most stable institutions in the era of managerialism have been those that guarantee the legitimacy of delegated authority: legislatures and courts. In America and in other countries as well, to the extent that their electoral politics involves the direct engagement of interest groups, elected officials will continue to be under pressure, when the legitimacy of the uses of delegated authority and resources is called into question, to enforce traditional modes and concepts of accountability. The same result is likely where the rule of law takes the form of a *Rechtsstaat*.

Against managerial institutions, and in a sense transcending them, then, stand the law and the courts that define and enforce it. "State power is the great antagonist against which the rule of law must forever be addressed," says H. W. Jones (1958, 144). As Anthony Bertelli notes, administrative law regimes exist to police the delegation of powers from sovereign authority to bureaus. "The commitment to uphold administrative law is made credible in most of the world by a third party[, notably] the courts" (Bertelli 2005, 151). But elected officials may decree other arrangements, such as ombudsmen or inspectors general or other entities possessing independent authority to review and report. Walter Kickert and Jan Hakvoort (2000, 251) note that the "all-pervasive dominance of administrative law, combined with the rational, deductive, comprehensive, systematic way of legal thinking, must have serious implications for the form of 'public management' that is adopted" in Continental countries dominated by civil law but in other countries as well.

This is not to say that inertia necessarily rules. In principle, certain kinds of state action (in America, for example, welfare entitlements or the operation of airport control towers) might come to be widely and authoritatively regarded as not inherently governmental functions, while other kinds of state action (again in America, commander-in-chief authority to detain and interrogate enemy combatants ungoverned by the Geneva Conventions or other statutes and treaties) might transform the relationships between state and society. Property (public lands, publicly owned industrial assets) and property rights (to determine modes of compliance with regulatory standards) might be transferred to the private sector. Public managers might be directed by law or executive order to consider or even make certain kinds of choices concerning eligibility for public services or for receipt of other public benefits and privileges (for example, to award grants to faith-based providers of social services). At the same time, delegations of authority might be broadened to allow for entrepreneurial strategies subject to non-traditional standards of performance.

Constitutions and constitutional institutions will continue to frame the evolution of states and, as a consequence, their managerial institutions, however. The overthrow of current constitutional arrangements is not in prospect. Within these institutional frameworks, institutions will continue to evolve. But, as noted above, the narrative of differentiation presages distinctive futures, not convergence, for national administrations. These futures may, over time, come to look different from the contemporary reality of public management, but only insofar as the central problematics of democratic governance are resolved in ways that sustain the constitutional legitimacy of state action.

NOTES

1 James D. Carroll (1998, 402) characterizes New Public Management in paradigmatic terms: "reducing and deregulating bureaucracy, using market mechanisms and simulated markets to conduct government action, devolving responsibility downward and outward in organizations, increasing productivity, energizing agencies, and empowering employees to pursue results, improve quality, and satisfy customers."

2 The new paradigms had scarcely more respect for republican institutions and electoral politics than did the traditionalists who sought separation of politics and administration, but they claimed to be more democratic in their fidelity to discovering and acting on "what citizens really want" expressed through consumer choice or in participatory forums.

3 Toonen (2004, 195) elaborates: "After a round of reforms at the operational and managerial levels of administrative systems, the process is very often lifted to the procedural (governance: accountability; responsibility; legitimacy) or even institutional levels (territorial reorganisation, constitutional reform, departmental reform, decentralisation, intergovernmental relations, etc.) of the government system." "New Labour" in Great Britain, for example, has instituted "constitutional" reforms following an era of managerial reforms. French reforms "created democratic political institutions in the regions some 20 years ago and are now gradually in the process of improving the managerial capacities of all levels of government."

4 The US Congress, for example, under heavy lobbying by provider interests, has steadily resisted efforts to change Medicare and Medicaid reimbursement policies in order to publicize and reward providers with superior records of performance. Federal legislation to do just that for public schools (the No Child Left Behind Act) has encountered stiff opposition from state and local officials, even though they can choose their own performance measures.

5 Howard Margolis (1993, 23) says of paradigmatic thinking, "[S]hared habits of mind are the only *essential* constituents tying together a community in the way that makes talk of sharing a paradigm fruitful. . . . [T]he essential component of a Kuhnian paradigm is an intrinsically invisible (though not undetectable) component, habits of mind. . . . A paradigm shift . . . is a special sort of change in habits of mind." Margolis distinguishes between "points of view," which an individual is conscious of, and "habits of mind," which an individual is unconscious of. He says we cannot identify complete paradigms and we do not need to; we need only identify "those habits of mind that are critical for distinguishing the community from outsiders or rivals" (26).

Michael Barzelay's definition of paradigm is drawn from Harmon (1970) and Barker (1985): "[T]he basic way of perceiving, thinking, valuing, and doing associated with a particular vision of reality. A dominant paradigm is seldom if ever stated explicitly; it exists as unquestioned, tacit understanding that is transmitted through culture and in succeeding generations through direct experience rather than being taught" (Barzelay 1992, 178).

6 Bounded rationality refers to decision makers' reducing the number of options they

consider to those that appear most feasible in recognition of the limitations both on the information available to them and on their capacity to process complexity.

7 Riggs argues (1997a, 347), "No bureaucracies, modern or traditional, are democratic; they are instead administrative and hierarchic." Of the emergence of the American administrative state, Barry Karl (1976, 503) notes that "the professionalization of administration created national interests among administrative specialists themselves, separating them from the local attachments their [Jacksonian] predecessors had understood so well," thus deepening the problems of democratic accountability. The consequences of professionalization may be even more evident in European democracies.

8 Another New Public Administration (capitalized this time) was proclaimed in the early 1970s, but this was a normative ideal rather than the assertion of a new administrative reality (Frederickson 1971).

9 "What distinguishes the privatizations of the last two decades of the 20th century from the long previous history of mostly incremental establishment and disestablishment of public enterprises," argue Wettenhall and Thynne (2002, 5), "is the sheer size of the recent movement and the ideological fervor with which it has been pushed."

10 According to Bevir, Rhodes, and Weller (2003a), "the central characters are central agencies – the elite of the elite – most commonly in the disguise of a ministry of finance or a prime minister's department. . . . Elite actors may launch reform, but other actors changed it markedly, constructing and reconstructing its meaning within their several traditions" (204). They continue: "[P]ublic service reform plays a key symbolic role for the elite. It is a token of authority as much as an indicator of change" (205).

11 Riggs (1997b, 254) has analyzed the differences between parliamentary and presidential regimes, arguing that "parliamentarist regimes can more easily solve many modern problems than can those based on the presidentialist model." In the former, control over the bureaucracy is strengthened by the fusion of powers; officials are responsible to an integrated center of authority. "Parliamentarist regimes have adopted the mandarin principle (with variations) and installed career officials who, following their appointment after taking academic tests, are rotated among posts in different locations and public agencies becoming experienced managers of public policies and trusted advisers to members of cabinet" (272). Parliament retains the interest of the general public without holding the government hostage; "public policy-making can proceed in tandem with dramatic legislative performances" (270). In the latter, it is necessary to centripetalize power enough so that voices of moderation based on centrist views can prevail in both the executive and the legislative branches. Single-member electoral districts, a holdover from the traditional British model, do this in America. In presidentialist regimes, bureaucrats cannot be seen as mandarins; their bureaucrats are more apt to be seen as career functionaries, retainers, or transients; otherwise they would rule, and their rule would be challenged in separation-of-powers regimes.

12 Convergence to at least some significant extent is a European Union goal. "The EAS represents an evolving process of increasing convergence between national administrative legal orders and administrative practices of Member States" (EPPA 1999, 6). The convergence is influenced by economic pressures from individuals and firms, regular and continuous contacts between public officials of member states, and the jurisprudence of the European Court of Justice.

13 Pollitt (2002) offers a four-stage model of "convergence" involving discursive

convergence, decisional convergence, practice convergence, and results convergence. His model is based on an original contribution by Brunsson (1989), who distinguished talk, decisions, and actions. One of Brunsson's points was that talk, decisions, and actions each have their own payoffs.

14 The discussion in this section is based on Lynn (2001a).

15 Despite its apparent enthusiasm for NPM, the OECD correctly observed that "there is no single model of reform, there are no off-the-shelf solutions" to the problems of the bureaucratic state (OECD 1995, 19).

16 Pollitt notes, however, that "[t]he most active participants [in discursive reform] have been the Anglophone countries, the Netherlands and the Nordic group. The others (for example, Germany, France, the Mediterranean states) have been much more cautious, even at the talk stage" (2002, 489). Within the Anglophone group, reform decisions have been noticeably more radical and far-reaching in New Zealand, Australia, and the UK than in Canada and the USA.

References

Aberbach, Joel D., and Tom Christensen. 2003. "Translating Theoretical Ideas into Modern State Reform: Economics-Inspired Reforms and Competing Models of Governance." *Administration and Society* 35: 491–509.

Aberbach, Joel D., and Bert A. Rockman. 1988. "Problems of Cross-National Comparison." In Donald C. Rowat, ed., *Public Administration in Developed Democracies: A Comparative Study*. 419–40. New York: Marcel Dekker.

——. 2001. "Reinventing Government or Reinventing Politics? The American Experience." In B. Guy Peters and Jon Pierre, eds., *Politicians, Bureaucrats and Administrative Reform*. 24–34. London: Routledge.

Aberbach, Joel D., Robert D. Putnam, and Bert A. Rockman. 1981. *Bureaucrats and Politicians in Western Democracies*. Cambridge, MA: Harvard University Press.

Albrow, Martin. 1970. *Bureaucracy*. New York: Praeger Publishers.

Allen, Jodie T. 1996. "Summary of Session Three: Managing for the Future: Seeking Solutions to Long-Range Problems in a World That Demands Immediate Action." Ministerial Symposium on the Future of Public Services, 5–6 March. Paris: OECD.

Allen, William H. 1908. "Instruction in Public Business." *Political Science Quarterly* 23: 604–16.

Allison, Graham T. 1983. "Public and Private Management: Are They Fundamentally Alike in All Unimportant Respects?" In James L. Perry and Kenneth L. Kraemer, eds., *Public Management: Public and Private Perspectives*. 72–92. Palo Alto, CA: Mayfield.

Allison, J. W. F. 1996. *A Continental Distinction in the Common Law: A Historical and Comparative Perspective on English Public Law*. Oxford: Clarendon Press.

Amos, Sheldon. 1874. *The Science of Law*. London: King.

Anderson, Eugene N., and Pauline R. Anderson. 1967. *Political Institutions and Social Change in Continental Europe in the Nineteenth Century*. Berkeley, CA: University of California Press.

Aucoin, Peter. 1990. "Administrative Reform in Public Management: Paradigms, Principles, Paradoxes and Pendulums." *Governance* 3: 115–37.

——. 1995. "Politicians, Public Servants, and Public Management: Getting Government Right." In B. Guy Peters and Donald J. Savoie, eds., *Governance in a Changing Environment*. 113–37. Montreal: McGill–Queens University Press.

Aucoin, Peter, and Ralph Neintzman. 2000. "The Dialectics of Accountability for Performance in Public Management Reform." *International Review of Administrative Sciences* 66: 45–55.

Babbage, Charles. 1832. *On the Economy of Machinery and Manufactures.* London: Charles Knight.

Badura, Peter. 2001. "The Constitutional Basis of Public Administration." In Klaus König and Heinrich Seidentopf, eds., *Public Administration in Germany.* 47–56. Baden-Baden: Nomos Verlagsgesellschaft.

Bagehot, Walter. 1949 [1867]. *The English Constitution.* London: Oxford University Press.

Barberis, Peter. 1995. "The Civil Service from Fulton to Next Steps and Beyond – Two Interpretations, Two Epistemologies." *Public Policy and Administration* 10: 34–51.

——. 1998. "The New Public Management and a New Accountability." *Public Administration* 76: 451–70.

Bardach, Eugene. 1987. "From Practitioner Wisdom to Scholarly Knowledge and Back Again." *Journal of Policy Analysis and Management* 7: 188–99.

——. 1998. *Getting Agencies to Work Together: The Practice and Theory of Managerial Craftsmanship.* Washington, DC: Brookings Institution.

Barker, Ernest. 1944. *The Development of Public Services in Western Europe: 1660–1930.* London: Oxford University Press.

Barker, Joel Arthur. 1985. *Discovering the Future: The Business of Paradigms.* St. Paul, MN: ILI Press.

Barlow, John, David Farnham, Sylvia Horton, and F. F. Ridley. 1996. "Comparing Public Managers." In David Farnham, Sylvia Horton, John Barlow, and Annie Hondeghem, eds., *New Public Managers in Europe.* 3–25. London: Macmillan.

Barnard, Chester I. 1968 [1938]. *The Functions of the Executive.* Cambridge, MA: Harvard University Press.

Barzelay, Michael (with Babak J. Armajani). 1992. *Breaking Through Bureaucracy: A New Vision for Managing in Government.* Berkeley, CA: University of California Press.

Beard, Charles A. 1926. *Government Research, Past, Present and Future.* New York: Municipal Administration Service.

Beattie, Alan, and Patrick Dunleavy. 1995. "Imperial Government and the Modern British Ministerial State." Online. Available http://www.psa.ac.uk/cps/1995/beat.pdf (accessed 12 February 2005).

Behn, Robert D. 1991. *Leadership Counts: Lessons for Public Managers from the Massachusetts Welfare, Training, and Employment Program.* Cambridge, MA: Harvard University Press.

Bélanger, Claude. 2001. "The British Constitution." Online. Available http://www2.marianopolis.edu/quebechistory/federal/british.htm (accessed 8 June 2004).

Bendix, Reinhard. 1977. *Max Weber: An Intellectual Portrait.* Berkeley, CA: University of California Press.

Benz, Arthur. 1993. "Commentary on O'Toole and Scharpf: 'The Network Concept as a Theoretical Approach.'" In Fritz W. Scharpf, ed., *Games in Hierarchies and Networks: Analytical and Empirical Approaches to the Study of Governance Institutions.* 167–74. Boulder, CO: Westview Press.

——. 1995. "Institutional Change in Intergovernmental Relations: The Dynamics of Multi-Level Structures." *The European Yearbook of Comparative Government and Public Administration.* 551–76. Baden-Baden: Nomos Verlagsgesellschaft.

Berman, Harold J. 1983. *Law and Revolution: The Formation of Western Legal Tradition.* Cambridge, MA: Harvard University Press.

Bertelli, Anthony M. 2004. "Strategy and Accountability: Structural Reform Litigation and Public Management." *Public Administration Review* 64: 28–42.

——. 2005. "Law and Public Administration." In Ewan Ferlie, Laurence E. Lynn, Jr.,

184

and Christopher Pollitt, eds., *Oxford Handbook of Public Management*. 133–55. Oxford: Oxford University Press.

Bertelli, Anthony M., and Laurence E. Lynn, Jr. 2003. "Managerial Responsibility." *Public Administration Review* 63: 259–68.

——. 2005. "Policymaking in the Parallelogram of Forces: Common Agency and Human Service Provision." *Policy Studies Journal* 32: 297–316.

——. 2006. *Madison's Managers: Public Administration and the Constitution*. Baltimore, MD: Johns Hopkins University Press.

Bevir, Mark, R. A. W. Rhodes, and Patrick Weller. 2003a. "Comparative Governance: Prospects and Lessons." *Public Administration* 81: 191–210.

——. 2003b. "Traditions of Governance: Interpreting the Changing Role of the Public Sector." *Public Administration* 81: 1–17.

Bezes, Philippe. 2004. "Bureaucrats and Politicians in the Politics of Administrative Reforms in France (1988–1997)." In Christopher Pollitt and Colin Talbot, eds., *Unbundled Government: A Critical Analysis of the Global Trend to Agencies, Quangos and Contractualisation*. 47–60. London and New York: Routledge.

Bogason, Peter, and Theo A. J. Toonen. 1998. "Introduction: Networks in Public Administration." *Public Administration* 76: 205–27.

Bonnin, Charles-Jean. 1812. *Principes d'Administration Publique*, 3rd edition, 3 vols. Paris: Chez Renaudière.

Box, Richard C. 1998. "Running Government Like a Business: Implications for Public Administration Theory and Practice." *American Review of Public Administration* 29: 19–43.

Bozeman, Barry. 1987. *All Organizations Are Public: Bridging Public and Private Organizational Theories*. San Francisco, CA: Jossey-Bass.

Brehm, John, and Scott Gates. 1999. *Working, Shirking, and Sabotage: Bureaucratic Response to a Democratic Public*. Ann Arbor, MI: University of Michigan.

Brennan, Kevin. 2004. "An MP's View of Future Reforms in the Civil Service." Online. Available http://www.epolitix.com/EN/MPWebsites/Kevin+Brennan/8d541295-fc20-49b2-8d10-1c9afe97a1aa.htm (accessed 14 December 2005).

Brunsson, Nils. 1989. *The Organization of Hypocrisy: Talk, Decisions, and Actions in Organizations*. New York: Wiley.

Caiden, Gerald E. 1991. *Administrative Reform Comes of Age*. New York: Walter de Gruyter.

——. 1999. "What Lies Ahead for the Administrative State?" In Keith M. Henderson and O. P. Dwivedi, eds., *Bureaucracy and the Alternatives in World Perspective*. 295–320. New York: St. Martin's Press.

Carpenter, Daniel P. 2001. *The Forging of Bureaucratic Autonomy: Reputations, Networks, and Policy Innovation in Executive Agencies, 1862–1928*. Princeton, NJ: Princeton University Press.

Carroll, James D. 1995. "The Rhetoric of Reform and Political Reality in the National Performance Review." *Public Administration Review* 55: 302–12.

——. 1998. Book Review. *American Review of Public Administration* 28: 402–7.

Chapman, Richard C. 1997. *The Treasury in Public Policy-Making*. London: Routledge.

Child, John. 1969. *British Management Thought: A Critical Analysis*. London: George Allen & Unwin.

Church, A. Hamilton. 1914. *Science and Practice of Management*. New York: The Engineering Magazine Co.

Cleveland, Frederick A. 1919. "Popular Control of Government." *Political Science Quarterly* 34: 237–61.

185

Cleveland, Harlan. 2000. "The Future Is Uncentralized." *Public Administration Review* 60: 293–7.

Cohen, Steven, and William B. Eimicke. 1995. *The New Effective Public Manager: Achieving Success in a Changing Government*. San Francisco, CA: Jossey-Bass.

Comer, John Preston. 1927. *Legislative Functions of National Administrative Authorities*. New York: Columbia University Press.

Common, Richard. 1998. "The New Public Management and Policy Transfer: The Role of International Organizations." In Martin Minogue, Charles Polidano, and David Hulme, eds., *Beyond the New Public Management: Changing Ideas and Practices in Governance*. 59–75. Cheltenham, UK: Edward Elgar.

Crainer, Stuart. 2000. *The Management Century: A Critical Review of 20th Century Thought and Practice*. San Francisco, CA: Jossey-Bass.

Creel, Harley G. 1964. "The Beginnings of Bureaucracy in China: The Origin of the Hsien." *Journal of Asian Studies* 23: 155–84.

——. 1974. *Shen Pu-Hai: A Chinese Philosopher of the Fourth Century B.C.* Chicago, IL: University of Chicago Press.

Crenson, Matthew. 1975. *The Federal Machine: Beginnings of Bureaucracy in Jacksonian America*. Baltimore, MD: Johns Hopkins University Press.

Crozier, Michel. 1967. *The Bureaucratic Phenomenon*. Chicago, IL: University of Chicago Press.

Crozier, Michel, and Erhard Friedberg. 1980. *Actors and Systems: The Politics of Collective Action*. Chicago, IL: University of Chicago Press.

Dahlberg, Jane. 1966. *The New York Bureau of Municipal Research: Pioneer in Government Administration*. New York: University of London Press.

Dale, H. E. 1941. *The Higher Civil Service of Great Britain*. Oxford: Oxford University Press.

Dandeker, Christopher. 1990. *Surveillance, Power and Modernity: Bureaucracy and Discipline from 1700 to the Present Day*. Cambridge: Polity Press.

Davy, Thomas J. 1962. "Public Administration as a Field of Study in the United States." *International Review of Administrative Sciences* 28: 63–78.

Deal, Terrence E., and Allan A. Kennedy. 1982. *Corporate Cultures: The Rites and Rituals of Corporate Life*. London: Penguin.

Deane, Phyllis. 1989. *The State and the Economic System: An Introduction to the History of Political Economy*. Oxford: Oxford University Press.

Derlien, Hans-Ulrich. 1987. "Public Managers and Politics." In Jan Kooiman and Kjell A. Eliassen, eds., *Managing Public Organizations: Lessons from Contemporary European Experience*. 129–41. London: Sage.

Dicey, A. V. 1885. *Introduction to the Study of the Law of the Constitution*. London: Macmillan.

Dickinson, H. T. 2002. "The British Constitution." In H. T. Dickinson, ed., *A Companion to Eighteenth-Century Britain*. 3–18. Oxford: Blackwell.

Dickinson, John. 1927. *Administrative Justice and the Supremacy of Law in the United States*. New York: Russell & Russell.

——. 1928. "Judicial Control of Official Discretion." *American Political Science Review* 22: 275–300.

——. 1930. "Democratic Realities and Democratic Dogma." *American Political Science Review* 24: 283–309.

DiMaggio, Paul J., and Walter W. Powell. 1991. "The Iron Cage Revisited: Institutional Isomorphism and Collective Rationality in Organization Fields." In Walter W. Powell and Paul J. DiMaggio, eds., *The New Institutionalism in Organizational Analysis*. 63–82. Chicago, IL: University of Chicago Press.

Dingwall, Robert, and Tim Strangleman. 2005. "Organizational Cultures in the Public Services." In Ewan Ferlie, Laurence E. Lynn, Jr., and Christopher Pollitt, eds., *The Oxford Handbook of Public Management*. 468–90. Oxford: Oxford University Press.

Douence, Jean Claude. 2003. "Recent Developments in the Laws Governing Local Public Services in France." *International Review of Administrative Sciences* 69: 83–97.

Downs, George W., and Patrick D. Larkey. 1986. *The Search for Government Efficiency: From Hubris to Helplessness*. New York: Random House.

Drucker, Peter. 1974. *Management: Tasks, Responsibilities and Practices*. New York: Harper & Row.

du Gay, P. 1996. *Consumption and Identity at Work*. London: Sage.

——. 2000. *In Praise of Bureaucracy: Weber, Organization, Ethics*. London: Sage.

du Gay, P., and G. Salaman. 1992. "The Cult(ure) of the Customer." *Journal of Management Studies* 29: 616–33.

Dunleavy, Patrick. 1992. *Democracy, Bureaucracy and Public Choice*. Englewood Cliffs, NJ: Prentice-Hall.

——. 1994. "The Globalization of Public Services Production: Can Government Be 'Best in the World'?" *Public Policy and Administration* 9, 2: 36–64.

Dunleavy, Patrick, and Christopher Hood. 1994. "From Old Public Administration to New Public Management." *Public Money and Management* 14: 9–16.

Dunsire, Andrew. 1973. *Administration: The Word and the Science*. New York: John Wiley.

——. 1990. "Policy Developments and Administrative Changes in the United Kingdom." In O. P. Dwivedi and Keith M. Henderson, eds., *Public Administration in World Perspective*. 261–305. Ames, IA: Iowa State University Press.

Eaton, Dorman. 1880. *Civil Service Reform in Great Britain: A History of Abuses and Reforms and Their Bearing upon American Politics*. New York: Harper.

Efficiency Unit. 1988. *Improving Management in Government: The Next Steps. Report to the Prime Minister*. London: Her Majesty's Stationery Office.

——. 1991. *Making the Most of Next Steps: The Management of Ministers' Departments and Their Executive Agencies*. London: Her Majesty's Stationery Office.

Eggertsson, Thráinn. 1990. *Economic Behavior and Institutions*. Cambridge: Cambridge University Press.

Elgie, Robert. 2003. "Governance Traditions and Narratives of Public Sector Reform in Contemporary France." *Public Administration* 81: 141–62.

Eliassen, Kjell, and Jan Kooiman. 1993. "Introduction." In Kjell Eliassen and Jan Kooiman, eds., *Managing Public Organizations: Lessons from Contemporary European Experience*. 5–16. London: Sage.

Ellwein, Thomas. 2001. "The History of Public Administration." In Klaus König and Heinrich Seidentopf, eds., *Public Administration in Germany*. 33–45. Baden-Baden: Nomos Verlagsgesellschaft.

Elton, Geoffrey. 1953. *The Tudor Revolution in Government: Administrative Changes in the Reign of Henry VIII*. Cambridge: Cambridge University Press.

Emmerich, Herbert. 1950. *Essays on Federal Reorganization*. University, AL: University of Alabama Press.

Epstein, David, and Sharyn O'Halloran. 1999. *Delegating Powers: A Transaction Cost Politics Approach to Policy Making under Separate Powers*. New York: Cambridge University Press.

187

European Principles for Public Administration (EPPA). 1999. SIGMA Paper No. 27 (CCNM/SIGMA/PUMA[99]44/REV1). Paris: Organization for Economic Cooperation and Development.

Fairlie, John A. 1920. "Administrative Legislation." In National Emergency. Hearings before the Special Committee on the Termination of the National Emergency of the United States Senate. 93rd Cong., 1st sess., Part 3 – Constitutional Questions Concerning Emergency Powers, 3 November 1973. 615–830.

——. 1935. "Public Administration and Administrative Law." In Charles G. Haines and Marshall E. Dimock, eds., *Essays on the Law and Practice of Governmental Administration: Essays in Honor of Frank Johnson Goodnow*. 3–43. Baltimore, MD: Johns Hopkins University Press.

Fenwick, Charles G. 1920. "Democracy and Efficient Government – Lessons of the War." *American Political Science Review* 14: 565–86.

Ferejohn, John. 1999. "Accountability and Authority: Toward a Theory of Political Accountability." In Adam Przeworski, Susan C. Stokes, and Bernard Manin, eds., *Democracy, Accountability and Representation*. 131–53. Cambridge: Cambridge University Press.

Fesler, James W. 1982. "The Presence of the Administrative Past." In James W. Fesler, ed., *American Public Administration: Patterns of the Past*. 1–27. Washington, DC: American Society for Public Administration.

Finer, Herman. 1940. "Administrative Responsibility in Democratic Government." *Public Administration Review* 1: 335–50.

——. 1942. "The Administrative Class: Past and Future." *Public Administration Review* 2: 259–65.

Finer, S. E. 1997. *The History of Government from Earliest Times,* 3 vols. New York: Oxford University Press.

Fitzneale, Richard. 1912. "Dialogue Concerning the Exechequer." In Ernest F. Henderson, ed., *Select Historical Documents of the Middle Ages*. 20–134. London: George Bell.

Follett, Mary Parker. 1918. *The New State: Group Organization the Solution of Popular Government*. New York: Longmans, Green.

Forbes, Melissa K., and Laurence E. Lynn, Jr. 2005. "How Does Public Management Affect Government Performance? Evidence from International Research." *Journal of Public Administration Research and Theory* 15: 559–84.

Forbes, Melissa K., Carolyn J. Hill, and Laurence E. Lynn, Jr. Forthcoming. "Public Management and Government Performance: An International Review." In George A. Boyne, Kenneth J. Meier, Laurence J. O'Toole, Jr., and Richard M. Walker, eds., *Public Services Performance: Perspectives on Measurement and Management,* Cambridge: Cambridge University Press.

Fosler, R. S. 1999. "The Global Challenge to Governance: Implications for National and Subnational Government Capacities and Relationships." In *The Challenge to New Governance in the Twenty-First Century: Achieving Effective Central–Local Relations*. 494–524. Tokyo: National Institute for Research Advancement.

Foster, C. D. 2001. "The Civil Service under Stress: The Fall in Civil Service Power and Authority." *Public Administration* 79: 725–49.

Frederickson, H. George. 1971. "Toward a New Public Administration." In Frank Marini, ed., *Toward a New Public Administration: The Minnowbrook Perspective*. 309–31. Scranton, PA: Chandler.

——. 1996. "Comparing the Reinventing of Government with the New Public Administration." *Public Administration Review* 56: 263–70.

——. 2005. "Whatever Happened to Public Administration? Governance, Governance Everywhere." In Ewan Ferlie, Laurence E. Lynn, Jr., and Christopher Pollitt, eds., *The Oxford Handbook of Public Management*. 282–304. Oxford: Oxford University Press.

Frederickson, H. George, and Kevin B. Smith. 2003. *The Public Administration Theory Primer*. Boulder, CO: Westview.

Freund, Ernst. 1915. "The Substitution of Rule for Discretion in Public Law." *American Political Science Review* 9: 666–76.

Friedrich, Carl J. 1939. "The Continental Tradition of Training Administrators in Law and Jurisprudence." *Journal of Modern History* 11: 129–48.

——. 1940. "Public Policy and the Nature of Administrative Responsibility." In Carl Friedrich and Edward Mason, eds., *Public Policy: A Yearbook of the Graduate School of Public Administration, Harvard University, 1940*. 3–24. Cambridge, MA: Harvard University Press.

——. 1946. *Constitutional Government and Democracy: Theory and Practice in Europe and America*. Boston: Ginn.

——. 1976. "Reflections on Democracy and Bureaucracy." In J. A. G. Griffith, ed., *From Policy to Administration: Essays in Honor of William A. Robson*. 39–54. London: George Allen & Unwin.

Friedrich, Carl Joachim, and Taylor Cole. 1932. *Responsible Bureaucracy: A Study of the Swiss Civil Service*. Cambridge, MA: Harvard University Press.

Fry, Geoffrey K. 1997. "Great Britain." Paper prepared for presentation at *Civil Service Systems in Comparative Perspective*, School of Public and Environmental Affairs, Indiana University, Bloomington, Indiana, 5–8 April 1997. Online. Available http://www.indiana.edu/~csrc/fry1.html (accessed 13 December 2005).

Fuhr, Harold. 2001. "Constructive Pressures and Incentives to Reform: Globalization and Its Impact on Public Sector Performance and Governance in Developing Countries." *Public Management Review* 3: 419–43.

Garvey, Gerald. 1997. *Public Administration: The Profession and the Practice*. New York: St. Martin's Press.

Gaus, John M. 1923–4. "The New Problem of Administration." *Minnesota Law Review* 8: 217–31.

——. 1931. "Notes on Administration: The Present Status of the Study of Public Administration in the United States." *American Political Science Review* 25: 120–34.

——. 1936. "The Responsibility of Public Administration." In John M. Gaus, Leonard D. White, and Marshall E. Dimock, eds., *The Frontiers of Public Administration*. 26–44. Chicago, IL: University of Chicago Press.

George, Claude S., Jr. 1972. *The History of Management Thought*. Englewood Cliffs, NJ: Prentice-Hall.

Gilmour, Robert S., and Laura S. Jensen. 1998. "Reinventing Government Accountability: Public Functions, Privatization, and the Meaning of 'State Action'." *Public Administration Review* 58: 247–58.

Gladden, E. N. 1972a. *A History of Public Administration*, Volume I: *From Earliest Times to the Eleventh Century*. London: Frank Cass.

——. 1972b. *A History of Public Administration*, Volume II: *From the Eleventh Century to the Present Day*. London: Frank Cass.

Goetz, Klaus H. 1999. "Between Autonomy and Subordination: Bureaucratic Legitimacy and Administrative Change in Germany." In Luc Rouban, ed., *Citizens and the New Governance: Beyond New Public Management*. 157–74. Amsterdam: IOS Press.

189

Goodnow, Frank J. 1886. "The Executive and the Courts." *Political Science Quarterly* 1: 533–59.

——. 1893 and 1902. *Comparative Administrative Law: An Analysis of the Administrative Systems National and Local, of the United States, England, France and Germany.* New York: G. P. Putnam's Sons.

——. 1967 [1900]. *Politics and Administration: A Study in Government.* New York: Russell & Russell.

——. 1905. "The Growth of Executive Discretion." *Proceedings of the American Political Science Association* 2: 29–44.

——. 1906. "Municipal Home Rule." *Political Science Quarterly* 21: 77–90.

Gore, Al. 1993. *From Red Tape to Results: Creating a Government That Works Better and Costs Less: Report of the National Performance Review.* Washington, DC: US Government Printing Office.

Grace, J. Peter. 1984. *Report of the President's Private Sector Survey on Cost Control.* Washington, DC: US Government Printing Office.

Graham, Andrew, and Alasdair Roberts. 2004. "The Agency Concept in North America: Failure, Adaptation, and Incremental Change." In Christopher Pollitt and Colin Talbot, eds., *Unbundled Government: A Critical Analysis of the Global Trend to Agencies, Quangos and Contractualisation.* 140–63. London and New York: Routledge.

Graves, W. Brooke. 1938. "Criteria for Evaluating the Effectiveness of State Government." *American Political Science Review* 32: 508–14.

Greve, Carsten, and Peter Kragh Jespersen. 1999. "New Public Management and Its Critics: Alternative Roads to Flexible Service Delivery to Citizens?" In Luc Rouban, ed., *Citizens and the New Governance: Beyond New Public Management.* 143–56. Amsterdam: IOS Press.

Groß, Thomas. 2000. "Monism(s) or Dualism(s)?: Germany." *European Review of Public Law* 12: 585–93.

Gulick, Luther, and Lyndall Urwick, eds. 1937. *Papers on the Science of Administration.* New York: Institute of Public Administration.

Gunn, Lewis. 1987. "Perspectives on Public Management." In Jan Kooiman and Kjell A. Eliassen, eds., *Managing Public Organizations: Lessons from Contemporary European Experience.* 33–46. London: Sage.

Haass, Richard N. 1999. *The Bureaucratic Entrepreneur: How to Be Effective in Government, the Public Sector, or Any Unruly Organization.* Washington, DC: Brookings.

Habermas, Jürgen. 1996. *Between Facts and Norms: Contributions to a Discourse Theory of Law and Democracy.* Cambridge, MA: MIT Press.

Haines, Charles G., and Marshall E. Dimock. 1935. "Introduction." In Charles G. Haines and Marshall E. Dimock, eds., *Essays on the Law and Practice of Governmental Administration: A Volume in Honor of Frank Johnson Goodnow.* i–xii. Baltimore: Johns Hopkins University Press.

Haldane, R. 1918. *Report on the Machinery of Government.* Cd. 9230. London: Her Majesty's Stationery Office.

Harmon, Willis. 1970. *An Incomplete Guide to the Future.* New York: W. W. Norton.

Hart, James. 1925. *The Ordinance Making Powers of the President of the United States.* Reprinted in Johns Hopkins University Studies in Historical and Political Science, Vol. XLIII, No. 3, pp. 1–359. Baltimore, MD: Johns Hopkins University Press.

Hay, Colin. 2004. "Theory, Stylized Heuristic or Self-Fulfilling Prophecy? The Status of Rational Choice Theory in Public Administration." *Public Administration* 82: 39–62.

Hayek, Friedrich von. 1945. "The Use of Knowledge in Society." *American Economic Review* 35: 519–30.

Hayward, Jack. 1982. "Mobilizing Private Interests in the Service of Public Ambitions: The Salient Element in the Dual French Policy Style?" In Jeremy Richardson, ed., *Policy Styles in Western Europe*. 111–40. London: George Allen & Unwin.

Hayward, Jack, and Vincent Wright. 2002. *Governing from the Centre: Core Executive Coordination in France*. Oxford: Oxford University Press.

Hazell, Robert, and David Sinclair. 2000. "The British Constitution: Labour's Constitutional Revolution." *Annual Review of Political Science* 3: 379–400.

Heady, Farrel. 1996. *Public Administration: A Comparative Perspective*, 5th edition. New York: Marcel Dekker.

——. 2001. *Public Administration: A Comparative Perspective*, 6th edition. New York: Marcel Dekker.

Heinrich, Carolyn J., Carolyn J. Hill, and Laurence E. Lynn, Jr. 2005. "Governance as an Organizing Theme for Empirical Research." In Patricia W. Ingraham and Laurence E. Lynn, Jr., eds., *The Art of Governance: Analyzing Governance and Administration*. 3–19. Washington, DC: Georgetown University Press.

Hennessy, Peter. 1989. *Whitehall*. New York: Free Press.

Herring, Pendleton. 1936. *Public Administration and the Public Interest*. New York: McGraw-Hill.

Heymann, Philip. 1987. *The Politics of Public Management*. New Haven, CT: Yale University Press.

Hill, Michael, and Peter Hupe. 2002. *Implementing Public Policy: Governance in Theory and Practice*. London: Sage.

Hogwood, Brian W., David Judge, and Murray McVicar. 2004. "Agencies, Ministers and Civil Servants in Britain." In Christoper Pollitt and Colin Talbot, eds., *Unbundled Government: A Critical Analysis of the Global Trend to Agencies, Quangos and Contractualisation*. 35–44. London and New York: Routledge.

Holliday, Ian. 2000. "Is the British State Hollowing Out?" *Political Quarterly* 71: 167–76.

Hood, Christopher. 1989. "Public Administration and Public Policy: Intellectual Challenges for the 1990s." *Australian Journal of Public Administration* 48: 346–58.

——. 1991. "A Public Management for All Seasons." *Public Administration* 69: 3–19.

——. 1999. "British Public Administration: Dodo, Phoenix or Chameleon?" In Jack Hayward, Brian Barry, and Archie Brown, eds., *The British Study of Politics in the Twentieth Century*. 287–311. Oxford: Oxford University Press.

Hood, Christopher C., and Michael W. Jackson. 1991a. "The New Public Management: A Recipe for Disaster?" *Canberra Bulletin of Public Administration* 64: 16–24.

——. 1991b. *Administrative Argument*. Aldershot, UK: Dartmouth Publishing Company.

Hsü, Leonard Shih-lien. 1975 [1932]. *The Political Philosophy of Confucianism: An Interpretation of the Social and Political Ideas of Confucius, His Forerunners, and His Early Disciples*. New York: Dutton.

Ignatieff, M. 2000. "The Man Who Was Right." *New York Review of Books* XLVII, 5: 35–7.

Ingraham, Patricia W. 1997. "Play It Again, Sam, It's Still Not Right: Searching for the Right Notes in Administrative Reform." *Public Administration Review* 57:

325–31.

Jacoby, Henry. 1973. *The Bureaucratization of the World*. Berkeley, CA: University of California Press.

James, Oliver. 2001. "Business Models and the Transfer of Businesslike Central Government Agencies." *Governance* 14: 233–52.

—— 2004. "Executive Agencies and Joined-up Government in the UK." In Christopher Pollitt and Colin Talbot, eds., *Unbundled Government: A Critical Analysis of the Global Trend to Agencies, Quangos and Contractualisation*. 75–93. London and New York: Routledge.

Jann, Werner. 1997. "Public Management Reform in Germany: A Revolution without a Theory?" In Walter J. M. Kickert, ed., *Public Management and Administrative Reform in Western Europe*. 81–100. Cheltenham, UK: Edward Elgar.

——. 2003. "State, Administration and Governance in Germany: Competing Traditions and Dominant Narratives." *Public Administration* 81: 95–118.

Jepperson, R. L., and J. W. Meyer. 1991. "The Public Order and the Construction of Formal Organizations." In Walter W. Powell and Paul J. DiMaggio, eds., *The New Institutionalism in Organizational Analysis*. 204–31. Chicago, IL: University of Chicago Press.

Jones, Bryan D. 2001. *Politics and the Architecture of Choice: Bounded Rationality and Governance*. Chicago, IL: University of Chicago Press.

Jones, Bryan D., Tracy Sulkin, and Heather A. Larsen. 2003. "Policy Punctuations in American Political Institutions." *American Political Science Review* 97: 151–70.

Jones, H. W. 1958. "The Rule of Law and the Welfare State." *Columbia Law Review* 58: 143–56.

Juran, J. M. 1944. *Bureaucracy: A Challenge to Better Management: A Constructive Analysis of Management Effectiveness in the Federal Government*. New York: Harper.

Kantorowicz, Ernst. 1931. *Frederick the Second, 1194–1250*. New York: Ungar.

Karl, Barry D. 1976. "Public Administration and American History: A Century of Professionalism." *Public Administration Review* 36: 489–503.

Kaufman, Herbert. 1977. *Red Tape: Its Origins, Uses and Abuses*. Washington, DC: Brookings Institution.

Keeling, Desmond. 1972. *Management in Government*. London: Allen & Unwin.

Kettl, Donald F. 1988. *Government by Proxy: (Mis?)Managing Federal Programs*. Washington, DC: Congressional Quarterly Press.

——. 2000. *The Global Public Management Revolution: A Report on the Transformation of Governance*. Washington, DC: Brookings Institution.

——. 2002. *The Transformation of Governance: Public Administration for the Twenty-First Century*. Baltimore, MD: Johns Hopkins University Press.

Khademian, Anne M. 2002. *Working with Culture: The Way the Job Gets Done in Public Programs*. Washington, DC: CQ Press.

Kickert, Walter J. M. 1997. "Public Management in the United States and Europe." In Walter J. M. Kickert, ed., *Public Management and Administrative Reform in Western Europe*. 15–38. Cheltenham, UK: Edward Elgar.

Kickert, Walter J. M., and Jan L. M. Hakvoort. 2000. "Public Governance in Europe: A Historical-Institutional Tour d'Horizon." In Oscar van Heflin, Walter J. M. Kickert, and Jacques J. A. Thomassen, eds., *Governance in Modern Society: Effects, Change, and Formation of Government Institutions*. 223–55. Dordrecht: Kluwer.

Kickert, W. J. M., E.-H. Klijn, and J. F. M. Koppenjan. 1997. "Introduction: A

Management Perspective on Policy Networks." In Walter J. M. Kickert, Erik-Hans Klijn, and Joop F. M. Koppenjan, eds., *Managing Complex Networks: Strategies for the Public Sector*. 1–13. Thousand Oaks, CA: Sage.

Knoke, David. 1994. *Political Networks: The Structural Perspective*. New York: Cambridge University Press.

König, Klaus. 1997. "Entrepreneurial Management or Executive Administration: The Perspective of Classical Public Administration." In Walter J. M. Kickert, ed., *Public Management and Administrative Reform in Western Europe*. 213–32. Cheltenham, UK: Edward Elgar.

Kooiman, Jan, and Kjell A. Eliassen, eds. 1993a. *Managing Public Organizations: Lessons from Contemporary European Experience*. London: Sage.

——. 1993b. "Preface." In Jan Kooiman and Kjell A. Eliassen, eds., *Managing Public Organizations: Lessons from Contemporary European Experience*. 1–4. London: Sage.

Kooiman, Jan, and Martijn van Vliet. 1993. "Governance and Public Management." In Kjell Eliassen and Jan Kooiman, eds., *Managing Public Organizations: Lessons from Contemporary European Experience*. 58–72. London: Sage.

Koppenjan, Joop, and Erik-Hans Klijn. 2005. *Managing Uncertainties in Networks: A Network Approach to Problem Solving and Decision Making*. London: Routledge.

Lachman, R., A. Nedd, and B. Hinings. 1994. "Analyzing Cross-National Management and Organizations: A Theoretical Framework." *Management Science* 40: 40–55.

Lane, Jan-Erik. 1987. "Public and Private Leadership." In Jan Kooiman and Kjell A. Eliassen, eds., *Managing Public Organizations: Lessons from Contemporary European Experience*. 47–64. London: Sage.

——. 1993. "Economic Organization Theory and Public Management." In Kjell Eliassen and Jan Kooiman, eds., *Managing Public Organizations: Lessons from Contemporary European Experience*. 73–83. London: Sage.

——. 1996. *Constitutions and Political Theory*. Manchester: Manchester University Press.

——. 2000. *New Public Management*. London: Routledge.

Laski, Harold Joseph. 1919. *Authority in the Modern State*. New Haven, CT: Yale University Press.

——. 1923. "The Growth of Administrative Discretion." *Journal of Public Administration* 1: 92–100.

Laver, Michael, and Kenneth A. Shepsle. 1999. "Government Accountability in Parliamentary Democracy." In Adam Przeworski, Susan C. Stokes, and Bernard Manin, eds., *Democracy, Accountability and Representation*. 279–96. Cambridge: Cambridge University Press.

Learned, H. B. 1912. *The President's Cabinet*. New Haven, CT: Yale University Press.

Lepawsky, Albert. 1949. *Administration: The Art and Science of Organization and Management*. New York: Knopf.

Light, Paul C. 1997. *The Tides of Reform: Making Government Work, 1945–1995*. New Haven, CT: Yale University Press.

Lindenfeld, David F. 1997. *The Practical Imagination: The German Sciences of State in the Nineteenth Century*. Chicago: University of Chicago Press.

Lindseth, Peter L. 2004. "The Paradox of Parliamentary Supremacy: Delegation, Democracy, and Dictatorship in Germany and France, 1920s–1950s." *Yale Law Journal* 113: 1341–1415.

Lipsky, Michael. 1980. *Street Level Bureaucracy: Dilemmas of the Individual in Public*

Services. New York: Russell Sage Foundation.

Lipson, Leslie. 1968 [1939]. *The American Governor from Figurehead to Leader.* New York: Greenwood Press.

Löffler, Elke. 2003. "The Administrative State in Western Democracies." In Jon Pierre and B. Guy Peters, eds., *Handbook of Public Administration.* 478–88. Newbury Park, CA: Sage.

——. n/d. "Germany." Online. Available http://www1.worldbank.org/publicsector/ civilservice /rsGermany.pdf (accessed 4 March 2005).

Lombard, Judith M. 2003. "Reinventing Human Resource Development: Unintended Consequences of Clinton Administration Reforms." *International Journal of Public Administration* 26: 1105–33.

Long, Norton E. 1949. "Power and Administration." *Public Administration Review* 9: 257–64.

——. 1952. "Bureaucracy and Constitutionalism." *American Political Science Review* 46: 808–18.

Louton, John. 1979. "Shen Pu-hai: A Misunderstood and Wrongly Neglected Thinker?" *Journal of the American Oriental Society* 99: 440–9.

Lupia, Arthur, and Mathew D. McCubbins. 2000. "Representation or Abdication? How Citizens Use Institutions to Help Delegation Succeed." *European Journal of Political Research* 37: 291–307.

Lynn, Laurence E., Jr. 1996. *Public Management as Art, Science and Profession.* Chatham, NJ: Chatham House.

——. 2001a. "Globalization and Administrative Reform: What Is Happening in Theory?" *Public Management Review* 3: 191–208.

——. 2001b. "The Myth of the Bureaucratic Paradigm: What Traditional Public Administration Really Stood For." *Public Administration Review* 61: 144–60.

——. 2003. "Public Management." In Jon Pierre and B. Guy Peters, eds., *Handbook of Public Administration.* 14–24. Newbury Park, CA: Sage.

——. 2005. "Public Management: A Concise History of the Field." In Ewan Ferlie, Laurence E. Lynn, Jr., and Christopher Pollitt, eds., *Handbook of Public Management.* 27–50. Oxford: Oxford University Press.

Lynn, Laurence E., Jr., Carolyn J. Heinrich, and Carolyn J. Hill. 2001. *Improving Governance: A New Logic for Empirical Research.* Washington, DC: Georgetown University Press.

Majone, Giandomenico. 1980. "An Anatomy of Pitfalls." In Giandomenico Majone and Edward S. Quade, eds., *Pitfalls of Analysis.* 7–22. Chichester, UK: John Wiley.

——. 1989. *Evidence, Argument, and Persuasion in the Policy Process.* New Haven, CT: Yale University Press.

Margolis, Howard. 1993. *Paradigms and Barriers: How Habits of Mind Govern Scientific Beliefs.* Chicago, IL: University of Chicago Press.

Martin, Daniel W. 1987. "Déjà Vu: French Antecedents of American Public Administration." *Public Administration Review* 47: 297–303.

Martin, Roscoe C. 1965. "Paul H. Appleby and His Administrative World." In Roscoe C. Martin, ed., *Public Administration and Democracy: Essays in Honor of Paul H. Appleby.* 1–14. Syracuse, NY: Syracuse University Press.

Mathews, John Mabry. 1917. *Principles of American State Administration.* New York: D. Appleton.

Meier, Kenneth J., and Gregory C. Hill. 2005. "Bureaucracy in the Twenty-First Century." In Ewan Ferlie, Laurence E. Lynn, Jr., and Christopher Pollitt, eds., *The Oxford*

Handbook of Public Management. 51–71. Oxford: Oxford University Press.

Merkle, Judith A. 1980. *Management and Ideology: The Legacy of the International Scientific Management Movement*. Berkeley, CA: University of California Press.

Metcalfe, Les, and Sue Richards. 1987. *Improving Public Management*. London: Sage.

——. 1993. "Evolving Public Management Cultures." In Kjell Eliassen and Jan Kooiman, eds., *Managing Public Organizations: Lessons from Contemporary European Experience*. 106–24. London: Sage.

Miewald, Robert D. 1984. "The Origins of Wilson's Thought: The German Tradition and the Organic State." In Jack Rabin and James S. Bowman, eds., *Politics and Administration: Woodrow Wilson and American Public Administration*. 17–30. New York: Marcel Dekker.

Milakovich, Michael E., and George J. Gordon. 2001. *Public Administration in America*, 7th edition. Boston: Bedford/St. Martin's Press.

Mill, John Stuart. 1861. *Considerations on Representative Government*. Online. Available http://www.constitution.org/jsm/rep_gov.htm (accessed 15 December 2005).

——. 1909 [1848]. *Principles of Political Economy with Some of Their Applications to Social Philosophy*, 7th edition. Ed. William James Ashley. London: Longmans, Green.

Millett, John D. 1949. "Post-War Trends in Public Administration in the United States." *Journal of Politics* 11: 736–47.

Milward, H. Brinton. 1994. "Nonprofit Contracting and the Hollow State." *Public Administration Review* 54: 73–7.

Milward, H. Brinton, and Keith G. Provan. 1993. "The Hollow State: Private Provision of Public Services." In Helen Ingram and Stephen R. Smith, eds., *Public Policy for Democracy*. Washington, DC: Brookings Institution.

Minogue, Martin. 1998. "Changing the State: Concepts and Practice in the Reform of the Public Sector." In Martin Minogue, Charles Polidano, and David Hulme, eds., *Beyond the New Public Management: Changing Ideas and Practices in Governance*. 17–37. Cheltenham, UK: Edward Elgar.

Moe, Ronald C. 1990. "Traditional Organizational Principles and the Managerial Presidency: From Phoenix to Ashes." *Public Administration Review* 50: 129–40.

——. 2001. "The Emerging Federal Quasi Government: Issues of Management and Accountability." *Public Administration Review* 61: 290–312.

Mommsen, Hans. 1991. *From Weimar to Auschwitz*. Princeton, NJ: Princeton University Press.

Moore, Mark H. 1984. "A Conception of Public Management." In *Teaching Public Management*. Proceedings of a Workshop to Assess Materials and Strategies for Teaching Public Management, Seattle, 9–11 May. 1–12. Public Policy and Management Program for Case and Course Development, Boston University.

——. 1995. *Creating Public Value: Strategic Management in Government*. Cambridge, MA: Harvard University Press.

Morstein Marx, Fritz. 1935. "Civil Service in Germany." In Leonard D. White, Charles H. Bland, Walter R. Sharp, and Fritz Morstein Marx, eds., *Civil Service Abroad: Great Britain, Canada, France, Germany*. 159–275. New York: McGraw-Hill.

——. 1940. *Public Management in the New Democracy*. New York: Harper.

——. 1945. "The Bureau of the Budget: Its Evolution and Present Role, I." *American Political Science Review* 39: 653–84.

——. 1948. "A Closer View of Organization." *Public Administration Review* 8: 60–5.

——. 1949. "Administrative Ethics and the Rule of Law." *American Political Science*

Review 43: 1119–44.

Mosher, Frederick C. 1975. "Introduction: The American Setting." In Frederick C. Mosher, ed., *American Public Administration: Past, Present and Future.* 1–10. University, AL: University of Alabama Press.

Muir, Ramsay. 1910. *Peers and Bureaucrats: Two Problems of English Government.* London: Constable.

Namier, L. B. 1929. *The Structure of Politics at the Accession of George III.* London: Macmillan.

Nash, Gerald D. 1969. *Perspectives on Administration: The Vistas of History.* Berkeley, CA: University of California, Institute of Governmental Studies.

National Academy of Public Administration (NAPA). 2000. *Report of the Priority Issues Task Force,* 10 January. Washington, DC.

Nelson, Michael. 1982. "A Short, Ironic History of American National Bureaucracy." *Journal of Politics* 44: 747–78.

Neustadt, Richard E. 1970. *Presidential Power: The Politics of Leadership.* New York: John Wiley.

Noordegraaf, Mirko. 2000. *Attention! Work and Behavior of Public Managers amidst Ambiguity.* Delft: Eburon Publishers.

North, Douglass C. 1990. *Institutions, Institutional Change, and Economic Performance.* New York: Cambridge University Press.

Norton, Philip. 1994. *The British Polity,* 3rd edition. New York: Longmans.

Olsen, Johan P. 2003. "Towards a European Administrative Space?" *Journal of European Public Policy* 10: 506–31.

Organization for Economic Cooperation and Development (OECD). 1993. *Public Management Developments. Survey 1990.* Paris: OECD.

——. 1994. *Public Management Developments: Survey 1993.* Paris: PUMA/OECD.

——. 1995. *Governance in Transition: Public Management Reforms in OECD Countries.* Paris: PUMA/OECD.

——. 1996. *Responsive Government: Service Quality Initiatives.* Paris: PUMA/OECD.

Osborne, David, and Ted Gaebler. 1992. *Reinventing Government: How the Entrepreneurial Spirit Is Transforming the Public Sector.* Reading, MA: Addison-Wesley.

O'Toole, Laurence J. 1984. "American Public Administration and the Idea of Reform." *Administration and Society* 16: 141–66.

Ott, J. Steven, Albert C. Hyde, and Jay M. Shafritz, eds. 1991. *Public Management: The Essential Readings.* Chicago, IL: Lyceum/Nelson-Hall.

Ouchi, W. G., and A. L. Wilkins. 1985. "Organizational Culture." *Annual Review of Sociology* 11: 457–83.

Overman, E. Sam, and Kathy J. Boyd. 1994. "Best Practice Research and Postbureaucratic Reform." *Journal of Public Administration Research and Theory* 4: 67–83.

Page, Edward C. 1992. *Political Authority and Bureaucratic Power: A Comparative Analysis.* Hemel Hempstead, UK: Harvester Wheatsheaf.

——. 1995. "Patterns and Diversity in European State Development." In Jack Hayward and Edward C. Page, eds., *Governing the New Europe.* 9–43. Cambridge: Polity Press.

Parris, Henry. 1969. *Constitutional Bureaucracy.* New York: Augustus M. Kelley.

Pascale, Richard T., and Anthony G. Athos. 1982. *The Art of Japanese Management.* London: Allen Lane.

Payre, Renaud. 2002. "A European Progressive Era?" *Contemporary European History* 11: 489–97.

Perrucci, Robert, and Harry R. Potter, eds. 1989. *Networks of Power: Organizational Actors at the National, Corporate, and Community Levels*. New York: Aldine de Gruyter.

Perry, James L., and Kenneth L. Kraemer. 1983. *Public Management: Public and Private Perspectives*. Palo Alto, CA: Mayfield.

Person, Harlow Stafford. 1977 [1926]. "Basic Principles of Administration and of Management: The Management Movement." In Henry C. Mecalf, ed., *Scientific Foundations of Business Administration*. 191–203. Easton, PA: Hive Publishing Company.

Peters, B. Guy. 1992. "Public Policy and Public Bureaucracy." In D. G. Ashford, ed., *History and Context in Comparative Public Policy*. 283–316. Pittsburgh, PA: University of Pittsburgh Press.

——. 1996. *The Future of Governing: Four Emerging Models*. Lawrence, KS: University Press of Kansas.

——. 1997. "A North American Perspective on Administrative Modernisation in Europe." In Walter J. M. Kickert, ed., *Public Management and Administrative Reform in Western Europe*. 251–66. Cheltenham, UK: Edward Elgar.

——. 2000. "Administrative Traditions." The World Bank Group. Online. Available http://www1.worldbank.org/publicsector/civilservice/traditions.htm (accessed 15 December 2005).

Peters, B. Guy, and Jon Pierre. 1998. "Governance without Government? Rethinking Public Administration." *Journal of Public Administration Research and Theory* 8: 223–44.

Peters, B. Guy, and Vincent Wright. 1996. "Public Policy and Administration, Old and New." In R. Goodin and H.-D. Klingemann, eds., *A New Handbook of Political Science*. 628–41. New York: Oxford University Press.

Peters, Thomas J., and Robert H. Waterman. 1982. *In Search of Excellence: Lessons from America's Best-Run Companies*. New York: Harper & Row.

Pfiffner, John M. 1935. *Public Administration*, New York: Ronald Press.

Pierre, Jon, and B. Guy Peters. 2000. *Governance, Politics and the State*. New York: St. Martin's Press.

Poggi, G. 1978. *The Development of the Modern State: A Sociological Introduction*. Stanford, CA: Stanford University Press.

Pollard, Harold R. 1974. *Developments in Management Thought*. London: Heinemann.

Pollitt, Christopher. 1990. *Managerialism and the Public Services: The Anglo-American Experience*. Oxford: Basil Blackwell.

——. 2000. "'Is the Emperor in His Underwear?' An Analysis of the Impacts of Public Management Reform." *Public Management* 2: 181–99.

——. 2002. "Clarifying Convergence: Striking Similarities and Durable Differences in Public Management Reform." *Public Management Review* 4: 471–92.

——. 2003. *The Essential Public Manager*. Maidenhead, UK: Open University Press.

Pollitt, Christopher, and Geert Bouckaert. 2004. *Public Management Reform: A Comparative Analysis*, 2nd edition. Oxford: Oxford University Press.

Pound, Roscoe. 1914. "Organization of the Courts." *Bulletin of American Judicature Society* VI: 1–28.

Powell, Walter W. 1990. "Neither Market nor Hierarchy: Network Forms of Organization." *Research in Organizational Behavior* 12: 295–336.

President's Committee on Administrative Management (PCAM). 1937. *Report of the Committee with Studies of Administrative Management in the Federal Government*.

197

Washington, DC: US Government Printing Office.

Price, Don K. 1959. "The Judicial Test." In Fritz Morstein Marx, ed., *Elements of Public Administration*. 475–99. Englewood Cliffs, NJ: Prentice-Hall.

——. 1985. *America's Unwritten Constitution: Science, Religion and Political Responsibility*. Cambridge, MA: Harvard University Press.

Prichard, Frank P. 1892. "The Study of the Science of Municipal Administration." *Annals of the American Academy of Political and Social Science* 2: 450–7.

Provan, Keith G., and H. Brinton Milward. 2001. "Do Networks Really Work? A Framework for Evaluating Public-Sector Organizational Networks." *Public Administration Review* 61: 414–23.

Putnam, Robert D., with Robert Leonardi and Raffaella Y. Nanetti. 1993. *Making Democracy Work: Civic Traditions in Modern Italy*. Princeton, NJ: Princeton University Press.

Raadschelders, Jos C. N. 1995. "The Use of Models in Administrative History, a Reply to Thuillier." In *The Influences of the Napoleonic "Model" of Administration on the Administrative Organization of Other Countries*. 263–7. Brussels: International Institute of Administrative Sciences. Working Group: History of Public Administration.

Raadschelders, Jos C. N., and Mark R. Rutgers. 1996. "The Evolution of Civil Service Systems." In Hans A. G. M. Bekke, James L. Perry, and Theo A. J. Toonen, eds., *Civil Service Systems in Comparative Perspective*. 67–99. Bloomington, IN: Indiana University Press.

——. 1999. "The Waxing and Waning of the State and Its Study: Changes and Challenges in the Study of Public Administration." In Walter J. M. Kickert and Richard J. Stillman, II, eds., *The Modern State and Its Study: New Administrative Sciences in a Changing Europe and the United States*. 17–35. Cheltenham, UK: Edward Elgar.

Raadschelders, Jos C. N., and Theo A. J. Toonen. 1999. "Public Sector Reform for Building and Recasting the Welfare State: Experiences in Western Europe." In James L. Perry, ed., *Research in Public Administration*. 39–62. Greenwich, CT: JAI Press.

Radin, Beryl A. 2001. "Intergovernmental Relationships and the Federal Performance Movement." In Dall Forsythe, ed., *Quicker, Better, Cheaper? Managing Performance in American Government*. 285–306. Albany, NY: Rockefeller Institute Press.

Rainey, Hal G. 1990. "Public Management: Recent Developments and Current Prospects." In Naomi B. Lynn and Aaron Wildavsky, eds., *Public Administration: The State of the Discipline*. 157–84. Chatham, NJ: Chatham House.

Rainey, Hal G., and Young Han Chun. 2005. "Public and Private Management Compared." In Ewan Ferlie, Laurence E. Lynn, Jr., and Christopher Pollitt, eds., *The Oxford Handbook of Public Management*. 72–102. Oxford: Oxford University Press.

Ranson, Stewart, and John Stewart. 1994. *Management in the Public Domain: Enabling the Learning Society*. Basingstoke, UK: Macmillan.

Redford, Emmette S. 1965. "Business as Government." In Roscoe C. Martin, ed., *Public Administration and Democracy: Essays in Honor of Paul H. Appleby*. 63–82. Syracuse, NY: Syracuse University Press.

Reich, Robert B. 1990. *Public Management in a Democratic Society*. Englewood Cliffs, NJ: Prentice-Hall.

Reichard, Christoph. 2003. "Local Public Management Reforms in Germany." *Public Administration* 81: 345–63.

Rhodes, R. A. W. 1994. "The Hollowing Out of the State: The Changing Nature of the

Public Service in Britain." *Political Quarterly* 65: 138–51.

——. 1996. "The New Governance: Governing without Government." *Political Studies* XLIV: 652–67.

——. 1997. "Reinventing Whitehall, 1979–1995." In Walter J. M. Kickert, ed., *Public Management and Administrative Reform in Western Europe*. 41–57. Cheltenham, UK: Edward Elgar.

Riggs, Fred W. 1997a. "Modernity and Bureaucracy," *Public Administration Review* 57: 347–53.

——. 1997b. "Presidentialism versus Parliamentarism: Implications for Representativeness and Legitimacy." *International Political Science Review* 18: 253–78.

——. 2002. "Globalization, Ethnic Diversity, and Nationalism: The Challenge for Democracies." *Annals of the American Academy of Political and Social Science* 581: 35–47.

Rohr, John. 1986. *To Run a Constitution: The Legitimacy of the Administrative State*. Lawrence, KS: University Press of Kansas.

——. 1987. "The Administrative State and Constitutional Principle." In Ralph Clark Chandler, ed., *A Centennial History of the American Administrative State*. 113–59. New York: Free Press.

——. 2002. *Civil Servants and Their Constitutions*. Lawrence, KS: University Press of Kansas.

Rosenberg, Hans. 1958. *Bureaucracy, Aristocracy and Autocracy: The Prussian Experience, 1660–1815*. Boston, MA: Beacon Press.

Rosenbloom, David H. 1998. *Understanding Management, Politics, and Law in the Public Sector*. New York: McGraw-Hill.

——. 2000. *Building a Legislative-Centered Public Administration: Congress and the Administrative State, 1946–1999*. Tuscaloosa, AL: University of Alabama Press.

Rouban, Luc. 1997. "The Administrative Modernisation Policy in France." In W. J. M. Kickert, ed., *Public Management and Administrative Reform in Western Europe*. 141–56. Cheltenham, UK: Edward Elgar.

Rourke, Francis E. 1987. "Bureaucracy in the American Constitutional Order." *Political Science Quarterly* 102: 217–32.

Rubin, Irene S. 1993. "Who Invented Budgeting in the United States?" *Public Administration Review* 53: 438–44.

Rugge, F. 2004. Personal communication.

Rutgers, Mark R. 2001. "Traditional Flavors? The Different Sentiments in European and American Administrative Thought." *Administration and Society* 33: 220–44.

Saalfeld, Thomas. 2000. "Members of Parliament and Governments in Western Europe: Agency Relations and Problems of Oversight." *European Journal of Political Research* 37: 353–76.

Saint-Martin, D. 1998. "The New Manageralism and the Policy Influence of Consultants in Government: An Historical-Institutionalist Analysis of Britain, Canada and France." *Governance* 11: 324.

Salamon, Lester M. 1981. "Rethinking Public Management: Third-Party Government and the Changing Forms of Public Action." *Public Policy* 29: 255–75.

——, ed. 2002. *The Tools of Government: A Guide to the New Governance*. Oxford: Oxford University Press.

Schlesinger, Rudolf B., Hans W. Baade, Peter E. Herzog, and Edward M. Wise. 1998. *Comparative Law*. 6th edition. New York: Foundation Press.

Schröter, Eckhard. 2004. "A Solid Rock in Rough Seas? Institutional Change and

Continuity in the German Federal Bureaucracy." In Christopher Pollitt and Colin Talbot, eds., *Unbundled Government: A Critical Analysis of the Global Trend to Agencies, Quangos and Contractualisation.* 61–72. London and New York: Routledge.

Schultze, Charles L. 1977. *The Public Use of Private Interest.* Washington, DC: Brookings Institution.

Schumpeter, Joseph A. 1994 [1954]. *History of Economic Analysis.* Oxford: Oxford University Press.

Seibel, Wolfgang. 2001. "Administrative Reforms." In Klaus König and Heinrich Seidentopf, eds., *Public Administration in Germany.* 73–87. Baden-Baden: Nomos Verlagsgesellschaft.

Seidman, Harold. 1998. *Politics, Position, and Power: The Dynamics of Federal Organization.* 4th edition. New York: Oxford University Press.

Sheldon, Oliver. 1979 [1924]. *The Philosophy of Management.* New York: Arno Press.

Short, Lloyd M. 1923. *The Development of National Administrative Organization in the United States.* Baltimore, MD: Johns Hopkins University Press.

Silberman, Bernard S. 1993. *Cages of Reason: The Rise of the Rational State in France, Japan, the United States, and Great Britain.* Chicago, IL: University of Chicago Press.

Silver, Robin, with Nick Manning. 2000a. "France." The World Bank Group. Online. Available http://www1.worldbank.org/publicsector/civilservice/francestudy.htm (accessed 15 December 2005).

——. 2000b. "United Kingdom." The World Bank Group. Online. Available http://www1.worldbank.org/publicsector/civilservice/ukstudy.htm (accessed 15 December 2005).

Simon, Herbert A. 1947. *Administrative Behavior: A Study of Decision-Making Processes in Administrative Organizations.* New York: Macmillan.

Simpson, J. R. 1949. "Improving Public Management." *Public Administration Review* 9: 100–6.

Skowronek, Stephen. 1982. *Building a New American State: The Expansion of Administrative Capacities, 1877–1920.* New York: Cambridge University Press.

Small, Albion W. 1909. *The Cameralists: The Pioneers of German Social Polity.* Chicago, IL: University of Chicago Press.

Stamp, Josiah C. 1923. "The Contrast between the Administration of Business and Public Affairs." *Journal of Public Administration* 1: 158–71.

Stever, James A. 1990. "Marshall Dimock: An Intellectual Portrait." *Public Administration Review* 50: 615–20.

Stillman, Richard J. II. 1982. "The Changing Patterns of Public Administration Theory in America." In Joseph A. Uveges, Jr., ed., *Public Administration: History and Theory in Contemporary Perspective.* 5–37. New York: Marcel Dekker.

——. 1999. "American versus European Public Administration: Does Public Administration Make the Modern State, or Does the State Make Public Administration?" In Walter J. M. Kickert, and Richard J. Stillman II, eds., *The Modern State and Its Study: New Administrative Sciences in a Changing Europe and the United States.* 247–60. Cheltenham, UK: Edward Elgar.

——. 2001. "Toward a New Agenda for Administrative State Research? A Response to Mark Rutgers's 'Traditional Flavors?' Essay." *Administration and Society* 33: 480–8.

Stokes, Donald C. 1986. "Political and Organizational Analysis in the Policy Curriculum." *Journal of Policy Analysis and Management* 6: 45–55.

Stone, Donald C. 1945. "Notes on the Governmental Executive: His Role and His

Methods." *Public Administration Review* 5: 210–25.

Strøm, Kaare. 2000. "Delegation and Accountability in Parliamentary Democracies." *European Journal of Political Research* 37: 261–89.

Suleiman, Ezra. 2003. *Dismantling Democratic States*. Princeton, NJ: Princeton University Press.

Swift, Elaine K., and David W. Brady. 1994. "Common Ground: History and Theories of American Politics." In Lawrence C. Dodd and Calvin Jillson, eds., *The Dynamics of American Politics: Approaches and Interpretations*. 83–105. Boulder, CO: Westview.

Talbot, Colin. 2004. "Executive Agencies: Have They Improved Management in Government?" *Public Money and Management* 24: 104–12.

Tarrow, Sidney. 1996. "Making Social Science Work across Space and Time: A Critical Reflection on Robert Putnam's *Making Democracy Work*." *American Political Science Review* 90: 389–97.

Taylor, Frederick W. 1911. *The Principles of Scientific Management*. New York: Harper.

Taylor, Sir Henry. 1958 [1836]. *The Statesman*. New York: New American Library.

Thoenig, Jean-Claude. 2003. "Nouvel article Note de lecture sur l'ouvrage de Hayward Jack et Vincent Wright, *Governing from the Centre: Core Executive Coordination in France*, Oxford University Press, 2002." Online (in English). Available http://www. melissa.ens-cachan.fr/article.php3?id_article=257 (accessed 15 December 2005).

——. 2004. "Sub-national Government of Public Affairs in France." Presented at the Conference on Modernizing State and Administration in Europe: A French–German Comparison, Goethe-Institute, Bordeaux, 14–15 May.

Thomas, Rosamund M. 1978. *The British Philosophy of Administration: A Comparison of British and American Ideas, 1900–1939*. London: Longman.

Thompson, James R. 2000. "Reinventing as Reform: Assessing the National Performance Review." *Public Administration Review* 60: 508–21.

Toonen, Theo A. J. 1998. "Networks, Management and Institutions: Public Administration as 'Normal Science'." *Public Administration* 76: 229–52.

——. 2001. "The Comparative Dimension of Administrative Reform: Creating Open Villages and Redesigning the Politics of Administration." In B. Guy Peters and Jon Pierre, eds., *Politicians, Bureaucrats and Administrative Reform*. 183–201. London: Routledge.

——. 2004. "The Comparative Dimension of Administrative Reform: Creating Open Villages and Redesigning the Politics of Administration." In Christopher Pollitt and Colin Talbot, eds., *Unbundled Government: A Critical Analysis of the Global Trend to Agencies, Quangos and Contractualisation*. 183–201. London and New York: Routledge.

Toonen, Theo A. J., and Jos C. N. Raadschelders. 1997. "Public Sector Reform in Western Europe." Background Paper for Presentation at the Conference on Comparative Civil Service Systems, School of Public and Environmental Affairs (SPEA), Indiana University, Bloomington, IN, 5–8 April 1997. Online. Available http://www.indiana.edu/~csrc/toonen1.html (accessed 20 December 2005).

Torres, Lourdes, and Vicente Pina. 2002. "Changes in Public Service Delivery in the EU Countries." *Public Money and Management* 22: 41–8.

Tribe, Keith. 1984. "Cameralism and the Science of Government." *Journal of Modern History* 56: 263–84.

True, James L., Bryan D. Jones, and Frank R. Baumgartner. 1999. "Punctuated Equilibrium Theory: Explaining Stability and Change in American Policymaking." In Paul Sabatier, ed., *Theories of the Policy Process*. 97–115. Boulder, CO: Westview.

Tsebelis, George. 2000. "Veto Players and Institutional Analysis." *Governance: An International Journal of Policy and Administration* 13: 441–74.

Turner, John. 1988. "'Experts' and Interests: David Lloyd George and the Dilemmas of the Expanding State, 1906–1919." In Roy MacLeod, ed., *Government and Expertise: Specialists, Administrators and Professionals, 1860–1919*. 203–23. Cambridge: Cambridge University Press.

Urwick, Lyndall. 1969 [1937]. "The Function of Administration, with Special Reference to the Work of Henry Fayol." In Luther Gulick and Lyndall Urwick, eds., *Papers on the Science of Administration*. 116–30. New York: Augustus M. Kelley.

Urwick, L., and E. F. Brech. 1945. *Thirteen Pioneers,* Volume 1: *The Making of Scientific Management*. London: Management Publications Trust.

US Government Accountability Office (USGAO). 2004a. *Results-Oriented Government: GPRA Has Established a Solid Foundation for Achieving Greater Results*. GAO-04-594T. Washington, DC.

——. 2004b. *Performance Budgeting: OMB's Program Assessment Rating Tool Presents Opportunities and Challenges for Budget and Performance Integration*. GAO-04-439T. Washington, DC.

Van Riper, Paul. 1990. *The Wilson Influence on Public Administration: From Theory to Practice*. Washington, DC: American Society for Public Administration.

Vivien, Alexandre François Auguste. 1859. *Études Administratives*. 3rd edition, 2 vols. Paris: Librairie de Guillaumin & Cie.

von Justi, Johann Heinrich Gottlob. 1760. *Die Grundfeste zu der Macht und Glückseligkeit der Staaten – oder ausführliche Vorstellung der gesamten Polizeiwissenschaft*. Königsberg/Leipzig.

von Stein, Lorenz. 1876. *Handbuch der Verwaltungslehre*. 2nd edition. Stuttgart: J. G. Cotta.

Wagner, Richard E. n/d. "The Cameralists: Fertile Sources for a New Science of Public Finance." Online. Available http://mason.gmu.edu/~rwagner/cameralist.pdf (accessed 20 December 2005).

Waldo, Dwight. 1984 [1948]. *The Administrative State: Second Edition with New Observations and Reflections*. New York: Holmes & Meier Publishers.

Wallace, Schuyler C. 1941. *Federal Departmentalization: A Critique of Theories of Organization*. New York: Columbia University Press.

Wamsley, Gary L., and Larkin S. Dudley. 1998. "From Reorganizing to Reinventing: Sixty Years and 'We Still Don't Get It'." *International Journal of Public Administration* 21: 323–74.

WEH (Web of English History). 2004. "The Poor Law Amendment Act, 1834." Online. Available http://www.historyhome.co.uk/peel/poorlaw/poorlaw.htm (accessed 10 January 2005).

Wettenhall, Roger, and Ian Thynne. 2002. "Public Enterprise and Privatization in a New Century: Evolving Patterns of Governance and Public Management." *Public Finance and Management* 2: 1–24.

White, Leonard D. 1924. "The Second International Congress of Public Administration." *American Political Science Review* 18: 384–8.

——. 1926. *Introduction to the Study of Public Administration*. New York: Macmillan.

——. 1927. *The City Manager*. Chicago, IL: University of Chicago.

——. 1933. *Trends in Public Administration*. New York: McGraw-Hill.

——. 1935a. "The British Civil Service." In Leonard D. White, Charles H. Bland, Walter R. Sharp, and Fritz Morstein Marx, eds., *Civil Service Abroad: Great Britain, Canada, France, Germany*. 1–54. New York: McGraw-Hill.

——. 1935b. *Introduction to the Study of Public Administration*, revised edition. New York: Macmillan.

Wilder, Gary. 2001. "Framing Greater France between the Wars." *Journal of Historical Sociology* 14: 198–225.

Willoughby, W. F. 1918. "The Institute for Government Research." *American Political Science Review* 12: 49–62.

——. 1919. "Democratization of Institutions for Public Service." In Frederick A. Cleveland and Joseph Schafer, eds., *Democracy in Reconstruction*. 146–61. Boston, MA: Houghton Mifflin.

——. 1927. *Principles of Public Administration*. Baltimore, MD: Johns Hopkins University Press.

——. 1936. *The Government of Modern States*. New York: D. Appleton-Century Co.

Wilson, James Q. 1975. "The Rise of the Bureaucratic State." *The Public Interest* 41: 77–103.

Wilson, Woodrow. 1885. *Congressional Government*. New York: Houghton Mifflin.

——. 1887. "The Study of Administration." *Political Science Quarterly* 2: 197–222.

Wollmann, Helmut. 2002. "German Local Government under the Impact of NPM Modernization and New Direct Democratic Citizen Rights." Prepared for the International Conference on Reforming Local Government, University of Stuttgart, 26–27 September. Online. Available http://www.uni-stuttgart.de/soz/avps/rlg/papers/Germany-Wollmann.pdf (accessed 21 December 2005).

World Bank. 1991. *The Reform of Public Sector Management: Lessons from Experience*. Washington, DC.

——. 1992. *Governance and Development*. Washington, DC.

Wren, Daniel A. 1979. *The Evolution of Management Thought*. New York: John Wiley.

——. 1987. *The Evolution of Management Thought*. 3rd edition. New York: John Wiley.

Wright, Deil S. 1987. "A Century of the Intergovernmental Administrative State: Wilson's Federalism, New Deal Intergovernmental Relations, and Contemporary Intergovernmental Management." In Ralph Clark Chandler, ed., *A Centennial History of the American Administrative State*. 219–42. New York: Free Press.

Wright, Susan, ed. 1994. *Anthropology of Organisations*. London: Routledge.

Wright, Vincent. 1994a. "Industrial Privatization in Western Europe: Pressures, Problems and Paradoxes." In Vincent Wright, ed., *Privatization in Western Europe: Pressures, Problems and Paradoxes*. 1–43. London: Pinter.

——. 1994b. "Reshaping the State: The Implications for Public Administration." In W. C. Muller and V. Wright, eds., *The State in Western Europe: Retreat or Redefinition?* 102–37. London: Frank Cass.

——. 1995. "Preface." In International Institute of Administrative Sciences, *The Influences of the Napoleonic "Model" of Administration on the Administrative Organization of Other Countries*. Working Group: History of Public Administration. 3–6. Brussels.

Wylie, J. Kerr. 1948. "Roman Law as an Element in European Culture." *South African Law Journal* LXV: 4–13, 201–13, 349–61.

Index

Aberbach, Joel D., 79, 100, 113, 130, 145
absolutism, 40, 43–8, 138–9
accountability: in democracies, 148–50, 154; interest in, 136; issues, 137, 138, 144–5; mechanisms, 139–42, 144, 150, 179; in new public management, 143, 144, 154, 178–9; in Old Public Administration, 142–3; political economy of, 145–54
administration: definitions, 5–6; history of concept, 5–6, 7; relationship to management, 4, 8–10, 30; separation from politics, 51, 54, 91, 93, 146–7
administrative law: American, 36–7, 86–7; British, 72–3; distinction from other types of law, 13; emergence of field, 6; French, 49, 59, 72, 140–1; functions, 179; German, 51
administrative science, 46–8, 50, 51, 56
agency theory, 149
Albrow, Martin, 49
Amos, Sheldon, 5
Articles of Confederation, 20–1, 80–1
Aucoin, Peter, 30, 114, 115–16, 136, 139, 142, 144, 146–7, 176, 177
Australia, 115

Babbage, Charles, 7
Bacon, Francis, 46–7
Bagehot, Walter, 66, 70, 86, 119
Barberis, Peter, 140, 141, 144, 154
Barker, Ernest, 6, 49
Barlow, John, 27, 66
Barnard, Chester I., 96
Barthélemy, Henri, 85
Barzelay, Michael, 110
Bentham, Jeremy, 67
Benz, Arthur, 153
Bertelli, Anthony M., 72, 88, 141, 179

Beveridge, William, 74
Bevir, Mark, 11–12
Bezes, Philippe, 125
Blair, Tony, 119–20
Bogason, Peter, 146, 153, 176
Bouckaert, Geert, 9, 24
Bozeman, Barry, 14
Brady, David W., 23
Brandeis, Louis, 7
Brehm, John, 148, 149, 151
Brennan, Kevin, 69
Brownlow Committee (Committee on Administrative Management), 8, 89, 95–6, 97
bureaucracy: advantages, 26; American, 161; British, 69–71, 161; criticism of, 25–6, 29–30, 49, 52, 70; French, 46; future of, 173–6; German, 161; origins, 41, 43, 160; of papacy, 43; positive views of, 25, 52; relationship to democracy, 29–30, 52, 69–70, 160–1, 169, 174–5, 177–8; state structure and, 171–2; values, 29, 31, 160; Weber on, 54
Burgess, John W., 88
Burke, Edmund, 65, 67, 86
Bush, George W., 112, 114

Caiden, Gerald E., 106
cameralism, 5, 6, 46, 47–8, 67, 116, 164–5
capitalism, 6–7, 53, 173–4
Carpenter, Daniel P., 83
Carroll, James D., 130
Catholic Church, 43
Chapman, Richard C., 74
Child, John, 7, 74–5, 86
Christensen, Tom, 145
Chun, Young Han, 14
Church, A. Hamilton, 92–3, 94

civil law systems, 33, 34, 128, 140
civil service: American, 29, 36, 84;
    British, 36, 63, 68–9, 71–2, 73–6,
    77, 118–19, 162–3, 164; Chinese,
    41; examinations, 41, 46, 54, 68;
    French, 50, 58; German, 34;
    professionalism, 69, 160; values, 29,
    71
Civil Service Reform Act of 1978 (US),
    98
Cleveland, Frederick A., 7, 85, 91
Clinton administration, rcinventing
    government effort, 25, 110–14, 130,
    152
Colbert, Jean Baptiste, 45
Comer, John Preston, 90
Committee on Administrative
    Management see Brownlow
    Committee
Common, Richard, 11, 175
common law tradition, 36, 62, 64, 72,
    128, 140, 142
Confucius, 41
Congress, US, 20, 37, 80–1, 100
constitutions, 48–9; British, 26, 35, 63,
    64–6, 76, 119, 164; European Union,
    127, 128; French, 32, 58; German,
    33, 34, 141–2; institutions and,
    179–80; United States, 21, 36, 37,
    79–80, 81, 90
Continental Europe see Europe; France;
    Germany
contracting, 108, 109, 118, 147, 178
courts, 140–1, 150
Creel, H. G., 41
Crozier, Michel, 169–70
culture, 172, see also organizational
    cultures

Dale, H. E., 71
Dandeker, Christopher, 171
Deal, Terrence E., 31
Deane, Phyllis, 47
Declaration of Independence, 80
delegation: chains, 143, 147–51, 152,
    154, 178; goals, 138; issues, 137,
    138; in new public management,
    143, 179; in United States, 101,
    see also accountability; principal-
    agent problems
democracy: accountability in, 148–50,
    154; development, 48–9, 160–1;
    horizontal, 152–3; parliamentary, 69,
    77, 116; relationship to bureaucracy,

29–30, 52, 69–70, 160–1, 169,
    174–5, 177–8
deregulation, 111
Descartes, René, 47
Dicey, A. V., 72, 140–1
Dickinson, John, 85, 87, 141
DiMaggio, Paul J., 170
Dimock, Marshall, 9, 30, 75
Downs, George W., 97
Drucker, Peter, 115
Dudley, Larkin S., 96
du Gay, Paul, 30
Dunleavy, Patrick, 146, 151, 173
Dunsire, Andrew, 56, 92

Eaton, Dorman, 68, 71, 86
Eggertsson, Thráinn, 148
Elgie, Robert, 126
Eliassen, Kjell A., 105
Ellwein, Thomas, 51, 54, 58, 124
entrepreneurial governance, 30
Epstein, David, 141
ethics, 30, see also values
Europe: absolutism, 40, 43–8, 53;
    feudalism, 40–1, 42–3, 44, 64,
    see also France; Germany; United
    Kingdom
Europe, public management in:
    differences from Britain and United
    States, 62, 67–8, 69–70, 99, 115,
    161; history, 40–58, 163; influence
    in US, 85–8; legacies, 58–60; new
    public management, 114–32, 166
European Administrative Space (EAS),
    128–9
European Court of Justice (ECJ), 128,
    150
European Union (EU): constitution, 127,
    128; economic policies, 122, 127;
    influences on public management in
    member countries, 122, 127–8;
    legislative decisions, 150; Maastricht
    criteria, 122; new public management
    in, 127–9
Executive Office of the President, 84, 96

Fairlie, John A., 6, 85, 88, 90, 176
Fayol, Henri, 7, 9, 85, 96
federalism, 33, 36, 124
Ferejohn, John, 148
Fesler, James W., 43
feudalism, 40–1, 42–3, 44, 64
Finer, Herman, 71, 96
Finer, S. E., 42

205

France: absolutism, 45; civil law system, 33; constitution, 32, 58; courts, 33; feudalism, 42; Fifth Republic, 26, 58
France, public management in: administrative law, 49, 59, 72, 140–1; bureaucracy, 46; citizen's relationship to state, 131; civil service, 50, 58; history, 45, 47, 49–50, 56, 163, 164; influence in US, 88; local governments, 126; Mitterrand reforms, 125; under Napoleon, 46, 49–50, 165; new public management, 124–7; overview, 32–3; training, 33, 58, 116–17
Frederick II, King of Lower Italy and Sicily, 41
Frederickson, H. George, 11, 12
Frederick the Great, King of Prussia, 45, 46, 51, 52
Frederick William (The Great Elector), 45
Frederick William I, King of Prussia, 45, 52
French Revolution, 50, 160, 165
Freund, Ernst, 90
Friedberg, Erhard, 169–70
Friedrich, Carl J., 46, 85, 96, 143, 174
Fry, Geoffrey K., 65, 67, 72, 76

Gaebler, Ted, 25, 110, 111, 166
Gates, Scott, 148, 149, 151
Gaus, John M., 7, 42, 43, 81, 85, 91, 163
General Accounting Office (GAO; US), 109, 112
George III, King, 68–9, 80
Germany: Basic Law, 33, 34, 141–2; civil law system, 34; courts, 34; reunification, 122; views of bureaucracy, 26; Weimar Republic, 33, 51, 55, 56, 161, see also Prussia
Germany, public management in: accountability issue, 141–2; administrative law, 51; bureaucracy, 51–2, 161; civil service, 34; history, 48–9, 50–2, 55, 163, 164–5; influence in US, 87–8; local governments, 122, 123; new public management, 121–4; New Steering Model, 122, 123–4, 144–5; overview, 33–4; as Rechtsstaat, 34, 59; in twentieth century, 55, 58
Gilmour, Robert S., 130
Gladden, E. N., 27, 42, 85, 138

globalization, 167, 168, 174
Goetz, Klaus H., 59, 124
Goodnow, Frank J., 6, 12–13, 14, 54, 86, 89–90, 91
Gore, Al, 25, 110–14
governance, 4, 10–12, 142, 175
Government Performance and Results Act (GPRA; US), 112
Grace Commission, 110
Graham, Andrew, 111–12
Graves, W. Brooke, 94
Greece, ancient, 41–2
Greve, Carsten, 129, 143–4, 175
Groß, Thomas, 142
Gulick, Luther, 96
Gunn, Lewis, 145–6

Habermas, Jürgen, 174
Hakvoort, Jan L. M., 23, 179
Hart, James, 82–3, 87, 90, 91
Hay, Colin, 147
Hayek, Friedrich von, 21, 173
Hayward, Jack, 126–7
Hazell, Robert, 119
Heady, Farrel, 42, 172, 178
Hegel, G. W. F., 26, 52, 79
Heinrich, Carolyn J., 11, 153
Hennessy, Peter, 72
Herring, Pendleton, 96
Hill, Carolyn J., 11, 153
Hintze, Otto, 52, 85
history see public management history
Holliday, Ian, 130
hollow state, 11, 130, 137
Hood, Christopher, 31, 48, 107, 108, 116, 129, 131, 167, 173, 176
Hoover Commissions, 89, 97
hybrid organizations, 98, 143, 147
Hyde, Albert C., 9

Indian civil service, 68
induced reforms, 158
industrialization, 6–7, 160
Ingraham, Patricia W., 167
institutional economics, 145, 148
interest groups, 174–5
international organizations, 1–2, 106

Jackson, Andrew, 83
Jackson, Michael, 48, 116, 129
Jacoby, Henry, 177–8
James, Oliver, 119
Jann, Werner, 12, 123, 178
Jensen, Laura S., 130

Jepperson, R. L., 170
Jespersen, Peter Kragh, 129, 143–4, 175
Jones, Bryan D., 159
Jones, H. W., 179
judicial branch, 140–1, 150
Juran, Joseph M., 27

Kantorowicz, Ernst, 41
Karl, Barry D., 86, 87–8
Keeling, Desmond, 28, 105
Kennedy, Allan A., 31
Kennedy, John F., 97
Kettl, Donald F., 10, 11, 107, 109, 137, 144, 166
Kickert, Walter J. M., 23, 99, 117, 153, 179
Klijn, Erik-Hans, 153
König, Klaus, 62, 107, 121, 130, 161, 176–7
Kooiman, Jan, 105
Koppenjan, J. F. M., 153
Kraemer, Kenneth L., 9, 106

Lane, Jan-Erik, 148
Larkey, Patrick D., 97
Laski, Harold, 73, 77, 85, 145
Laver, Michael, 149
law, 13, *see also* administrative law; civil law systems; common law tradition; constitutions; courts
Lepawsky, Albert, 41–2
Le Play, Frederick, 52
Light, Paul C., 97, 108–9, 110
Lindenfeld, David F., 54
Lindseth, Peter L., 56, 59
Lipsky, Michael, 151
Löffler, Elke, 158, 166
Lombard, Judith M., 113
Long, Norton E., 101, 141, 150–1
Louis XIV, King of France, 45, 47
Lupia, Arthur, 150, 152
Lynn, Laurence E., Jr., 9, 11, 88, 153

Majone, Giandomenico, 28
Major, John, 117–18
management: history of concept, 6–8; relationship to administration, 4, 8–10, 30; theories, 7, *see also* scientific management
management, private: business schools, 28; differences from public management, 4, 12–15, 30; methods used in public management, 110, 115,

118; similarities to public management, 14
Management by Objectives (MBO), 57, 97
managerialism: definitions, 10; development, 95; in Europe, 27, 114–17, 121–9; future of, 175–6; increased interest in, 2, 105–7, 165–6; justification, 178; politics/administration dichotomy, 146–7; state-society relationships, 3, 11, 12, *see also* new public management
Martin, Daniel W., 50, 88
Martin, Roscoe C., 9, 27
McCubbins, Mathew D., 150, 152
merit systems, 36, 48, 51, 73
Merkle, Judith A., 47, 68, 71, 74, 160, 161
Metcalfe, Les, 14, 105, 130
Meyer, J. W., 170
Miewald, Robert D., 51, 86
Mill, John Stuart, 5, 21, 70, 120
Milward, H. Brinton, 152–3
Minogue, Martin, 106, 129, 167
Mitterrand, François, 125
Moe, Ronald C., 143
Mommsen, Hans, 55
Moore, Mark H., 10, 27, 106
Morstein Marx, Fritz, 7, 30–1
Mosher, Frederick C., 84, 88
Muir, Ramsey, 21, 70–1
Mulroney, Brian, 25
municipal research bureaus, 7, 91, 93–4

Napoleon Bonaparte, 46, 49–50, 165
Nash, Gerald D., 43
National Health Service (UK), 31, 74, 117
National Performance Review (NPR; US), 113–14, *see also* reinventing government effort
Neintzman, Ralph, 136, 139, 142, 144, 177
Nelson, Michael, 83
Netherlands, Tilburg reforms, 122, 123
networks, 152–3, 170–1
Neustadt, Richard E., 97
New Deal, 84, 95–6, 164
new governance, 11
new management, 7, 93
new public management (NPM): accountability, 143, 144, 154, 178–9; in Britain, 117–20, 129, 166–7;

criticism of, 123, 129–31, 143–4, 178–9; definitions, 107; delegation, 143, 179; early development, 98–9, 116, 165–6; in Europe, 114–32, 166; evidence of change, 19, 157–8; future of, 158; increased interest in, 157; lack of political support, 158; models, 107; national differences, 131–2, 161, 166–7, 168, 179–80; relationship with old public administration, 3, 137; in United States, 108–14, 166–7; use of term, 2, 107–8, *see also* managerialism
New Steering Model (NSM; Germany), 122, 123–4, 144–5
New York Bureau of Municipal Research, 91, 93–4
New Zealand, 115
Next Steps Reform (UK), 111, 117, 118–19
Nixon, Richard M., 97, 98
non-delegation doctrine, 141
Noordegraaf, Mirko, 28
North, Douglass C., 22, 169
Northcote-Trevelyan Report, 21, 67, 68–9, 96, 164
NPM *see* new public management

OECD *see* Organization for Economic Cooperation and Development
Office of Personnel Management (US), 36, 113
O'Halloran, Sharyn, 141
Old Public Administration, 3, 76, 137, 142–4, *see also* public management history
Olsen, Johan P., 12, 105, 127, 128–9, 142
organizational cultures, 31–2, 151
Organization for Economic Cooperation and Development (OECD), 1, 2, 174–5
Osborne, David, 25, 110, 111, 166
Ostrom, Vincent, 152
O'Toole, Laurence J., 89
Ott, J. Steven, 9

Page, Edward C., 100
paradigm shifts, 166
para-modernism, 175
path dependence, 22, 23, 158, 162–3, 168, 169, 172
Performance Based Organizations (PBOs), 111–12

Perry, James L., 9, 106
Peters, B. Guy, 11, 26, 111, 144, 146, 158, 173, 174
Peters, Thomas J., 31, 110
Pfiffner, John M., 85, 163
Pierre, Jon, 11
Planning–Programming–Budgeting System (PPBS), 57, 97, 109, 123
pluralism, 174–5
Poggi, Gianfranco, 169
Pollitt, Christopher, 9, 24, 27, 28, 30, 31, 105–6, 115, 168
post-bureaucratic state, 173
Pound, Roscoe, 141
Powell, Walter W., 170–1
President's Management Agenda (PMA), 112, 114
Price, Don K., 14, 76, 80
principal-agent problems, 92, 119, 144, 145, 147, 149, 151
privatization, 98, 117, 127, 131, 147
Program Assessment Rating Tool (PART), 112, 114
Provan, Keith G., 152–3
Prussia: absolutism, 45–6, 53; bureaucracy, 48, 50–1, 52, 53, 70, 164
public choice theory, 22–3, 115, 116, 130, 146, 148, 151
public interest, 14, 47, 130, 131, 143, 148
public management: alternatives to, 20–1; convergence in, 167–8; craft emphasis, 27–9; definitions, 24; distinction from public administration, 9; future of, 179–80; interest in, 1–2; meaning, 4; relationship to governance, 4; structures and processes, 24–7; three-dimensional view, 24–32; values, 14, 29–32, 142–3
public management field, 19; in Britain, 75–6; in Europe, 57; in France, 116–17; future of, 177; internationalization, 176–7; theoretical developments, 169–73; training, 27, 28, 57; in United States, 6, 27, 28, 106, 109
public management history, 20–3, 58–60; ancient world, 20, 40–2; in continental Europe, 40–58; continuity in, 159, 162–3; debates on, 21–3; origins, 40; paradigm shifts, 159, 162; punctuated equilibrium

narratives, 159, 165; relationship with administrative history, 26–7
Putnam, Robert D., 100, 172

quasi-governments, 143, 147

Raadschelders, Jos C. N., 9–10, 42–3, 44, 55, 112, 120, 121, 123, 132, 142, 144, 166, 168, 177
Rainey, Hal G., 9, 14, 106
Ranson, Stewart, 24
rational choice models, 147
Reagan, Ronald, 25, 110, 113
Rechtsstaat: criticism of, 54; emergence, 48–9, 52–3, 163, 165; Germany as, 34, 59; limits on managerialism, 59; strengths, 121
Redlich, Josef, 52
red tape, 83, 111
Reichard, Christoph, 123, 144–5
Reinventing Government (Osborne and Gaebler), 25, 110, 166
reinventing government effort (US), 25, 110–14, 130, 152
Rhodes, R. A. W., 11–12, 129, 130
Richards, Sue, 14, 105, 130
Riggs, Fred W., 160–1, 175
Roberts, Alasdair, 111–12
Rockman, Bert A., 79, 100, 113, 130
Roger II, King of Lower Italy and Sicily, 41
Rohr, John, 35, 58, 73, 82, 100, 112, 127
Roman civilization, 41–2
Roosevelt, Franklin, 8, 89, see also New Deal
Roosevelt, Theodore, 84
Rosenberg, Hans, 43–4
Rosenbloom, David H., 30
Rouban, Luc, 59, 126
Rourke, Francis E., 97–8
rule of law, 66, 174, see also Rechtsstaat
Rutgers, Mark R., 42–3, 44, 59, 99, 177

Saalfeld, Thomas, 147
Salamon, Lester M., 11, 109
Schlesinger, Rudolf B., 72
Schmoller, Gustav, 54
Schröter, Eckhard, 122, 124
Schultze, Charles L., 109
Schumpeter, Joseph A., 48
scientific management: British views, 74–5; in France, 47; history of concept, 7; influence on public

management, 94–5; in United States, 92–5, 96, 100, 109, 164; values, 93
Seibel, Wolfgang, 122–3
separation of powers: accountability and, 140; in Germany, 33; in United States, 28, 36, 79–80, 90, 100, 101, 111–12, 162
Shafritz, Jay M., 9
Sheldon, Oliver, 8, 9
Shen Pu-hai, 41
Shepsle, Kenneth A., 149
Silberman, Bernard S., 171–2
Simon, Herbert A., 28, 95, 146
Simpson, J. R., 8
Sinclair, David, 119
Small, Albion W., 47
Smith, Adam, 53, 67
Smith, Kevin B., 11
sovereignty: accountability and, 138–9; administration and, 20, 21, 44–6; national, 49; parliamentary, 65, 66, 141; popular, 54–5, 138
Spencer, Herbert, 70
spoils system, 68, 83, 163
Staatswissenschaften see cameralism
Stamp, Josiah C., 13
state: development, 169–73; relationships with society, 3, 11, 12, see also sovereignty
Stever, James A., 9
Stewart, John, 24
Stillman, Richard J., II, 79
Strøm, Kaare, 149–50
subsidiarity, 108, 147
Suleiman, Ezra, 29–30, 113, 130, 131, 160, 168
Supreme Court, US, 36
Swift, Elaine K., 23

Taft, William Howard, 84, 96
Talbot, Colin, 118–19
Taylor, Frederick W., 7, 92, 93, 94, 95, 145, 164, see also scientific management
Taylor, Sir Henry, 5
Thatcher, Margaret, 25, 26, 110, 115, 117–19
third-party government, 11
Thoenig, Jean-Claude, 125
Thomas, Rosamund M., 8, 75
Thompson, James R., 113–14
Thynne, Ian, 175–6
Tilburg reforms, Netherlands, 122, 123
Tocqueville, Alexis de, 79, 83

Toonen, Theo A. J., 9–10, 55, 106, 107, 112, 120, 121, 123, 132, 142, 144, 146, 152, 153, 158, 166–7, 168, 176
transactions costs, 148, 169
Truman, Harry, 97
Tsebelis, George, 150

United Kingdom: common law tradition, 36, 62, 64, 72, 128; constitution, 26, 35, 63, 64–6, 76, 119, 164; courts, 36; Crown, 35, 36, 64; feudalism, 42, 64; parliament, 36, 64, 65, 66, 119, 120
United Kingdom, public management in: accountability issue, 136, 140–1, 142; administrative law, 72–3; bureaucracy, 69–71, 161; civil service, 36, 63, 68–9, 71–2, 73–6, 77, 118–19, 162–3, 164; civil service values, 29, 71; colonial rule of America, 80; differences from Continental Europe, 62, 67–8, 69–70, 161; differences from United States, 7–8, 75, 76–7, 161; Economic Reform Movement, 67; Fulton Report, 72, 74, 77, 118, 164; Haldane Report, 72, 73–4; history, 7–8, 21, 49, 63–76, 162–3, 164; influence in US, 86–7; Labour governments, 74, 77, 119–20; legacies, 76–7; local governments, 119, 120; MacDonnell Commission, 69, 73; management philosophy, 74–5; managerialism, 105; new public management, 117–20, 129, 166–7; Next Steps Reform, 111, 117, 118–19; Northcote-Trevelyan reforms, 21, 67, 68–9, 96, 164; overview, 35–6; reforms, 26, 72, 74, 77, 115, 117–19; training, 68, 71, 75–6; in twentieth century, 69, 72, 73–6; welfare state, 74
United States: Articles of Confederation, 20–1, 80–1; common law tradition, 36, 62; Constitution, 21, 36, 37, 79–80, 81, 90; judicial branch, 36–7, 86–7
United States, public management in: accountability issue, 136, 141, 142; administrative law, 36–7, 86–7; anti-formalism, 89; budgets, 91, 97, 109, 112, 114; bureaucracy, 161; civil service, 29, 36, 84; differences from Europe, 62, 99, 115, 161; European

influences, 85–8; executive power, 84, 95–6, 97; founding views, 80–2; history, 6–7, 21, 80–99, 162, 163–4; legacies, 99–101; new public management, 108–14, 166–7; overview, 36–8; pre-bureaucratic era, 82–4; as profession, 88–9; reform movements, 84–91, 108–9, 164; reinventing government effort, 25, 110–14, 130, 152; relationship to legislature, 100; state and local governments, 36–7, 84, 89, 93–4; uniqueness, 79, 99; values, 30–1
Urwick, Lyndall, 74–5, 96

values: bureaucratic, 29, 31, 160; civil service, 29, 71; institutionalized, 4, 29–32; public management, 14, 29–32, 142–3; scientific management, 93
Van Riper, Paul, 9
Vauban, Sebastien Le Prestre, Seigneur de, 47
vom Stein, Freiherr, 51, 53
von Justi, Johann, 47
Von Seckendorff, Veit Ludwig, 44–5
von Stein, Lorenz, 26, 52, 54, 85

Waldo, Dwight, 83, 86, 87, 146
Wallace, Schuyler C., 68, 99
Wamsley, Gary L., 96
Washington, George, 81
Waterman, Robert H., 31, 110
Webb, Sidney and Beatrice, 73, 75
Weber, Max, 26, 54, 171, 174
welfare states, 54, 57, 69, 74, 95, 121, 132
Weller, Patrick, 11–12
Westminster model, 69, 116, 142
Wettenhall, Roger, 175–6
White, Leonard D., 6, 7, 13, 23, 30, 83–4, 92, 93, 163, 176
Willoughby, W. F., 6, 85, 87, 91, 94
Wilson, Woodrow, 9, 85, 86, 92, 161
Wollman, Helmut, 122
World Bank, 1, 105, 175
World War I, 55, 56, 91
World War II, 56–8, 59, 121
Wright, Susan, 31
Wright, Vincent, 108, 126–7, 131, 144, 146

Zero-Based Budgeting (ZBB), 57, 97
Zincke, Georg, 5